MIGRANT MEDIA

NEW ANTHROPOLOGIES OF EUROPE

EDITORS

Daphne Berdahl, Matti Bunzl, and Michael Herzfeld

Migrant Media

Turkish Broadcasting and Multicultural Politics in Berlin

KIRA KOSNICK

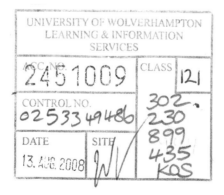
INDIANA UNIVERSITY PRESS

Bloomington & Indianapolis

This book is a publication of

Indiana University Press
601 North Morton Street
Bloomington, IN 47404-3797 USA

http://iupress.indiana.edu

Telephone orders   800-842-6796
Fax orders   812-855-7931
Orders by e-mail   iuporder@indiana.edu

The paper used in this publication meets the minimum requirements of
American National Standard for Information Sciences—Permanence of
Paper for Printed Library Materials, ANSI Z39.48-1984.

Manufactured in the United States of America

Library of Congress Cataloging-in-Publication Data

Kosnick, Kira.
Migrant media : Turkish broadcasting and multicultural politics in Berlin
/ Kira Kosnick.
p. cm. — (New anthropologies of Europe)
Includes bibliographical references and index.
ISBN-13: 978-0-253-34948-4 (cloth)
ISBN-13: 978-0-253-21937-4 (pbk.)
1. Ethnic broadcasting—Germany—Berlin. 2. Turks—Germany—
Berlin. 3. Social integration—Germany—Berlin. I. Title.
PN1991.8.E84K67 2007
302.23089'9435043155—dc22
                                                  2007013959
1 2 3 4 5 12 11 10 09 08 07

for Laura Poitras

CONTENTS

ACKNOWLEDGMENTS

This book is the result of debates, insights, and controversies that I've had the privilege to share with many people across different continents. Most importantly, I have benefited from the great generosity and openness of many broadcasting activists in Berlin, without whom few of these pages could have been written. I hope that I can justify their trust, and contribute to their ongoing efforts to sustain inspiring debates against violence and enforced silences. I would also like to thank Jürgen Linke at the OKB and Friedrich Voß at Radio MultiKulti, both for inviting me into their respective institutional contexts and for their openness to criticism.

I could not have embarked upon the research for this book without the financial support of the Wenner-Gren Foundation for Anthropological Research, which enabled me to carry out my fieldwork in Berlin with a pre-dissertation research grant. Their support is gratefully acknowledged.

At Indiana University Press, I thank my editor Rebecca Tolen and particularly Matti Bunzl, series editor of New Anthropologies of Europe, for his commitment to this project. I am also greatly indebted to Dominic Boyer and Martin Stokes for their helpful suggestions and criticisms as external readers. Their comments have made this a better book.

My thinking around many crucial issues of this book was inspired by the teaching of Brackette F. Williams. I thank her for opening many intellectual doors for me, including the one that led me into anthropology. The former members of the Department of Anthropology at Johns Hopkins University, most importantly Michel-Rolph Trouillot and Katherine Verdery, encouraged me to pursue my own intellectual trajectory even as it led me away from their department.

At the New School for Social Research, I thank M. Jacqui Alexander and the participants of the Mobilization for Real Diversity, Democracy, and Economic Justice who importantly challenged me to think about both political and spiritual implications of my academic work. I am also greatly indebted to the members of my dissertation committee at the New School for the intellectual inspiration they provided, as well as for their perseverance and support over the years. In particular, I thank Steven Caton for his unfailing support, and for taking on the sometimes arduous work of supervising the completion of my Ph.D. even after leaving the Graduate Faculty of Political and Social Science. I am grateful to Rayna Rapp for her careful reading of different manuscript versions and for her astute criticism. Talal Asad provided essential intellectual guidance in the early phase of conceptualizing my research project. Victoria Hattam generously agreed to engage with its outcomes. Margarita Alario has been a crucial friend and intellectual interlocutor in the process of writing up my thoughts.

I thank Faye Ginsburg for her ongoing encouragement and advice, as well as for the opportunity to present my thoughts at the Program in Culture and Media at New York University. Thanks is also due to Dorle Dracklé and all the participants of the Media Anthropology Summer School in Hamburg, for their supportive criticism and their efforts to transform the discipline of anthropology. To the OKB seminar group at Humboldt University in Berlin, including Anke Bentzin, Jeanine Dağyeli, Ayfer Durdu, Riem Spielhaus, and Gerdien Jonker, I am grateful for inviting me into your debates and for giving so much to a shared project. I also thank Thomas Faist, Eyüp Özveren, and the participants of the Turkish-German Summer Institute for their insights and support of young scholars.

As a Marie-Curie Research Fellow at the University of Sussex, I have greatly benefited from Ralph D. Grillo's persistent support and engaged criticism at crucial junctures. Richard Black, Russell King, and Nancy Wood provided me with a supportive environment during my stay at the Centre for Migration Research. I thank Nicole Wolf, Anniken Hagelund, Charlotte Sever, and Nicola Mai for their intellectual companionship and laughter. Roger Bromley and my former colleagues at Nottingham Trent University have made possible the impossible task of coping with both writing and teaching responsibilities. I would like to thank Gary Needham and Olga Guedes-Bailey for their ongoing encouragement. Thanks to my parents for putting many things into perspective.

In Istanbul, I thank Özüm Basmaz, Özlem Kanpara, and İdil Gülbalkan for their unconditional friendship, generosity, and patience with my never-ending questions uttered in imperfect Turkish.

In Berlin, Shermin Langhoff, Martina Priessner, Hanna Keller, and Tuncay Kulaoğlu taught me lots about teamwork, cultural-political activism, and sticking together in difficult times. They made crucial contributions to my postdoctoral research in the context of the European Union Fifth-Framework Project "Changing City Spaces," as did Brigitta Busch, Kevin Robins, Asu Aksoy, Heidi Armbruster, and Nadia Kiwan. To Stefanie Jordan, Tijen Durkut, İpek İpekçioğlu, and Hülya Karcı, thanks for offering manifold challenges, explanations, and assistance. Above all, I thank Claudia Krams, for being there with all her love, political passion, sharp intellect, and sense of justice.

MIGRANT MEDIA

1

Introduction

It was hot on a late summer evening in Berlin in 1994. The living room windows of Deniz and Zerdi's[1] apartment were wide open, facing a busy street in the western district of Schöneberg. The kids had just gone to bed, after an hour of exchanging banter with me in English at their parents' request. The English lesson was over, and we were to move on to the Turkish part, with me as the student. Yet, Deniz and Zerdi, both in their early 30s, were firmly placed in front of the television, channel-zapping as they tried to catch news on the Kurdish rally that had taken place earlier that day in Frankfurt. They had wanted to go, but could not leave their newspaper store, where they worked long hours six days a week. Deniz got lucky with the German public service channel ARD, which briefly covered the rally in its evening news program. The report stated that 15,000 people had attended the rally from all over Germany. Deniz exclaimed, "Not true—there were twice as many!" Zerdi told me that they had heard about the numbers who attended the rally from relatives who had participated. "But television always lies," Deniz said, adding that "the Turkish channels are fascist anyhow, and the only place where you can get the truth is the Kurdish programs on the Open Channel." There were lots of programs produced by migrants from Turkey on Berlin's open access television channel, they told me, and some of their friends were broadcasting there as well.

At that time, the summer of 1994, Berlin was teeming with migrant media projects that used television to proclaim their own truths and speak for different kinds of constituencies. These projects broadcast against the grain of large network television stations in both Germany and Turkey. Five years later, Berlin became the first city outside of Turkey to have its own twenty-four-hour Turkish radio station. Satellite dishes have appeared in migrant neighborhoods all over the city, providing access to television channels from Turkey, but also to transnational Kurdish channels broadcasting from Western Europe. Yet, local migrant media production has continued unabated. This book explores the reasons for the vitality of Berlin's Turkish-language broadcasting landscape, and migrants' efforts to represent their lives with a difference.

Migrant Media

The movement of people and the flow of mediated cultural representations across nation-state boundaries are key features of globalization processes in the contemporary world. At no point in human history have there been more people on the move, experiencing new forms of liminality and transience, but also creating new patterns of settlement and diversity. At the same time, we are witnessing an unprecedented increase in media production and circulation on a global scale, incorporating new technological developments and reaching out to increasingly dispersed audiences.

At a time when cross-border migratory movements render social formations across the globe increasingly diverse and culturally complex, the politics of representing such diversity and complexity take on growing importance. Mass media such as radio and television constitute central public technologies and arenas in which cultural representations are formed, contested, and disseminated. In a historical period that is marked by increasing engagement with such media on a worldwide scale, and through the integration of these media into "new media" circuits (Bolter and Grusin 1999), the question of access to such technologies and arenas is of ever more urgent cultural and political consequences. Developments such as the emergence of transnational media conglomerates, increasing commercialization, and concentration of ownership threaten to limit such access and result in mass media monopolies of ideas (Bagdikian 2004; McChesney and Schiller 2003). However, media landscapes have also diversified, with new social groups gaining access to media production. New technologies help these groups to articulate positions that are marginalized or entirely absent from dominant mass media circuits.

Migrant media form part of this diversification of media production, albeit a largely unacknowledged one (Husband 2005). Immigrant populations across the world contribute to transnational and diasporic[2] audiences, and are often deliberately targeted by cross-border media as members of deterritorialized national or religious imagined communities. But migrants also engage in media production themselves, addressing not just fellow migrants but wider audiences that participate in national as well as transnational public spheres. Such media production is rarely backed up by financial resources or state interests that would allow for the emergence of prominent media ventures. Instead, migrant media tend to flourish in the marginal and often unstable spaces opened up by the erosion of public service and state broadcasting monopolies, by the development of new communication technologies, and by the uncertainties of political regulation that often still characterize new transnational media infrastructures.

Marginal as it might be, migrant media activism is nevertheless politically central when it comes to debating issues of democratic empowerment and minority participation in immigration countries. These are key issues in Western European nation-states at the beginning of the twenty-first century, where fears over the alienation of Muslim migrant populations in particular and the alleged failure of integration policies dominate political agendas. While the curbing of immigration and the containment of dissent might be the primary objective of these agendas, immigrant groups across Western Europe have become increasingly vocal in their demands for greater participation and empowerment. Migrant media activism is an obvious starting point to look for such "voices," and to try to understand both their emergence and reach.

Just twenty years ago, migrant populations in Western Europe had little or no access to media offerings that targeted them as audiences, and even less representation in the mass media. Nowadays, particularly in metropolitan centers such as London, Paris, and Berlin, locally produced radio and television programs target migrants in a variety of languages and complement cross-border satellite imports. Often small in scale, migrant broadcasting production appears to exemplify the democratizing potential of new media technologies and infrastructures and contributes to a "pluralization" of voices in mass-mediated public spheres. Migrant and ethnic minority media production is increasingly being discovered as a crucial resource for collective agency and self-representation in European social formations and beyond (Busch 2004; Cottle 2000; Silverstone and Georgiou 2005).

While migrant populations have begun to make use of new mass media opportunities in many Western European countries, this appearance has nowhere been more pronounced than in Germany. Turkish-language media production is thriving, particularly in the capital city of Berlin, which is home to the largest Turkish population outside of Turkey. Berlin's largest group of immigrants is served by a twenty-four-hour Turkish television channel and a twenty-four-hour Turkish radio station, by a wide range of open-access television programs broadcast in Turkish, by Germany's only radio station with an explicitly "multicultural" orientation, and by several small commercial television projects that share a cable frequency. All of these radio and television programs are produced in Berlin for immigrant audiences, and thus have a "local" character. They complement, and at times deliberately compete with, the mass media imports from Turkey that became available all over Germany via satellite and cable during the 1990s. The multitude of local programming also manages to compete with German mainstream radio and television, indicating that migrant media thrive in niches that major state-supported or commercial media players have failed to occupy.

Radio and particularly television, despite the advance of "second media age" technologies such as the Internet (Poster 1995), far outrank all other options as the mass media of choice for migrants from Turkey in Germany. Even though daily newspapers from Turkey are available across German newsstands in regions with immigrant populations, their circulation numbers are low. Efforts to establish print publications aimed at Turkish readers in Germany have almost all been doomed to failure.[3] Print media cannot compete with the vibrant arenas of Turkish-language radio and television broadcasting.

This book presents an in-depth study of Turkish-language radio and television production in Berlin, based on ethnographic research that I carried out in the city between 1998 and 2003. Prompted by my curiosity at Berlin's thriving and at times politically explosive migrant broadcasting landscape, I set out to investigate the vexing dilemmas of minority representation in "multicultural" and transnational contexts that—as will be shown—go far beyond the urban space of Berlin. I have been concerned with the cultural practices of (self-)representation that migrants from Turkey engage in, and with the political struggles over who can authoritatively "speak for" an immigrant population whose presence in Germany is still highly contested.

The grounds for such contestation have shifted historically since the beginnings of labor migration in the 1960s. Initially, both citizenship laws and dominant imaginaries of the German nation had made the integration and naturalization of labor migrants neither desirable nor conceivable. But in the early twenty-first century, long-term immigrants are encouraged to take on German citizenship, and their social and cultural integration is high on the political agenda as never before. As will be discussed in more detail below, migrants from Turkey constitute not only the largest ethnic minority population in the country but also the one that is considered most difficult to integrate. German policy debates across the political spectrum and national tabloid headlines concur in their views that the overwhelmingly Muslim immigrant group constitutes a problematic minority in both cultural and religious terms. The explicit encouragement of naturalization has in a sense made the project of incorporating migrants more precarious, since any developments among immigrants that run contrary to integrative aims now indicate trouble at the very heart of German society, and not just at its margins. And these troubles are amplified in the context of the European Union, in which the search for a common cultural core goes hand in hand with concerns over the compatibility of Islam with "Western civilization."

This explains why the topic of Turkish migrant media is politically explosive in German integration debates: while some positions see migrant media activism as a form of public engagement and democratic participation that signals integration, others regard it as potentially and uncontrollably promoting segregation, undemocratic values, and religious fanaticism. Just how different are "the Turks," and how different do they want to be? Should migrants be allowed to "speak for themselves," and what do they have to say?

The investigation of immigrant representation in electronic mass media contexts inevitably raises issues concerning the relationships among categorical identities, cultural production, and power. Categorical identities that classify human collectivities along ethnic or religious lines are never just innocent labels for objectively existing groups. They are mobilized to legitimate group claims, and to ascribe differential worth to those categorized as different. Categorical identities justify both exclusionary and integrationist practices and defend differential rights to belonging, particularly when it comes to national communities (Williams 1989). In Germany, categorical identities, such as "Turkish," figure as central signifiers of essentialized cultural, ethnic, and religious difference.

Dominant cultural classifications have powerful consequences for the forms of exclusion and inclusion that prevail in ethnically and religiously diverse countries. In turn, these forms shape the opportunities for engaging in the politics of cultural (self-)representation. Defined as Germans' stereotypical "Other," Turkish cultural production in Germany is forced to be continuously concerned with transforming, challenging, or confirming migrant identity labels. Since such labels and the meanings they carry have palpable consequences, affecting laws, policies, and everyday interactions, migrants cannot afford to ignore them. Yet, the power to objectify, to produce cultural classifications and to intervene in public discourses of cultural identity is unevenly distributed among minority and majority groups, and is a highly political issue (Werbner 1997). Who can "speak for" whom, by what means, and who is listening or watching? Seen in this light, Turkish migrant radio and television broadcasting in Berlin has an important role to play in circulating representations that challenge the range of ethnic and religious stereotypes of migrants pervasive in dominant media discourses—not just in Germany, but also in Turkey. Migrant media are of prime importance as arenas for producing and circulating identity claims in order to intervene in the politics of representation.

Questions of media representation cannot be asked without considering the socioeconomic conditions under which mass media function as cul-. tural technologies, political instruments, and profit-generating economic sectors. Analysts of media globalization have pointed out that increasing market concentration, multisectoral involvement, and transnational corporate engagement are strengthening the links between dominant political and economic interests. This in turn negatively affects both access to mass media and the production and availability of critical media contents, particularly when it comes to radio and television broadcasting (Leidinger 2003).

Migrant media practices run counter to this tendency, and examining them in detail can illuminate the conditions under which "alternative voices" can be represented in mass-mediated public spheres—voices that articulate critical forms of knowledge, contest hegemonic representations of reality, and offer different sources of identification and empowerment in a particular context. It is only by moving among production practices, producers' motivations, media contents, and the structural conditions of production that the points of convergence, determination, and conflict among the economic and the cultural dimensions of such "subaltern voices" can be explored. As of yet, few studies exist that link these different levels of analysis, combining a focus on the political economy of media production, and on data gathered during participant observation of production practices, with close semiotic analysis of media programs, interviews, and conversations with media producers, as well as with an investigation into the historicity of broadcasting by and for migrants. Such linkage is central, however, for exploring the subversive potential of migrant media production and the dilemmas of representation that migrant producers cannot escape from. These dilemmas are tied to the wider contexts in which apparently local Turkish media production is embedded, contexts that have national as well as transnational dimensions. Migrant media engagement in Berlin cannot be fully made sense of unless the dominant cultural politics toward migrants and minorities in both Turkey and Germany are taken into account. Migrant media production unfolds at the intersection of two different national arenas, their discursive fields and political-cultural practices.

In the lives of Berlin's migrants from Turkey, and in the media representations they produce of themselves, their positioning as members of an ethnic and religious minority in Germany and their belonging to different groups within Turkey are simultaneously at issue. Just how this multiple implication in different hegemonic structures and ongoing state formation processes should best be navigated—for example, by claiming a local identity, the importance of national belonging, or by asserting the priority of diasporic affiliations—is a highly contested issue that motivates and structures migrant broadcasting practices. The landscape of broadcasting produced locally in Berlin is both strongly divided and stratified, with different constituencies making radically divergent claims regarding the proper representation of migrant life, and with different resources and discursive means at their disposal to do so.

Migrants from Turkey in Berlin

Turkish migration to Berlin goes back centuries, with Turkish-Ottoman elites establishing trade relations and training at educational institutions in the city (Greve and Çinar 1997). However, up until the 1960s, their presence was never a very prominent one. The fact that Berlin is now home to the largest population of migrants from Turkey anywhere in Europe is owed largely to a historical coincidence. Spurred by the strategic political interest of the Western Allies after World War II, the Federal Republic of Germany was experiencing a postwar economic boom, with labor power becoming a scarce resource. Workers were to be recruited from abroad, the so-called *Gastarbeiter* (guestworkers)—not just to sustain economic expansion, but also as a useful industrial "reserve army" that would keep union demands at bay (Nikolinakos 1973). Just as the West German government was about to sign a labor recruitment agreement with Turkey, following earlier agreements with Italy (1955), Spain (1960), and Greece (1960), the GDR cut off West Berlin from its surroundings by building the Berlin Wall. On August 13, 1961, the GDR closed all remaining border checkpoints through which thousands of people had been streaming to leave the socialist German state. Given the spatial distribution of workforce and industry in the city, West Berlin factories suddenly found themselves without employees, many of whom were stuck on the Eastern side of the wall. When a few months later the newly opened Istanbul branch of the West German Federal Employment Office began to recruit and send workers abroad, Berlin was a prime destination.

Turkish interest in working abroad was huge: like most of the other sending countries, Turkey was facing strong population growth, high unemployment among unskilled workers, and pronounced rural to urban migration. The bulk of migrants to Germany thus originated from Turkey's rural regions, with some having migrated first to the growing urban centers in the west of the country. Between 1961 and 1973, more than 700 000 people were recruited from Turkey, initially on short-term contracts that

Map 1. Map of Germany. *Courtesy of Jürgen Frohnmaier, www.yoyus.com.*

usually lasted two years. Employers soon realized that the "rotation principle" (*Rotationsprinzip*), which forced labor migrants to return to Turkey
after two years, was disrupting productivity, and thus they successfully lobbied the government to abandon it in 1964. Initially, only a small percentage of those recruited were women, but their numbers eventually rose to 30
percent by 1968 (Treibel 1990). Women were given preference in the recruitment process, since many branches of industry, such as textiles, were
relying on a predominantly female workforce. The gender balance was
equalized even more as workers began to bring the families they had left behind in Turkey. Even though labor recruitment came to a sudden end with

the oil crisis in 1973, family reunions remained a legal migration route, and many workers decided to have family members join them in Germany rather than return to Turkey. Thus, even though the number of Turkish employees in the West German workforce declined, the number of immigrants from Turkey continued to rise.

Close to two million individuals with a Turkish passport now reside officially in Germany, according to the latest figures of the German Federal Agency for Statistics.[4] Turkish citizens thereby constitute 25.6 percent of more than 7 million foreign nationals living in the country, forming the largest immigrant group among a total population of about 82 million. This figure does not include the number of those who have adopted German citizenship, more than a half-million between 1995 and 2003 alone (Beauftragte der Bundesregierung für Migration, Flüchtlinge und Integration 2004).

Foreign labor recruitment in the postwar era was initially perceived and intended as a strictly economic measure to boost the West German *Wirtschaftswunder* (economic miracle). Despite the racist horrors of the Nazi era, West German citizenship law had remained tied to the principle of *jus sanguinis* (Latin for "right of blood"), meaning that blood relation rather than place of birth determined access to citizenship. The labor migrant populations that began to settle in West Germany after 1959 remained for decades more or less excluded from citizenship and also from the nation as a symbolic construct (Mandel 1994, 1995; Räthzel 1990). This was reflected in the pervasive use of the term *Ausländer* (foreigner) to refer to immigrants up until the 1990s, a label that was employed even in antiracist and pro-immigration discourses of the Left and the newly constituted Green Party movement. The foreigner label had taken over from the earlier term *Gastarbeiter* (guestworker) when it became clear that the so-called guests were there to stay.

Concerns about integration first arose in the mid-1970s, when family reunions and new patterns of settlement together with the suddenly diminished need for labor power turned migration into a social issue. However, it took until the 1980s before the political establishment acknowledged that the labor migrant populations were "here for good" (Castles 1984). This acknowledgment did not yet amount to an admission that West Germany had become a country of immigration (*Einwanderungsland*). Even children born to the first and second generations of labor migrants remained *Ausländer,* most of them legally but all of them also symbolically, regardless of their actual citizenship status. The *Ausländer* burden was similarly carried by people of color who might have no immigration background at all. Children born to "biracial" parents used to be routinely categorized as foreigners, an exclusion that was all the more painful as many of them grew up in White German surroundings with few sources for positive identification as Black German or other (Oguntoye, Opitz, and Schultz 1986). Thus, the term "foreigner" was never simply an issue of citizenship, but a highly racialized category. Racialized perceptions of who could claim belonging to the German nation in turn influenced the politics of integration and migration.

West German government policies during the 1980s focused more or less unsuccessfully on encouraging the return of labor migrants and their families, seeing integration as a pragmatic task in order to minimize social conflicts where they arose. It was only during the late 1990s that attention shifted toward a different kind of integration—not just in terms of labor markets and social services, but also symbolically in terms of how Germany could be imagined as a multicultural and multiethnic society.

The city of Berlin has for several decades been at the forefront of changing integration politics. The Berlin Senate was the first federal state government to appoint a Deputy for Foreigner Affairs (*Ausländerbeauftragte*) in 1982, a position that is now common across Germany. And even though this deputy was to deal with the concerns of people who were still labeled foreigners, the deputy's office quickly began with campaigns to reshape the public image of Berlin as a city of immigration. When at the national level, categorical identities common today, such as German Turks (*Deutschtürken*) or Turkish Germans (*Türkische Deutsche*), still appeared like a contradiction in terms, immigrants in Berlin were invited to see themselves as Berliners of different backgrounds and colors. Immigrants and people of color living in Berlin still carried the *Ausländer* label, foreigners in terms of symbolic national belonging, but they could be presented as part of the city—a city that was increasingly trying to represent itself as the multicultural and cosmopolitan capital of a reunited Germany.

By the end of 2005, more than 460,000 foreign nationals were officially counted among the inhabitants of Berlin, stemming from 183 different countries.[5] Together, they constitute 13.8 percent of the population. Of these, 121,696 have a Turkish passport, making Berlin the city with the largest Turkish population outside of Turkey. However, Berlin is also the German city with the highest number of naturalizations. Since 1980, more than 45,000 Turkish residents have adopted German citizenship, with a steep increase in the number of naturalizations since 1999. That year, the Social Democratic–Green government made good on its promise to change Germany's notorious naturalization laws (Brubaker 1992), encouraging long-term foreign residents to acquire German citizenship. One can thus estimate a total of about 180,000 Berliners with "roots" in Turkey, and if one adds the estimated number of undocumented Turkish citizens residing in Berlin, the figure is likely to be closer to 200,000. Their numbers are more than twice that of residents from other European Union countries (a third of them Polish) and the substantial refugee population from the former Yugoslavia, to name the three largest groups. They are followed in size by Russian citizens, though many of the Russians have also taken on German citizenship as part of the *Aussiedler* population that claimed German ancestry to leave the former Soviet Union, or as Jewish refugees. Many more are thought to be undocumented (Ohliger and Raiser 2005).

The settlement pattern of Berlin's largest and most established immigrant group has not changed much since the beginnings of labor migration. In search of cheap, affordable housing, the majority of migrants from Turkey eventually settled in rather poor, dilapidated inner-city districts of West Berlin, many of them close to the Wall that divided the city until 1989. This pattern has continued into the present, despite efforts by the city government to limit the influx of foreign residents into certain neighborhoods for fear of "ghettoization."[6] This concentration facilitated the emergence of a complex Turkish infrastructure, ranging from shops, restaurants, and banks to mosques, sports associations, medical practices, insurance agents, and auto mechanics. The Turkish Yellow Pages (*Altın Sayfalar*) for the city lists about 4,000 entries, of an estimated 5,000 Turkish businesses in the city alone. Some are geared specifically toward the needs of Turkish migrants, providing *helal* foods, translation services, Turkish music imports, and the like, but most have a wider clientele. Small fruit-and-vegetable markets in all areas of the city now tend to be run by Turks, as well as fast-food shops that sell the famous *Döner Kebap*, pieces of roasted meat served with salad between puffy white bread with a crunchy crust.

Integration Fears

The success of the *Döner Kebap* as Germany's fast food of choice (Seidel-Pielen 1996) has not been replicated on a wider scale for other aspects of Turkish immigrant culture. Surveys show that Turks are widely considered the culturally most "alien" group of immigrants in Germany (Ogelman 2003). Integration failures are diagnosed when it comes to violence in schools with a high percentage of immigrant children, or when the topic of forced marriages and the oppression of women is discussed. A spate of much-publicized events has raised the specter of migrants' potential unwillingness to integrate. The case of the Rütli High School in Berlin, where a young male student with a Turkish background hit his female German teacher, made for nationwide newspaper headlines and a flurry of television talk shows in which politicians lamented the failures of laissez-faire multiculturalism. Several books written by young women with Turkish migrant backgrounds revealed deplorable facts about women forced into marriage in Turkish Islamist circles (for example, see Kelek 2005), revelations that strengthened the links made between Turkishness, Islam, and gender oppression in the German media. The hostile and segregationist teachings of a self-appointed Islamic "Caliph" in Cologne and his community of Turkish Islamist followers, the statistics concerning the predominance of viewing Turkey-imported television in migrant households, violence in schools, and a number of so-called honor-killings of young migrant women by family members all seemed to indicate the failure of the German multiculturalist project in the early twenty-first century. Terrorist attacks and violence in the name of Islam in other European Union countries have heightened such fears.

As a consequence, the task of integrating immigrant populations in cultural terms is very high on the German political agenda, as the conservative-led debate on *Leitkultur* has shown. In response to fears over integration, center-right politicians argued for a stronger emphasis on German culture, perceived as a necessary "guiding culture" in the mix of cultures produced by immigration. While the concept itself was quickly rebuffed for its nationalist impetus, there is widespread fear across the political spectrum that an apparently uncritical acceptance of cultural differences in the context of multiculturalism has led to immigrants' segregation and the flourishing of hostile attitudes toward "basic Western values." Germany's Turkish population is the prime suspect for a refusal to integrate and a preference for living in so-called parallel societies (*Parallelgesellschaften*). These views have been compounded by fears over Muslim extremism in the wake of the September 11 attacks in the United States and the so-called War On Terror. Despite the fact that migrants from Turkey often endorse secularist principles and show a complex range of orientations toward Islam, their Muslim religiosity is increasingly seen as the culprit for the alleged integration failures.

Experts and public figures such as prominent scholar Bassam Tibi warn that these failures render Muslims vulnerable to fundamentalist Islamism and threaten Germany's "inner peace" (Tibi 2002). Others go further and speak of a "deadly threat" posed by Muslim ghettos in Germany, where the "Western values" of tolerance and freedom of opinion find no acceptance (Lachmann 2005). The failure to integrate has produced a marginalized, "fanaticized" generation, Lachmann claims, having fallen prey to a Neo-Islamism which now aims to subjugate European societies by terrorist means.

Such fears are echoed across the European Union, and news of incidents that seem to confirm them travel quickly across the European Union's internal borders. Events such as the murder of filmmaker Theo Van Gogh in the Netherlands, killed for his alleged filmic desecration of the Koran, have received great attention in German print and broadcasting media. Together with so-called honor killings, forced marriages, and headscarf debates, the dominant media representations of Turks focus on Islamism in the context of intolerance and violence.

I make no effort here to evaluate these alleged threats, nor to explore the connections and distinctions among Islam, different practices of Islam, and political violence. While a significant part of the material I present in this book deals with Islamic broadcasting, this material reveals a wide range of religious orientations and understandings of Islam. It is analyzed primarily with regard to the different communicative approaches, aims, and strategies of representation that migrant broadcasters adopt. Rather than denying or confirming instances of oppression and violence committed in the name of religion, this study highlights very different aspects of Islamic practice in Germany, and will thus hopefully contribute to more nuanced discussions about the presence of Islam and Muslim populations in Europe.

The European dimension is relevant also because the claims regarding a basic cultural incompatibility of Islam with "Western values" are increasingly articulated in supra-national terms. Matti Bunzl has claimed that the contemporary "Islamophobia" in Western European nation-states is substantially different from earlier nineteenth-century forms of antisemitism and racism, because it "functions less in the interest of national purification than as a means of fortifying Europe" (Bunzl 2005). In the early twenty-first century, European civilization has taken the place of the earlier national community that was to be protected from allegedly harmful "outsiders." The logic of exclusion that was fueled by racism has by and large disappeared from mainstream politics in Western Europe, claims Bunzl. The new exclusionary project is European both in its scope and in its explicit orientation, not seeking to protect ethno-national purity, but as a particular civilization conceptualized as European. Turkish Muslims appear as a threat in this context not because of their ethnic belonging, but because of their religion. For conservative and right-wing political forces across the European Union, the prospect of Turkey's potential membership in the European Union threatens its cultural core precisely because of its Muslim populace.

In Germany, where European unification has also evoked political hopes of shedding some of the historical burden of Nazism and the Holocaust (Boyer 2005b), it is certainly more acceptable to speak of European values than of German values—a term that has been thoroughly discredited since the period of National Socialism. Yet, as the debate on *Leitkultur* has shown, invocations of the national continue to exert an influence upon German politics. What is more, racist criteria linked to the stereotypical embodiments associated with "foreigners" determine who is perceived as Muslim in everyday contexts. Racism and the logic of national culture thus continue to play a role in the configuration of integration fears and Islamophobia.

THE DILEMMAS OF MINORITY REPRESENTATION

It is not just ethno-religious stigmatization that migrants from Turkey have had to contend with over the past years in Germany. Once recruited predominantly for the low-wage and unskilled end of the labor market, labor migrants and their families have been disproportionately affected by the country's economic crisis, with high levels of poverty and unemployment particularly among young people (Troltsch 2002). While a growing number of small-scale entrepreneurs have set up businesses, many of which cater to the special needs of migrants from Turkey, their economic future looks grim. Statistics that measure the labor market participation of resident aliens against that of German citizens show that the latter are much more likely to hold full-time jobs that offer insurance, and that resident aliens are twice as likely to be affected by unemployment. The unemployment rate is highest among those with Turkish citizenship, with over a quarter registered as unemployed in 2003 (Beauftragte der Bundesregierung für Migration, Flüchtlinge und Integration 2005).

Given this grim economic situation, it is all the more surprising that the range of locally produced media offerings aimed at Turkish immigrants has expanded since the late 1990s rather than contracted. This expansion has partly to do with German corporations' discovery of Turkish immigrants as a distinctive consumer group, leading to new "ethno-marketing" strategies that provide advertising revenues to commercial Turkish media ventures (Çağlar 2004).[7] But as will become evident, the expansion is also closely linked to the increasing political importance attached to migrant media production in Germany.

The issue of migrants' media consumption has received increasing political attention in Germany since the arrival of satellite television. Turkish households watch more and more programming imported from Turkey, raising fears among policymakers that this might negatively affect integration by orienting migrants toward the country of origin (Weiß and Trebbe 2001; Zentrum für Türkeistudien 1997). In contrast, local media produced by and for migrants at their place of residence tend to be regarded in a much more positive light, as an "authentic voice" of the respective migrant community and a response to its special needs. It is widely assumed that migrant media will almost naturally have a local community focus, instead of addressing their audience as extensions of a "homeland" audience the way that media imports do. Migrant media are expected to provide migrants with a mass-mediated forum of self-representation that reflects their needs and interest by virtue of being "their own" (Cottle 2000; King and Wood 2001).

The early beginnings of foreign-language media in Germany were informed by a very different agenda. Foreign-language radio programs for so-called guestworkers were initially instituted in the West German public service domain of broadcasting in order to facilitate their insertion into the labor market. Labor migrants had to be acquainted with their German environment, with formal rules and informal expectations that they would encounter during and after work. The radio programs also featured music and information from "back home" as an antidote to homesickness. The questions of who was to produce such foreign-language programs and whether or not the positions articulated in these programs represented the opinions and interests of the respective labor-migrant population were initially deemed irrelevant. With regard to the labor migrant population in West Germany, the aim was to provide educative services, information, and entertainment, and certainly not to provide them with a "voice."

This question came to the fore only during the 1980s, a decade that witnessed not only the crumbling of the public service broadcasting monopoly and the rapid increase of radio and television channels at local, federal, and national levels, but also a shift in political discourse toward the recognition of (West) Germany as a multicultural society (Bloomfield 2003). With the commercialization of broadcasting and new communication technologies that multiplied the channels of mass communication, new spaces for "ethnic programming" outside of the public service domain opened up. The question of representation became an issue within public service broadcasting as well, with increasing calls for the inclusion and promotion of immigrant and ethnic minority journalists in German media institutions, and for an "ethnic point of view" as a contribution to wider German public debates. This went hand in hand with an increasing presence of ethnic minorities—most often second- or third-generation descendants of labor migrants—in programs on private channels, as characters in soap operas, as guests and moderators of afternoon talk shows. In the cultural politics of representation, this marked an important moment for the symbolic construction of German society: young people of Turkish origin could for the first time appear on television to talk about relationship problems, hairdos, and the like rather than having to comment solely on their identity as Turks in Germany. By including ethnic minority youths in staged studio debates, however much choreographed, private channels began to break with the engrained broadcasting practice of (re)presenting migrants or people with migrant backgrounds only when ethno-cultural difference is at issue.

Together with the increasing inclusion of ethnic minorities as participants in mass-mediated public debates went the much less debated conviction that immigrants or ethnic minorities are best serviced by programs they produce themselves. Programs for migrants should be produced by migrants, thereby guaranteeing that they reflect their needs and concerns. If having an immigrant background authorizes the statements of journalists as an ethnic minority point of view in the mainstream German media, the particular "representativeness" of ethnic broadcasters is all the more taken for granted in the production of programs for ethnic minority audiences. Policymakers across Western Europe regard migrant media production as a way to articulate and defend ethnic minority identity, but also as a chance for migrant groups to "speak for their own community" in the national public spheres of their countries of residence (Frachon and Vargaftig 1995). Such views are backed up in most of the academic literature on ethnic minority media from a variety of disciplines and theoretical traditions (Husband 1994; Riggins 1992).

This study will show that the assumptions shared in European policy discourses and many academic studies regarding the ability of ethnic minorities to represent themselves, and to use mass media as tools for "cultural preservation" or for the "defense of identity," are deeply problematic. While almost always informed by the well-meaning intent to empower disadvantaged minorities, the dominant debates on ethnic media fail to ask how the "voices" of minority communities actually come into being. As the following chapters will demonstrate, a closer look at the media articulations of Turkish migrant producers in Berlin reveals a baffling variety of competing migrant "voices." All of them claim to authoritatively speak for a constituency which in the dominant parlance of Western European integration politics features quite unproblematically as "the Turkish community." While some of these "voices" enjoy the support of German political institutions and are, as I will show, partially constructed through them, other migrant articulations constitute a major embarrassment to the proponents of minority media access. Among the former, we find Turkish producers at Berlin's public service radio station Radio MultiKulti, who produce programs for an enlightened and self-avowedly "multicultural" audience of Turkish Berliners. Most prominent among the latter are the Turkish Islamist television producers at Berlin's open access channel OKB, whose amateur productions regularly incense viewers and the city's parliament alike.

Approaches to ethnic and migrant media that do not critically examine the representational claims of minority media articulations cannot make sense of the diversity of Turkish migrant broadcasting in Berlin. Neither can they claim to seriously advocate the empowerment of subaltern immigrant minorities: who exactly is to be empowered, for what purpose, and by what means? There is a dearth of serious investigation and research on specific migrant media practices, and on the conditions under which migrant media operate (Sreberny 2001). Instead, many proponents of ethnic and migrant media remain content to discuss minority empowerment in rather abstract terms, presupposing the existence of homogeneous immigrant "communities" that are simply waiting for a chance to raise their voices. Such assumptions are pervasive not just in academic discourses, but also in the political and institutional environment within which ethnic minority media have developed in Germany over the past decades. It is therefore important not just to criticize the presupposition of authentic minority voices as instances of "wrong thinking,"[8] but to reveal how this thinking operates as an integral part of multicultural policymaking and political discourses in Germany. As will be seen, such assumptions have shaped decisions pertaining to the licensing of radio and television projects, the philosophy of public service broadcasting for immigrant groups, the feeding of satellite television into the Berlin cable system, the policies of open access channels, and the political debates on integration that conceptualize Berlin as a multicultural or cosmopolitan city.

THE TRANSNATIONAL AND THE LOCAL

Apart from exploring the vexed problems of minority representation and the "voices" that come to be constructed in migrant media practices, this study also draws attention to their transnational dimensions. While dominant academic and political debates on minority media conceive of immigrant populations almost exclusively as ethnic minorities, the analysis of Turkish-language media in Berlin reveals the importance of cross-border ties and orientations that link migrants to people and institutions, conflicts, and debates in Turkey and beyond. The neglect of migrants' transnational and diasporic affiliations in Western European integration discourses and ethnic media policies is often deliberate: the aim is to integrate migrants at their place of residence and to encourage local identifications. As will be seen in the discussion of broadcasting strategies at Radio MultiKulti, migrant identification as part of the multicultural mosaic of Berlin is regarded as evidence of successful integration, whereas orientation toward Turkey is seen as "backward" and politically undesirable.

Expedient as the neglect of transnational and diasporic orientations in migrants' lives might be, it is politically short-sighted and keeps us from understanding the actual complexities of migrant media production. The production of migrant programs is implicated not only in the formation and representation of an ethnic minority community that is part of the "multicultural" city Berlin but also in wider networks and discursive formations that pertain to two different nation-states and sometimes beyond. The local dimensions of migrant media are nevertheless important, and will be discussed at different levels: in the context of a discourse of locality that is central to multiculturalist policies in German broadcasting and the arts, in the context of cultural hierarchies and dominant schemes of classification that prevail in Germany and Turkey respectively, and in the context of migrant cultural practices that have local, national, and transnational dimensions.

At a time when not just anthropology but many academic disciplines resound with talk of the global, of transnationalism and border-crossing flows and diasporic formations, it is worth thinking through the implications for the local. As Anna Tsing has argued in her analysis of "social science globalisms" and their charisma, the local is often unproblematically invoked as the "stopping point of global circulations" in such discourses, where space easily falls into place, and becomes bounded and particular (Tsing 2000). Whereas "the global" is thought of in terms of movement, the local appears as a fixed location, a place of stability, tradition, and secure identity. Such dichotomies preclude the analysis of how places are made and imagined in particular localities, and how they are articulated with wider spaces and flows (Massey 2005; Morley and Robins 1995). Just as important, they also preclude an analysis of how the local is invoked in what Tsing calls "ideologies of scale" that relate to cultural claims about the local and its appropriate place and function in the world. Such an analysis is crucial for an understanding of the conditions under which migrant broadcasting operates in Berlin.

In chapters 2 and 3, I argue that contemporary German multiculturalist discourses and policies that impact migrant broadcasting in Berlin rely on "the local" as an ideology of scale. The success or failure of the desired social and cultural integration process is seen to hinge upon the degree to which migrants can be turned into locals. Given the discourse of locality associated with migrant cultural production, local broadcasting activities are assumed to promote and at the same time be an indicator of the local affiliations and affective ties that bind immigrants to the multicultural social formation. The "local" is therefore not only a descriptive term that designates the geographical focus of this study, it is a key concept that needs to be analyzed with regard to its ideological implications in the media representations of Turkish migrant culture and identity in Germany. Chapter 4 takes the discussion of locality to another domain of policymaking in Berlin, and examines the consequences of the ideological link between ethnic minorities and local sociocultural diversity for immigrant artists in the city.

With a focus on "migrant voices" linked to the locality of Berlin, this book at first sight appears to continue traditions within anthropology that focus on the local and on subaltern cultural practices as both context and topic. Yet, my study of Turkish migrant broadcasting in a single European city takes the local as well as the marginality of migrant media "voices" as points of departure in order to investigate both questions of scale and of dominant power relations that shape media practices and representations. The concept of the local will not only be problematized as the taken-for-granted scale for subaltern oppositional practices, it will also be examined as both ideological trope and as a factual context for transnational hegemonic interventions.

By addressing the politics of migrant cultural production at local, national, and transnational levels, the anthropology of migrant media can provide both challenges and new impulses to the existing anthropological literatures on national media cultures and indigenous media production. The focus on how migrant media production is mobilized to represent and speak for ethnic minorities can provide a new perspective on specific politics of nation-building and national cultural formation. These politics have been admirably explored elsewhere through a focus on media production that is placed at the symbolic center rather than at the margins of national cultural life (for example, Abu-Lughod 2005; Mankekar 1999; Spitulnik 1998). Yet, the marginal struggles of Turkish migrant broadcasters reveal much about the contemporary project of German nation-building that could not be glimpsed from an engagement with mainstream media production alone.

The anthropological literature on indigenous media production has mainly addressed it as a particular form of local cultural activity in community contexts of "first peoples" (Ginsburg 1991, 1993; Michaels 1994; Tini Fox 1993; Turner 1990, 1991, 1992). As in the literature on ethnic media, this activity has primarily been conceptualized as a sign of vitality and opposition on the part of locally rooted cultures against the obliteration of national or even transnational influences. Yet, anthropologists have also taken note of contrary evidence that complicates the notion of authentic cultural (re-)production. Research on indigenous media production has noted the influence of dominant media environments that often define what is to qualify as indigenous cultural production (Ginsburg, Abu-Lughod, and Larkin 2002). Asking about both the ideological construction of the local and the implication of national and transnational influences in local practices, this study can contribute to a critical contextualization of locality and discourses of nativity.

An anthropology of migrant media can further explore the connections between ethnic and diasporic/transnational media practices. While these have developed as two distinct fields of inquiry, this study shows that media activism that has been politically or academically labeled "ethnic" might well have transnational or diasporic dimensions. On the other hand, it is worth considering diasporic media not just in terms of cross-border flows, but also within the context of nation-state policies that might consider diasporic media producers as ethnic minorities only. Thus, Kurdish amateur producers at Berlin's open access television station would love to broadcast material produced in other parts of Europe, but are prevented from doing so by broadcasting regulations that are to protect "local" content.

Positionings

An awareness of the transnational dimensions of migrant broadcasting crucially depends on understanding the cultural frames of reference, histories, networks, and politics that inform local broadcasting practices from "elsewhere," most significantly from Turkey. Had I not lived in Turkey prior to beginning fieldwork in Germany, I would have missed and certainly not understood most of the manifold cultural, social, and political references to Turkey that pervade Turkish broadcasting in Berlin. Focusing on the cultural production of Turkish-language broadcasts in Berlin, the material I present and my analysis of it constantly move beyond the single city context within which it unfolds. Chapter 5 in particular deals with the challenge that migrant broadcasting activities pose to the Turkish state, and prompting state responses at a transnational level in return. Since much of migrant broadcasting in Berlin comments upon political developments in Turkey, it is important to outline the national terrain of cultural and political conflict that they are referring to.

This study can thus best be described as a case of what George E. Marcus has termed a "strategically situated single-site ethnography" (Marcus 1995). While my object of analysis is based in a single city, it is crucially embedded in a multisited context. Awareness of the multiple frames of reference and transnational connections that migrant broadcasters draw upon in their work enables in turn a different perspective on the multicultural politics of integration in Germany. The political strategy of addressing migrants as locals and encouraging local identifications can be seen not just as a form of misrecognition regarding transnational attachments, but as a form of sometimes deliberate intervention against apparently competing loyalties and seemingly "imported" conflicts (Østergaard-Nielsen 2003).

I embarked upon fieldwork as a nonimmigrant female German student with affiliations to an American university and some experience of having lived in Turkey. My status as a nonimmigrant German aligned me with the dominant "unmarked majority" against which immigrants from Turkey and their descendents have been positioned as *Ausländer,* foreigners. This alignment shaped a priori the kinds of relationships I could establish in the field, giving me access to a certain "cultural capital" (in Bourdieu's sense, 1984) as well as introducing expectations and power dynamics that determined in many ways my encounters with people, organizations, and institutions.

At times, I benefited from the complicity that was assumed particularly in German institutional contexts when I spoke with policymakers and broadcasting officials, but also when talking to Turkish secularists and modernists who expected me to share a certain worldview. The former expected me to approach topics with a disinterested objectivity that those with a Turkish background could never be expected to muster, while the latter assumed that I must share the alleged average German's discomfort at watching Islamist "preachings" on television. This positioning was of course also highly significant in my work with immigrant producers, who were understandably asking themselves, and who asked me directly on many occasions, about the potential dangers and benefits of providing me with different kinds of information. This has particular relevance for the context of open access broadcasting at Berlin's Open Channel (OKB), where many immigrant producers were aware of, or assumed, negative public and institutional attitudes toward their work. Many of them challenged me to think about the political implications of my work, and weighed the dangers of talking to me against the potential benefits. I was an outsider, a disinterested observer, and a commentator only in a representational, highly politicized sense. Over the course of fieldwork, I realized—at times very uncomfortably so—that I was myself intervening and mobilized to intervene in the representational politics of Turkish broadcasting: by acting as a journalist for different media projects, as an academic imbued with the power to speak with a qualified authority about matters of culture, or as a representative of a wider German public, in need of enlightenment with regard to, for example, Islam when I was invited as a studio guest on television.

"Participant observation" thus meant, in the context of my research project, increasing involvement in the very politics of representation that I tried to analyze, and this book itself will become—and to some extent already is—part of these politics. In the early stage of fieldwork, I conducted formal interviews with broadcasting and immigration officials, consulted archives, and traced internal papers as well as official publications pertaining to migrants and broadcasting. I became more closely involved with producers when I began to work as an intern and freelance journalist for different broadcasting projects, and participated in the production of media representations of migrant life in the city and beyond. To start my work with amateur producers at the Open Channel, where the politically most "problematic" and marginal Turkish-language programs were being produced, turned out to be a fortuitous choice. I contacted the producers of all Turkish-language programs via the OKB in writing, explaining in Turkish and German about my research and asking them for an interview. Almost all of them—twenty-seven out of thirty-two—replied and readily agreed to meet with me. Thus, for the first six months of my fieldwork, I was busy watching OKB programs, and visited amateur producers at the Open Channel studios, at mosques, at *cem evis*,[9] or most often at their homes. Some of them I visited repeatedly, witnessing live broadcasts in the studio or recordings elsewhere, and sometimes also appearing as a guest on their programs. Only the most pertinent part of the extensive material gathered in these contexts could be included in this book.

While I openly stated that I was interested in talking to all kinds of Turkish-language broadcasters across political and religious divides, in the course of fieldwork my activities were met with increasing disapproval on almost all sides of the "cultural camps" I was dealing with. Once they had explained their positions and aims to me, my assumed political innocence could no longer figure as an excuse for my crossing of different divides. As I began to be known in the relatively small world of Turkish-language broadcasting in Berlin, my engagement with different broadcasting projects constituted and was eventually perceived as a form of alignment that made it increasingly difficult to "cross lines" again as a disinterested observer from an "outside" position with no knowledge of Turkish politics. I was no longer assumed not to know the difference between "Turkish migrants" and "migrants from Turkey," for example.

While in this book I will often use the term "Turkish migrants" to speak about people involved in the production of Turkish-language broadcasting and their audiences, it is important to note that the use of this term is highly contested. Its contested dimension leads right into the heart of the problematic that will emerge with greater clarity below: at issue in the use of the term is the difficult relationship of migrants to the symbolic community of the nation and the states that claim to represent it. To equate migrants from

Turkey with Turkish migrants is to adopt the political logic of the Turkish state, which argues that there is no room for ethnic difference within its territorial borders and its diaspora of citizens living abroad. Many of those with a migrant background from Turkey refuse to be called "Turkish," even if they hold Turkish citizenship. For them, Turkishness evokes the history of violent suppression that ethnic minorities have endured in Turkey. Instead, they might describe themselves as "stemming from Turkey," as Kurdish, or as Anatolian, to name the most common alternative identifications.

With regard to the German context, to speak of Turks similarly runs the danger of replicating dominant schemes of ethnic classification that see migrants from Turkey and their descendants as eternal "foreigners" (*Ausländer*), regardless of their citizenship status. "German Turks" or "Turkish Germans" are terms that are becoming increasingly common, but are by no means endorsed by all of those concerned. Thus the term "Turkish" renders invisible in its ethnic use all those who have a Turkish passport but do not identify politically as Turks, and in its formal political use all those former Turkish nationals who have adopted German citizenship, as well as their descendants, who increasingly are born with it. I therefore prefer to speak of Turkish-language broadcasting rather than Turkish broadcasting as the main focus of study in this book, and hope that the detailed discussion in the following chapters will reveal the complexities of the term "Turkish migrants" to an extent that will permit me to nevertheless use it as a concept referring to all immigrants from Turkey and their descendants residing in Germany. Young people of Turkish background in fact increasingly resent being referred to as immigrants or migrants, even if qualified in terms of generation. To label them as second- or third-generation migrants describes them in reference to the first generation, and prioritizes "arrival" over the fact of their having been born and raised in Germany. Since the turn of the millennium, young artists and intellectuals with a family background from Turkey increasingly refer to themselves as "postmigrants," a term that retains the connection to a prior migration event, but at the same time emphasizes a distance. I will occasionally use this term when describing the distinctive position and activities of younger people with migration backgrounds.

Open Questions

The work I present here opens up many questions that it leaves unanswered. As a contribution to media anthropology, it does not reveal much about how the broadcasting activities of producers constitute part of their daily lives and other forms of cultural activity not geared toward public representation. Had I become more intimately involved with a certain group of producers, I might have been able to better situate media production as a particular form of political cultural activity in the complexity of migrants' lives both locally and transnationally. Instead, I have focused on the politics of cultural struggle over the meaning of migrant identity and life in Berlin, exploring its conflictual dimensions. Limiting myself to a single production context would have presented the danger of missing an essential fact that characterizes Turkish-language media production in the city: its profoundly referential character.

Much of Turkish migrant media production is intended to intervene in what its producers see as certain political, social, and cultural fields that have an impact on migrant audiences. Most producers are acutely aware of the dominant positions that shape these fields, and thus intentionally model their work of representation and education as a response to these positions. It is therefore important—whether one approaches these responses as a form of public dialogue or as part of a cultural struggle over representation—to see them as interrelated and to try and explain what characterizes their interrelations. In order to understand why, for example, certain Islamic positions are broadcast on Berlin's Open Channel instead of public service or commercial stations, it is necessary to analyze the patterns of dispersal that link specific media representations to particular institutional locations in the city. These patterns of dispersal have everything to do with the conflicts and cultural hierarchies that intersect in the lives of migrants both locally and transnationally.

While it might have been possible to illuminate those conflicts and hierarchies from the vantage point of the complexity of everyday life as it is lived by one particular social and political group of migrant broadcasters, I was better positioned to cross the lines that divided different groups of broadcasters and talk to many, though not all of them. The so-called Kaplan group in Germany, whose founder Cemaleddin Kaplan declared himself Caliph[10] and advocated the violent struggle for an Islamic state in Turkey, has isolated itself even from other Turkish-Islamic groups and keeps all contacts with "nonbelievers" to a minimum. My written request for an interview was met with a swift and polite refusal. The broadcasters of the cable television project TFD, Türkisches Fernsehen Deutschland, did not explicitly refuse to talk to me, but kept me in a state of waiting without ever finalizing a date for a meeting. Affiliated with Millî Görüş (National View), the European branch of the Islamic Fazilet Partisi (Virtue Party) that has been outlawed and regrouped in Turkey,[11] the broadcasters had reason to be suspicious of German journalists who they felt had misrepresented them as extremists in the past. At the point at which I contacted them, I had already begun to work for Radio MultiKulti, a station arguably less than sympathetic to political Islam. However, other broadcasters active at the Open Channel who were affiliated with Millî Görüş mosques or sympathetic to their positions readily talked to me, so that almost all of the cultural-political "camps" that are engaged in politics of cultural struggle in Turkey as well as in the migration context were represented in my interviews.

Another absence in this study concerns the actual audiences of the migrant broadcasting discussed here. Since the 1990s, cultural studies approaches and media anthropology in particular have emphasized the importance of studying "reception" as an active cultural engagement with media that is itself a signifying practice (Ang 1989; Dickey 1997; Ginsburg 1991; Spitulnik 1993). The strict analytical separation of media production and reception as more or less unrelated cultural activities can itself be traced back to the specific historical development of mass media that have rendered these processes hardly interactive. In the history of Western European mass media, control over production and circulation has been associated with state or religious elites (Eisenstein 1980). The relatively young broadcasting media of radio and television were in most countries initially controlled by the state. Production was in the hands of professional specialists, and communication was until quite recently seen as a one-way flow of information, education, and entertainment.[12] This unidirectional dissemination could not guarantee how audiences would make sense of what they received, but their active intervention was limited. New communication technologies related to the Internet and digital television promise to strengthen the input of audiences, allowing them to "communicate back" and directly influence the production of media representations. In the traditional domains of radio and television, the "feedback possibilities" are still generally rather small, with the notable exception of open access broadcasting.

While audiences by and large cannot directly intervene in the production of programs and are not known in detail to producers, they do figure importantly in production activities as imagined entities, measured statistically in ratings, through representative sampling methods, or through "letters to the editor" (Das 1995). From a theoretical perspective that considers the contexts of production and reception to be important dimensions of mass media programs, any neglect of one of these dimensions therefore has to be qualified.

While certain instances of "reception" and audience response to migrant producers will be discussed in this book, few generalizable statements on migrant audiences can be deducted from them. Little will be said in terms of statistical information on viewers or listeners, in terms of ethnographic description of media uses among audiences, or in terms of audience statements about Turkish-language programs. The reasons for this neglect are partly methodological: statistical information such as ratings tends to be gathered for marketing purposes. Since the bulk of Turkish-language programs produced in Berlin tends to be of a noncommercial character or small in scale, broadcasting projects have little incentive and options to produce information on their audience as a marketable product to be sold to potential advertisers. For a single researcher, it is simply not realistic to embark on such a project.

However, this study does not ignore the question of the audience: it is the audience as an imagined entity that figures prominently in the production work and program results that form the center of attention here. Producers of mass media—media that are obviously intended for public consumption—are deeply concerned about the reach and possible impact of their programs. The potential size, composition, and response of their audience is a constant issue to be considered, and significantly shapes the production process. It is in the producers' own conceptualizations of the migrant population as a distinct kind of audience with specific needs and expectations, and in the forms of address and representation they employ in their programs, that alternative and often conflicting visions of community and identity emerge with particular clarity.

2

The History of Broadcasting for
Migrants in Germany

> I know lots of young people, when they hear that jingle from
> Radio Cologne they start shaking! Because when they were
> kids and that music came on, everybody had to be quiet
> and listen to the Turkish program. I'm traumatized, too.
> At nine P.M., that was it! The end! The kids couldn't go on
> playing, you either listened or were sent to bed. Just imagine,
> all the Turkish households must have come to a standstill.
> That was a true mass medium back then.
>
> —Zonya, freelance journalist and second-
> generation immigrant from Turkey[1]

The development of mass communication technologies and the breakdown of broadcasting monopolies in many nation-states have greatly increased the media options of immigrant audiences all over Western Europe, and particularly for migrants from Turkey. Before privatization and the advent of satellite technologies, public service broadcasting was the main and almost only source of programming in migrants' native languages in Germany. As of the turn of the millennium, a large part of foreign-language programs produced in the country still emerged from public service broadcasting. However, the classical rationale for foreign-language programs in the public service domain has been called into question by the transformations that have taken place over the last three decades. Old arguments that justified these programs as "orientation help" and a "bridge to home" no longer hold. As the former guestworkers have turned into ethnic minorities, broadcasters have reconceptualized the mission and responsibility of public service broadcasting toward immigrants and the "multicultural society" as a whole. This shift reflects the changing political logic by which migrants have been discursively transformed from "guestworkers" to "foreigners" and then into "ethnic minorities," marking their gradual emergence as a problematic group that has to be integrated into society and into the German nation.

Turkish-Language Media in Berlin

In the early days of labor migration, Berlin's migrant population was starved for mass media offerings in Turkish, with very limited airtime on public service radio and only an occasional program on German television. Print media such as daily newspapers from Turkey had become available during the 1970s, and remained until the mid-1980s the main source of home country information for the migrant population. However, print media were (and still are) used by migrants from Turkey to a much lesser extent than in the nonmigrant population, and circulation numbers have been steadily declining since the 1990s. In the case of visual media and television consumption, the extent and intensity[2] of use has greatly increased (Zentrum für Türkeistudien 1992, 1997). As Gunnar Roters described the situation in his study of the Turkish video market during the 1980s, the emergence of video technology led to a booming commercial sector in Germany, with migrants renting or buying tapes of material imported from Turkey (Roters 1990). Migrants are also credited with having introduced video technology to Turkey, buying VCRs in Germany and bringing them to relatives "back home" on their annual summer vacations.

In Berlin, the 1985 appearance of the first Turkish-language television channel in Western Europe, TD-1 (short for Türkisch-Deutsches Fernsehen), caused an immediate slump on the video market. The founder of the channel, Atalay Özçakır, had made his fortune with renting and selling tapes on the Turkish *Bazar* in the West Berlin neighborhood of Schöneberg, housed in an old subway station aboveground that once led (and now leads again) into East Berlin. He had also acquired the broadcasting rights to a large number of Turkish and Indian films that TD-1 later became known for. Turkish migrants signed up for cable access at a much higher rate than the rest of the Berlin population, and the channel became a moderate commercial success. Its main source of revenue was and continues to be advertising from small Turkish-owned and -operated businesses that have sprung up all over the city, but particularly in those areas with large migrant populations. It is the small to middle-sized Turkish businesses that provide the advertising revenue for TD-1 and several other commercial broadcasting projects in Berlin. Not only can advertisers be sure to reach their target audiences (though increasingly less so, due to the competition from imported channels), TD-1 offers advertising time for only a fraction of the price that advertisers would have to pay at other television channels. Television advertising is generally far out of reach for the small businesses represented on TD-1, but due to the very low operating costs of the station, prices can be kept moderate.

The German business world has also discovered migrant populations as social groups with increased buying power, and has begun "ethnic marketing," targeted particularly toward Turkish migrants (Çağlar 2004). Corporations like the German Telecom advertise in European editions of Turkish newspapers such as *Hürriyet, Sabah,* and the like and air commercials on television stations such as TRT-International and Kanal D. They also give their business to locally produced media like TD-1 or the more recent radio station Metropol FM, on air in Berlin since 1998. A number of ethnic advertising agencies has sprung up, claiming special cultural expertise and the ability to mediate between German companies and Turkish customers. Their approach is exemplified by a German-language advertisement in the Turkish Yellow Pages of 1999, placed by BEYS Marketing and Media GmbH and directed toward German companies:

> The right tone for your advertising—the market potential of the Turkish population in Europe is growing continuously and has become an important issue in the media. Many companies have realized the importance of advertising in ways appropriate to their targeted audience. But a simple linguistic translation of communicative content can by no means do justice to such efforts. We are a young, dynamic team of creative communication professionals that is up to the task. Our German-Turkish background has provided us with the right sensibility toward our fellow countrymen. In close cooperation with you, we develop the right strategy and find the right solutions in order to reach Turkish customers successfully. (İş Rehberi 1999, 227)

Statistical evidence of the need for German companies to concentrate on ethnic advertising was provided in 1994 by a much-noted survey published by the marketing company IPA Plus, depicting the Turkish migrant population as avid consumers with a preference for Turkish-language media (IPA Plus 1994). In the wake of this survey, large companies such as the car manufacturer Mercedes-Benz did their own research and started advertising campaigns that targeted Turkish audiences (Kern 1996).[3] The discovery of Turkish migrants as consumers and target audiences for advertising has thus made Turkish-language broadcasting for migrants commercially viable, particularly in Berlin, where the largest audience for advertising is concentrated. Yet, a different kind of reasoning had already led to the emergence of Turkish-language programs before the introduction of private broadcasting in the 1980s, and this reasoning continues to inform political decisions and institutional practices that support a wide range of noncommercial programming for migrants in the city.

Early Beginnings

The building of the Berlin Wall not only brought large numbers of labor migrants from Turkey to Berlin, Germany's division also prompted the start of foreign-language programming in the public service domain of broadcasting. The event, and the ensuing confrontation between the Western Allies and Soviet forces, caused great concern among the West German labor migrant population, even prompting some to return to their home countries in fear of another war. West German politicians and broadcasting officials responded:

> Back then it was realized that the foreign workers, unfamiliar with the German situation, interpreted political situations differently, sometimes wrongly, and that therefore, a particular need for informational foreign-language broadcasts arose. (Rissom et al. 1977, 20)

Only two months later, the public service broadcasting corporation of the Saarland region started the *Mezz'ora Italiana,* a half-hour radio program broadcast each Saturday. Two other regional broadcasting corporations followed later that year with radio programs for Italian workers. Greek and Spanish broadcasts were begun in 1962, and a Turkish program produced in Cologne started in 1964. That same year, it was decided at a meeting of public service broadcasting corporations to expand programming for the largest groups of foreign nationals, and to broadcast the programs produced by certain regional corporations in other regions as well.[4] Given the federal structures of public service broadcasting, regional corporations with large migrant populations within their area of transmission were the most active, such as the Bavarian BR and the West German broadcasting corporation WDR in Cologne. In his presentation of "guestworker programming" in a public service broadcasting yearbook, a WDR official acknowledged that the Berlin Wall and its aftermath prompted broadcasters to consider the broadcasting needs of labor migrants. As he stated, "Guestworkers not only stand at the assembly line or sweep the streets, they also try to understand their new surroundings" (Rotter 1969, 96). The migrants needed someone to explain conditions to them, he concluded, and preferably, this should be done by German public service broadcasters.

By 1961, others were trying to give explanations as well. Eastern Bloc countries had in fact taken the initiative in producing radio programs targeting the labor migrant population in the young Federal Republic of Germany. Radio Prague was addressing Italians and Spaniards, Radio Budapest produced programs for Turks and Greeks. The Cold War thus provided another motive for introducing public service programs for labor migrants: West German broadcasting needed to compete with the "propaganda" from abroad. When the West German side began its public service programs, "There was a veritable war on the airwaves going on, competing for political influence on the guestworkers in the Federal Republic," analysts concluded, with broadcasters trying to provide a "defense against undesired political influences" (Brüning and Nax 1975; see also Diller 1975; Stelzle 1980).

The "war on the airwaves" was of course not only directed at migrant workers. The radio programs aimed at them from the Eastern Bloc were part of a wider effort to influence public opinion in the West. In the reverse direction, radio stations like Radio Liberty and Radio Free Europe were similarly Cold War weapons, broadcasting since the 1950s from Munich and up until 1972 covertly funded by the U.S. Central Intelligence Agency. They were complementing the already existing Voice of America, which had its headquarters in the United States and quite explicitly claimed to be "America's voice abroad." In the divided city of Berlin, the Western radio station RIAS competed with the Eastern Berliner Rundfunk.[5] By 1976, the activities of Eastern Bloc broadcasters had diminished or ceased altogether, due to the lessening of tensions between East and West.

The extent to which political motivations played a role in the further development of foreign-language programming in the German public service domain is difficult to establish. Certainly, the engagement for labor migrants could be justified in other terms as well, most importantly in terms of the general mission of public service broadcasting in the Federal Republic, which required it to reflect a plurality of social groups and interests. This argument gained importance as migrants slowly came to be regarded as a permanent part of German society—though not yet of the nation (Mandel 1995).

The broadcasting system was established under the control of the Western Allies after World War II. In an effort to preclude the political instrumentalization of broadcasting by the state as had happened under National Socialism, the newly founded regional broadcasting corporations were tied to the federal states, the *Länder*. The corporations were financially self-sufficient, self-administered, and had editorial independence within the boundaries of federal broadcasting laws. The different broadcasting corporations established the Association of Public Broadcasting Corporations in the Federal Republic of Germany, known as the ARD.[6]

The foreign-language programs of the ARD were met with great enthusiasm by migrant audiences. They achieved ratings that "regular" German programs could not even dream of, to the delight of broadcasters. One official claimed a unique fact in the history of broadcasting: the number of listeners among Turks and Greeks could almost be equated with the figures given as the official number of labor migrants from the respective countries issued by the Federal Employment Agency (Rotter 1969). A study on labor migrants and mass media commissioned by UNESCO stated that by 1975, still more than 75 percent of foreign workers in the Federal Republic were listening regularly to the ARD programs, about half of them daily (Rissom et al. 1977).

The producers did not have to rely on statistics alone: their desks were flooded with letters from listeners. In 1974 at WDR, for example, the Italian program received about 1,500 letters per month, and more than a thousand arrived for the Turkish editors. Many writers asked for concrete advice on work, health, and housing issues. One ARD official explained that "for many listeners, the daily program is the only place they know they can turn to. They know the staff by name, and they expect them to help" (Coulmas 1975, 87). Letters addressing questions of general concern would often be read and answered in the programs, but most were answered on an individual basis by special staff members. Given this active listener response, editors had a good sense of what their target group wanted to hear, and could plan their programs accordingly. At the same time, they could show the letters to their respective broadcasting corporations as proof that their programs were indeed fulfilling their function as an "orientation help" (Rissom et al. 1977, 29).

While orientation help provided the main motive, the programs served another officially acknowledged function. Building a "bridge to home" (*Brücke zur Heimat*), mainly by informing about events taking place in the sending countries, but also through music, readings, and so on, provided the second main justification and task for foreign-language programming in the public service sector, which was extended to television in 1965. A German producer at the ZDF (Second German Television) program for migrants claimed that initially the programs were nothing but "homesick-consolation and help-providers for the foreign men living in Germany, who sat in their barracks and just waited for a chance to hear an Italian pop-song . . . or see a familiar landscape from back home again" (quoted in Huth 1981, 64). During the first phase of foreign-language programming, broadcasts were thus guided by the attempt to uphold "relatively unreflected" connections with the home country (ibid.).

However, this phase did not last very long. It was soon realized that the representation of home culture, let alone the reporting on current events in the home country, was politically highly charged. With the decision to provide a "bridge to home," public service broadcasting had inevitably entered a dangerous political terrain: foreign governments felt strongly that their subjects abroad should receive only that information from and about their countries that did not "interfere" with their own internal politics. Yet, the producers of foreign-language programs in the German public service context often seized the opportunity to be openly critical of regimes back home (Huth 1981). Several of the sending countries that had signed labor recruitment treaties with the Federal Republic experienced periods of nondemocratic rule: most prominently, the Franco dictatorship, which lasted until 1975, and military rule in Greece, which lasted from 1967 to 1974. While mass media in their respective countries were censored, native journalists working in public service broadcasting had a chance to publicly denounce nondemocratic rule. This oppositional stance was backed up by a mass media culture and broadcasting laws in West Germany that defined broadcasting as independent of the state, and upheld the right to criticize it. Public service broadcasting thus inadvertently facilitated the beginnings of a transnational mass-mediated public sphere in which political opposition could be articulated and broadcast by nonstate actors. As will be shown in chapter 5, such opportunities have been greatly expanded by satellite technologies and new communication infrastructures, but the early *Gastarbeiter* broadcasts in West German public service broadcasting already provided a platform for transnational migrant activism.

The journalist Manuel Moral, who built up the Spanish program at the Bavarian broadcasting corporation BR, was very clear about its political objectives:

> We wanted to get our Spanish listeners who had lived under the dictatorship used to democracy and the exercising of their rights. Of course, for the regime back then . . . our program was "subversive" and "anti-Spanish." . . . We were engaged for a parliamentary democracy in Spain, and were able to thwart all efforts by the Spanish powers to use the Spanish program for their propaganda. (Diaz-Diaz 1989, 18)

The Greek program at the Bavarian broadcasting corporation was similarly engaged against military rule in Greece. But the broadcasters were not immune to political pressures. The German head of foreigner programs at the BR was called to Madrid and asked by the Spanish Ministry of Information to "leave politics aside."[7] In 1971, protests of both Spanish and Greek diplomats led the German Foreign Office (*Auswärtiges Amt*) to contact the Bavarian broadcasting corporation and ask them to discontinue certain programs, since they were seen to "seriously jeopardize the foreign policy and economic interests of the Federal Republic of Germany" (quoted in Lohr-mann and Manfrass 1974, 302).

One year later, the protests reached their objective at least temporarily when the commentary sections were cut out of the Spanish and Greek programs, due to intervention by BR officials. An outcry resulted in the German press, who saw the incident as a tampering with the freedom of the press.[8] In a major German weekly, the editor of the Greek program termed the interventions an attack on the freedom of information protected in the constitution and in German broadcasting laws, and polemically asked whether a basic constitutional right should be sacrificed to the pressure of foreign dictators and German corporate interests (Bakojannis 1972).

The foreign editors finally prevailed in the conflict. But the debate provided support for those who questioned editorial control lying in the hands of foreign journalists. At the WDR broadcasting corporation, responsible at the time for the production of Turkish, Serbo-Croatian, and Italian programs, having a native German as editor-in-chief was justified as a protective measure, with the explanation that "foreign"—especially Turkish—journalists were facing intense political pressures from home governments and emigrant organizations (Coulmas 1975). The Spanish journalist Manuel Moral was an example: he was banned from entering Spain, a ban that was finally lifted one year after Franco's death. This "protective measure" at the WDR in fact meant that a German editor had the last word with regard to the content of programs. However, at this time most of the immigrant journalists at ARD broadcasting corporations were employed as freelance staff (*freie Mitarbeiter*), which meant that editorial control was not in their hands anyway (Brüning and Nax 1975). The Bavarian model was still an exception.

The sending countries could exert greater influence on the television programs produced by public service broadcasters. While foreign-language radio programs that focused on life in the Federal Republic did not rely on program imports, the weekly television broadcasts of the ARD and the ZDF cooperated much more closely with television producers in the sending countries.[9] The ARD program *Your Home—Our Home* (*Ihre Heimat—Unsere Heimat*), produced by the WDR in Cologne since 1965, started as an information program providing mainly news from the sending countries. Initially, only ten minutes were offered daily, addressing a different migrant group each day of the week. Visual material was generally obtained from the state broadcasting corporations of the respective countries. It therefore tended to reflect official positions rather than critical evaluations of current political issues. What is more, the reliance on material from abroad created a dependency that made it difficult or even impossible to utter criticism, Ebers and Erdoğmus charged:

If a commentary is the least bit critical of the political conditions which prevail in a country, that country will tend to react by blocking the delivery of material, and limit or stop the transmission of information. . . . It needs to be stated that the necessities of production and the intertwined nature of interests hardly allow for a critical approach, in fact even prohibit such an approach. (Ebers and Erdoğmus 1975, 11)

In the case of the ZDF series *Neighbors in Europe* (*Nachbarn in Europa*), the reliance on foreign states was even more pronounced: its broadcasts in Italian, Spanish, Serbo-Croatian, Turkish, and Greek were produced entirely in the sending countries. In 1975, the ZDF began to add its own ten-minute information segment intended to offer "orientation help for the stay in the guest-country," as the ZDF yearbook put it. The bulk of material still came from abroad, and tended to reflect the respective government's perspective.

The problems associated with the reliance on state broadcasting finally had to be acknowledged by the ZDF in the early 1980s. The channel was seeking to reduce the reliance on foreign broadcasting corporations, due to the influence that their respective governments could exert on their programs. The ZDF wanted to avoid "political indoctrination" (Koschinski 1986). The discomfort of ZDF officials at the time was in fact related to the Turkish military coup of 1980 and its aftermath, which affected the program imports from Turkey. When the Turkish state television sent film material in which the military leader, General Evren, called on Turks abroad to report regime critics, ZDF editors refused to broadcast it. After Turkish diplomats and immigrant organizations pressured ZDF officials, the material was finally broadcast in March 1981, even if in a "somewhat tempered" version. It took two more years to change the structure of the ZDF program, which now included a German-speaking host who led through the program and more self-produced material that addressed ethnic minority issues in the Federal Republic. These changes were made not just to avoid political influences from abroad, but also in response to the changing conditions of migration.

From Guestworkers to Ethnic Minorities

The oil crisis had already brought labor recruitment to a sudden halt in 1973. Contrary to public expectations, however, the "guests" from abroad did not go home again. Many decided to stay at least temporarily, and brought family members to Germany who had initially stayed behind. By the early 1980s, the composition of the migrant population had changed significantly, and so had the public discourse on labor migration that increasingly defined migrants as a social problem. They were now discussed primarily in terms of "integration' issues, such as the danger of "ghettoiza- tion" in urban neighborhoods, the education problems of the second gen- eration, and the formation of an ethnic underclass (Berger 1990).

Migrants were presumed to have an actual—and potentially danger- ous—impact on German society. It was no longer the "lonely guestworker" that public service programs were addressing. As the original function of providing orientation help seemed somewhat out of date, in the 1980s public service broadcasters sought to adapt their programs to new realities. A study commissioned by a public service research institute that evaluated the German broadcasting landscape for migrants in 1981 came to the con- clusion that broadcasting had an important role to play in realizing integra- tion aims, "however these might be conceptualized" (Huth 1981, 66). Ori- entation help was becoming integration-help, with the aim of preparing migrants for a permanent life in the Federal Republic. Providing migrants with particular kinds of information was no longer a matter of regulating a foreign labor force, but a matter affecting the very fabric of German society.

While the mission to "integrate" migrants suggested a stronger empha- sis on issues related to life in Germany, surveys among migrant audiences indicated that they were much more interested in news and entertainment from the country of origin (Huth 1981; Darkow et al. 1985; Eckhardt 1987). This indication of a potential split between migrant expectations and political objectives in the public service domain had not been much of an issue in the early 80s, when the official government strategy was to en- courage return migration. Migrants' ongoing interest in former home- country affairs was seen as much more problematic by the end of the decade, when the political objectives shifted toward achieving "integration" at their place of residence. As will be shown in the following chapters, transnational orientations toward the country of origin were believed to hinder such integration. In the early 1980s, however, providing migrants with a "bridge to home" in public service broadcasting could still be justi- fied in terms of helping migrants to think about their return.

A director of radio programs at the WDR, Walter Stelzle, stated in 1980 that the "double mission" of foreign-language programs was still valid. Programs at the ARD were on their way to become "a family program for national minorities," yet at the same time, they also responded to the de- mand for more reporting on "home country" issues: "In the spirit of the re- turn movement, all of these issues are of considerable interest to the Ger- man side as well. They therefore have recently . . . received more attention in the programs" (Stelzle 1980, 64). "Home country" reporting was deemed relevant also for the second generation, which became of increasing concern during the 80s. The argument was that young people needed to develop an understanding for their parents' language and culture, and also a national consciousness. Foreign-language programs were thus promoting a particular form of integration for migrants, "without losing a feeling of belonging and a language connection with the country of origin to which many . . . in the end do want to return" (Stelzle 1980, 65).

The political effort to encourage return migration was more or less abandoned by the government in the second half of the 1980s. The migrant population had not shrunk in size, and while the government of the Federal Republic was still refusing to acknowledge that (West) Germany had become an immigration country, the permanence of immigration slowly came to be seen as an established fact in the debates on public service broadcasting for migrants. These were taking a new turn. Starting in 1979, the relatively scarce and spotty quantitative data on the audiences of foreign-language programs were indicating a slow decline of interest. In the face of an obvious diversification of the migrant population and its changing position in German society, the rationale for such programming was no longer as evident as it used to be. With language competence becoming less of a barrier that kept migrants from using German media, a main justification for foreign-language programs was slowly eroding.

The public service broadcasters ARD and ZDF responded by commissioning a large-scale survey that was to determine the current meaning and importance of foreign-language programs for migrants (Darkow et al. 1985). More than 3,000 interviews were carried out all over the Federal Republic, making it the first comprehensive attempt to determine media use among different migrant groups. From a public service perspective, the study came to a comforting conclusion: ratings were declining somewhat, but not dramatically enough to call the programs themselves into question. Migrants increasingly had a better command of the German language, and made more use of German mass media. Also, daily newspapers from countries of origin became increasingly available at West German newsstands. Still, demand for mother-tongue broadcasting was high, just with a different emphasis. Orientation help had become less important, while information from the home country was still in strong demand. The study identified the Turks as occupying a special position among the different labor migrant groups: they were most strongly attached to the public service programs, most isolated in sociocultural terms, and least "willing to be integrated" (Darkow et al. 1985, 54).

The study did not discuss what it would actually mean to integrate migrant populations, and through what kind of programs public service broadcasting could contribute to this process. These issues were taken up more explicitly in the second half of the 1980s, in discussion forums and at conferences that public service broadcasters organized in cooperation with different government institutions. In 1986, the editors of the Italian program at the WDR broadcasting corporation organized a conference together with the Deputy of the Federal Government for the Integration of Foreign Employees and Their Families on the issue of "foreigners and mass media" (Bundeszentrale für politische Bildung 1987). The conference marked an important shift with regard to the concept of integration: integration was no longer a process that concerned migrants alone, but a process that pertained to inter-ethnic relations. It was at this point that German audiences became of concern as well. The first part of the conference was devoted to the increasingly pressing issue of "hostility against foreigners' (*Fremdenfeindlichkeit*), the German euphemism for racist attitudes among the majority population, and to the ways in which German mass media dealt with the "foreigner issue." The second part of the conference was concerned with migrants as a target audience of special public service programs. The underlying assumption was quite clear: integration could only be the result of inter-ethnic tolerance, based on a mutual understanding that public service broadcasting had the duty to promote by providing information for and about the "other." The WDR editors of the Italian program outlined the new challenge:

> In this changed and changing situation, media offerings in the mother-tongue gain importance as a central contribution toward respecting the cultural identity of the minorities and toward promoting intercultural encounters in the receiving country. . . . Teaching tolerance . . . can only be understood and realized as an integrated mission of the German information system and especially of the public-service corporations. . . . Mother-tongue programs, target group programs, and general programs in German should face . . . this new collective challenge, and thus overcome the barriers of an outdated information for and about "guestworkers." (Zambonini and Barbi 1987, 103)

Given the political climate of rising hostility against "foreigners," broadcasters argued that the integrative mission of public service programming could not disregard the German audience in their efforts to teach people about ethnic difference. As a consequence, producing programs *for* "foreigners" and producing them *about* "foreigners" became conceptually less and less distinct in the public service domain. In the domain of television, the magazine-format show *Nachbarn* began to dub or provide subtitles for foreign productions in order to reach German audiences. The rationale for the program had changed. Though *Nachbarn* continued to rely on foreign program imports, director Hans-Heinz Röll defined its new aim as wanting to be "a colorful magazine for the multicultural society," and stated for the so-called foreigner programs in general that they were to

> uncover and fight against tendencies of discrimination and intolerance among the population of the host country, awaken understanding for the difficulties of the host countries, and try to teach respect for the culture of the other in order to enable a harmonious living-together and a mutual cultural enrichment. (Röll 1985, 115)

The ARD program *Your Home, Our Home* followed suit in the course of the 1980s and introduced German subtitles in order to attract German viewers. Apart from the "intercultural" educative aim of this measure, the issue of audience ratings also became of growing concern to public service broadcasters. This had to do with the fundamental transformation of the German broadcasting landscape in the late 1980s. Several landmark rulings by the German Constitutional Court opened the way for private broadcasting in both radio and television (Blumer and Hoffmann-Riem 1992). The transformation of broadcasting structures and new communication technologies brought new competitive pressures for the public service sector (Müller 1990; Nowell-Smith and Wollen 1991). The competition from private broadcasters introduced incentives to streamline public service programs in order to attract larger audiences. Against these pressures, the proponents of foreign-language broadcasting were (and still are) on the defensive.[10] Producers battled against financial cutbacks and unattractive time slots and frequencies.

It was the changing political climate toward accepting (West) Germany's status as an immigration country that provided public service broadcasting for migrants with a new lifeline. In the wake of this change, the concept of "foreigner" had replaced the term "guestworker," a term that continued to exclude migrants from symbolic belonging to the German nation. The cumbersome official concept of "foreign fellow-citizens" (*ausländische Mitbürger*) that now became dominant was a contradiction in terms. Yet its common usage did grant migrants the status of social minorities whose rights had to be protected. This became evident in the Constitutional Court's ruling that public service broadcasting was still needed to ensure "pluralist diversity" in the media (Humphreys 1990). Broadcasters could defend minority programming on the basis of the public service principle that "regional and ethnic divisions in society were to be fully catered to and respected" (Humphreys 1990, 141).

As a result, special public service programs could now be justified in different terms: the migrant population was part of the tax-paying general public which provided the funds for public service broadcasting. They were thus entitled to programs, just like any other social group. And since migrants seemed to lose out in the commercialization of German broadcasting (Becker 1998b), it fell to the public service domain to cater to their programming needs. At a 1988 conference that continued the discussion on "foreigners and mass media" that the WDR had initiated two years earlier, the participants warned against the demise of public service broadcasting. As a representative of the group Turkish Community Germany (*Türkische Gemeinde Deutschland*) argued in his talk, it was precisely this institution that could serve as a model for the multicultural future of Europe, with its integrative aim of building bridges—not just "to home," but now also "between cultures" (Keskin 1989, 62).

Seeking the Multicultural Audience

At the turn of the 1990s, the term "integration" in public service broadcasting gained a new dimension with the fall of the Berlin Wall and the difficult incorporation of the former GDR into the Federal Republic. Political restructuring in Eastern Europe also brought a new stream of immigrants, many of whom could claim German ancestry and thus (under the citizenship laws at the time) immediate rights to citizenship. One year after the borders were opened, public service broadcasters met to continue the discussion on migrants and media, this time with the participation of journalists from the *neue Länder,* the new federal states, as the former GDR came to be called. The title of the conference suggested the new general orientation: *Programme gegen Fremdenfeindlichkeit* (programs against antiforeigner hostility) indicated a turn toward mainstream German audiences, now including those in the East (Kilgus and Meier-Braun 1991). The organizers focused on the recent increase of racism and racist violence, particularly in the former GDR, and stressed the media's responsibility to work against it. A panel discussing the future of foreigner programs in the united Germany identified the most important task as treating foreigner issues in the context of "regular programming." They stated that "reports for and about foreigners need to become a normality, just like the presence of foreign fellow-citizens in daily life" (Kilgus and Meier-Braun 1991, 119).

New statistical data on audience figures that were presented at the conference reassured the participants that the special foreign-language programs instituted for labor migrant groups were still in demand (Eckhardt 1991). Another survey presented at the conference on the media use of Turks in Berlin, however, gave an indication of drastic and imminent changes affecting the media landscape for ethnic minorities in Germany. Gunnar Roters's presentation (Roters 1991) outlined the new developments that had given Turkish-speaking Berliners access to Turkish media outside the public service domain. With the advent of video technology, a large Turkish video market had already come into existence by the early 1980s, providing films and entertainment that public service broadcasting did not offer (Klitzke 1980, 1981). But it was the advent of cable technology and the subsequent start of a private Turkish cable television channel (TD-1) in Berlin that radically transformed the media habits of the Turkish population there. Roters's survey showed that the large majority of Turkish households already had or were trying to obtain access to cable, the main motive being the availability of Turkish-language television (Roters 1991). In cable-television households, the new television channel TD-1 was watched more than any other German channel, public service or private, and the use of foreign-language programs offered by public service broadcasters declined significantly. It was a sign of things yet to come.

At the time the survey was conducted (1989), TD-1 was showing mainly programs taken from the Turkish state television corporation TRT, complemented by its own rather amateur productions and 1970s films from India and Turkey. In mid-1990, TRT was itself given a license to feed its channel TRT-International into the Berlin cable system. This channel, TRT-Int, became available in most regions of Germany with Turkish-speaking immigrant populations. Though available in Turkey as well, it was a channel explicitly created for those in the Turkish diaspora, with the quite explicit aim of tying migrant populations closer to the "home country" (Zentrum für Türkeistudien 1997). The commercial channels that came into existence in Turkey after the state-broadcasting monopoly broke down the following year did not share this political objective (Şahin and Aksoy 1993). Via satellite they soon also became available to migrants in Western Europe. A WDR survey conducted in 1995, again for migrant groups in the federal state of North Rhine-Westphalia, came to the conclusion that 95 percent of Turkish respondents were able to receive at least one channel from Turkey (Eckhardt 1996). Satellite technology has enabled Turkish migrants abroad to receive most of the same channels the inhabitants of major Turkish cities are watching (Aksoy and Robins 2000, 2002). For the migrant population in Germany as a whole, the 1993 survey established figures for cable access at 44 percent, for satellite access at 38 percent. Though not specified, it is likely that the figures for the Turkish group were even higher, and have significantly risen since then.

Already in 1995, the WDR survey states that 47 percent of the Turkish respondents preferred channels from Turkey (Eckhardt 1996). A more comprehensive study for the whole of Germany conducted by the Center for Turkey Studies in 1996 was to examine whether the feared *mediale Abschot-*

tung, media isolation, was actually taking place. It came to the conclusion that almost 40 percent of Turkish respondents watched exclusively Turkish programs on television (Zentrum für Türkeistudien 1997),[11] and others put the figures even higher (Ünüz 1998). For public service broadcasters, the findings were alarming. The 1995 study had asked quite explicitly about the link between media imports and the use of public service migrant programs. Comparing audience ratings for the ARD foreign-language radio programs with the figures from 1990, the study spoke of a "dramatic decline" (Eckhardt 1996). The programs had lost about half of their audience—but disproportionately so among migrant groups well serviced by media imports from the former home countries, Italians and above all Turks. With regard to the Turkish program, the study diagnosed a "veritable deterioration of use" (455). While in 1990, 52 percent claimed to listen daily, that figure had dropped to only 5 percent in 1995.

> While back then the Turks . . . formed the largest audience for the ARD foreign-language programs among the five nationalities, they nowadays rarely make use of them. This is directly linked to the fact that the Turks . . . since the introduction of satellite television programs from the home country are completely fixated on this new media offering. (Eckhardt 1996, 455)

The majority of Turks living in the state of North Rhine–Westphalia had turned away not just from the special public service programs intended for them, but from German broadcasting generally, the study claimed.[12] It concluded that this development was "certainly detrimental to the desired integration of this large national group into German society" (Eckhardt 1996, 461). Other voices echoed this fear. At another public service broadcasting conference in Cologne in 1997, an editor at the WDR Turkish program warned against the "fatal consequences" of the migrant turn to satellite broadcasting. Programs from Turkey, he argued, rarely reported on events that concerned the German lifeworld of migrants.

> It is a strange fact in our much-praised global village that for example the Turks living on the left bank of the Rhine river in Cologne are "informed" about what happens on the other side only through the eyes of journalists in Turkey, 2000 kilometers away. . . . at the thought of what this "isolation" might lead to, observers of the Turkish media simply feel queasy. (Okkan 1998, 14)

Given the increasing importance of transnational media from Turkey, the representations of migrant life in Germany and of the country itself in such media have become of growing interest to German media analysts and integration experts. The Federal Press Office (*Bundespresseamt*), which commissioned the survey on Turkish migrant media use in 1996, also asked for an analysis of the "image of Germany" that television programs from Turkey conveyed. Researchers concluded that very few programs had any connection with Germany or the Turkish migrants living there, and the same held true for the Turkish press. Apart from major news events, the scarce reporting that explicitly dealt with migrant life generally conveyed at best a feeling of loss, sometimes even alienation, in terms of an alleged cultural, religious, and moral distance of migrants from the German majority population (Zentrum für Türkeistudien 1997; see also Heinemann and Kamcılı 2000). Other observers went further, suggesting that some media representations might actually foster negative attitudes among migrants toward German society, and often introduce political conflicts from Turkey that polarize the migrant population.[13]

The increasing marginalization of their programs in terms of viewer and listener interest forced public service broadcasting to respond. Far from concluding that their work had become superfluous, however, broadcasters claimed that there was an urgent need to compete with media imports from former home countries. In order to prevent the feared media isolation that is seen to result from the turn to satellite programs, public service broadcasting had to make a "counter-offer" (Okkan 1998). The turn to media from the respective "home" countries has been interpreted as a sign of the German failure to sufficiently address immigrant populations as an audience (Schweitzer 1998), and in the same vein the authors of the 1996 WDR study concluded that migrants with access to satellite television needed "a lot more media attention from the German side than has been given so far" (Eckhardt 1996, 461).

While the boom of satellite television left public service broadcasters scrambling for their immigrant audiences, events of a different nature in the recently united Germany challenged the integrative mission they were aiming for. A surge of racist violence directed at immigrants, coupled with a political climate of rising hostility, made the ideal of a multicultural society that had been articulated in the 1980s seem like a remote utopia. Therefore, educating the German majority population about immigrant groups and generally furthering intercultural understanding was identified as an urgent task by public service broadcasters. It guided the restructuring of public service programs that had started as foreign-language programming for guestworkers. In the domain of television, a reorientation toward reaching German audiences had already begun in the 1980s. At the ZDF, the program *Nachbarn* began to increase its own productions in German in 1992, and stopped program imports entirely in 1995. By that time, programs were a half-hour long and focused on a single topic, generally having to do with migrant life inside Germany (Jordanova-Duda 1997). In 1998, the program was renamed *BlackRedMulti-Colored* (*Schwarzrotbunt*), transforming the third color of the German flag so as to symbolize the multiethnic and multicultural Germany the program wanted to represent.

The ARD program *Ihre Heimat, Unsere Heimat* was transformed and renamed *Babylon* in 1993. The old title and the *Heimat* concept was seen to be out of touch with the times. Instead of nostalgia for the lost homogeneity and boundedness of the nation that the *Heimat* concept carried with it (Morley 2000; Morley and Robins 1995), the new point of reference for these television magazines was to be the conflictual reality of Germany as an immigration country. Departing from the public service philosophy of objective, nonpartial, and balanced broadcasting, *Babylon* quite explicitly wanted to take sides: as the head of the program, Aysim Alpman, stated at a conference on intercultural television in 1998, *Babylon* wanted to represent minority interests and thus needed to be "one-sided" at times, given migrants' relative lack of power in German society. Unattractive screening times for both programs and limited regional distribution were already an indication, however, that the lobby for "multicultural" television at ARD and ZDF was facing opposition within public broadcasting corporations. By 2002, both programs had been phased out for an alleged lack of audience interest. In the domain of radio broadcasting, similar discussions started in the 1990s on how to adapt the public service foreign-language programs to meet the challenges of satellite imports, new immigration, and increasing racism. Rising numbers of asylum seekers were sensationalized in the tabloid press as a "tidal wave" threatening to submerge Germany. In Rostock, a right-wing arson attack on a building housing asylum seekers was meet with cheers from local bystanders. The racist murders in the West German cities of Mölln and Solingen finally provided the calls for an antiracist, multicultural broadcasting strategy with a new urgency. In Berlin, the SFB public service broadcasting corporation finally received the go-ahead for a new radio station, Radio MultiKulti (Vertovec 1996a). Providing a twenty-four-hour program broadcast on a terrestrial frequency in the city, MultiKulti has the double aim of servicing different immigrant groups and increasing understanding among the German majority population (Busch 1994; SFB 4—MultiKulti 1995). The station's ambitious effort to combine broadcasting for and about immigrants has been widely regarded as a success. Conceived as a "model experiment" in 1993, the station was finally assured permanent funding in 1997. Apart from a positive audience response the station claims to have,[14] it has won acclaim as a unique and innovative approach to intercultural broadcasting and has received numerous prizes, both nationally and internationally.

Similar deliberations to establish a nationwide radio station with a multicultural profile have taken place at the ARD level since 1993. There, too, it was the urge to provide a public service response to the racist violence that set the discussion in motion. Broadcasting officials at the WDR, the large regional broadcasting corporation that has played a major role in foreign-language programming since its early days, suggested integrating the foreign-language programs with German-language programs produced jointly by "foreigners" and "Germans." A commission was formed by the ARD which developed a plan and conception for a new radio station that went by the name Funkhaus Europa (Guglielmi 1999). Inspired by the activities of Radio MultiKulti, the new station was to offer more nuanced foreign-language programs and link them to German-language programs, with a common focus on Germany as the shared center of life and communication (Breuer-Ücer and Zambonini 1996).

When the commission presented its suggestions in 1996, the different regional corporations united in the ARD were unable to agree on even partial reforms (Kammann 1997). While there was a consensus that the current structure of foreign-language programming at the ARD was less and less able to answer to changing conditions of immigration and media use, some regional corporations seemed hesitant to transfer editorial control or financial means for a joint project (Guglielmi 1998). In the meantime, other corporations have begun their own reforms. The WDR, for example, started its own small-scale Funkhaus Europa in September 1998. Initially broadcasting only between 6 P.M. and 6 A.M., the station now offers "multicultural magazines" in German, its traditional foreign-language programs in the afternoon, and evenings with programs from other German and European radio stations. It cooperates closely with Radio MultiKulti in Berlin. The SWR corporation has similarly started a multicultural program for one hour on weekends, using digital technology to broadcast in different languages simultaneously. Other initiatives have begun at local stations outside the structure of public service broadcasting, often in the context of Open Channel broadcasting or so-called citizens' radio (*Bürgerfunk*) (Breunig 1998; Lendzian 1999).

Multiculture

Over the past thirty-eight years, public service programming for Germany's immigrant population has undergone considerable changes. "Public service" in this context has always meant much more than serving the particular broadcasting needs of migrant populations. Broadcasting for and about migrants served different missions at different points in time: its efforts were directed toward countering undesired political influences both internally and from abroad; facilitating the insertion of foreign labor power into the West German economy; offering a "bridge to home" that migrants were expected to cross again; promoting intercultural understanding in the interest of a society increasingly imagined as multicultural; encouraging identification as an ethnic minority; and, increasingly, competing with foreign national and transnational media imports in the effort to strengthen migrants' ties to local or regional communities of residence. Migrant programming in the public service domain has always been linked to wider public debates and historical changes that transformed the conditions of migrant life in the Federal Republic.

The discourse of multiculturalism that has gained ground during the 1990s was initially limited to urban centers with large immigrant populations such as Berlin and Frankfurt, meaning that a community of urban residents could be imagined as being composed of different cultures and ethnic groups. This image did not yet extend to the national community. Being a German Turk or a Turkish German still seemed to be a contradiction in terms. Toward the end of the 1990s, however, the new Social Democratic–Green government coalition publicly acknowledged Germany's having become a country of immigration. Laws were changed to facilitate naturalization and redefine German citizenship, away from its "blood and soil" legacy.[15]

Campaigns were started to encourage immigrants to become German citizens, aiming at the same time at a transformation of consciousness among the nonimmigrant population. In Berlin, public poster campaigns were started in 1989 that stressed the multicultural and multiethnic composition of its population. The most prominent campaign presented portraits of smiling people displaying phenotypically recognizable "ethnic" and cultural differences under the headline "*Wir sind Berlin—Wir sind helle und Dunkle!*" ("We are Berlin—We are bright and Dark!").[16]

The huge posters were shown in subway stations and on a few public busses in the Western part of the city. After the Wall came down, the campaign was quickly extended to the Eastern part as well, "for the first time confronting East Berliners with advertising for an open society," as the press material put it. The later, nationwide campaigns associated with the new citizenship laws similarly portrayed people who would represent stereotypical racialized embodiments of "foreigners" in Germany, under the heading of, for example, *Sie ist Deutsche* (She is German), or *Typisch Deutsch* (Typically German). The office of the national Commissioner for Migration, Refugees and Integration (*Beauftragte der Bundesregierung für Migration, Flüchtlinge und Integration*) uses these poster campaigns to encourage naturalization under the new citizenship laws.

FIGURE 1. 1990s poster campaign, "We are Berlin," initiated by the Commissioner for Foreigners' Affairs of the Berlin Senate. *Reprinted with kind permission of the Commissioner for Integration and Migration of the Senate of Berlin.*

In the year 2000, a nongovernmental political organization, "Germans against Right-Wing Violence" (*Deutsche gegen rechte Gewalt*), started a nationwide, much-acclaimed poster campaign that played on right-wing rhetoric and symbolism. Initiated by a well-known public relations firm and supported by prominent TV stars, politicians, and others, the campaign showed images of young men stereotypically classified as "foreigners" who sported T-shirts with the notorious extreme right slogan: "I am proud to be German" (*Ich bin stolz, ein Deutscher zu sein*). They were displayed in various public spaces in Berlin, such as in subway stations and on billboards.

The organizers were provocatively trying to lay claim to the very symbolic territory of national belonging that so-called foreigners had so far been excluded from, and to—quite problematically—promote a "new national consciousness" that would not be associated with right-wing extremism. The grounds for the imagining of the German nation have definitely shifted, now explicitly incorporating ethnic difference. This has opened up a new symbolic terrain on which ethnic minority claims can be legitimated

FIGURE 2. 2000 poster campaign, "Proud to be German,"
initiated by the NGO Germans against Right-Wing Violence.
Photo by Matthias Koslik for Scholz & Friends.

on the basis of belonging. Thus, while most people with immigrant background from Turkey would still call themselves "German Turks" (*Deutschtürken*) rather than "Turkish Germans," the combination of the two labels
no longer appears as an oxymoron. Rather, it has become thinkable within
the new multicultural imagining of German society that has become official government policy over the past decade.

The root cause of ethno-cultural difference in the context of Western European societies is most often conceived as one of encounter: international

migration is assumed to be responsible for formerly unconnected groups with diverse "cultures" confronting each other, thereby highlighting their differences. Cultural difference is thus understood to preexist the encounter, but is more or less irrelevant as long as the diverse groups that are bearers of different cultures do not coexist and interact in close proximity, particularly within the same nation-state.

Culture in this approach appears as a quality of ethno-national groups that defines them as such, not in relation to other groups. Put in semiotic terms, culture figures as a stable signifier that seems to exist only in relation to the signified—as a "natural isolate," as Ulf Hannerz has put it (Hannerz 2000). People appear to "have culture" or live a "whole way of life" in ways that define them, but do not necessarily distinguish them from one another. Distinction, or cultural difference, is here rather associated with the idea of "culture contact": a secondary phenomenon that in temporal terms always follows and presupposes the prior existence of different cultures as separate and unrelated entities. Migration is the classic mode by which culture contact is deemed to come about, leading at least initially to a kind of "cultural mosaic" in which cultures mix analogous to groups of people (Taylor 1992).

This assumption problematically blurs the difference between the cultural and the social. Yet it is the implicit or explicit starting point for most theories of multiculturalism, whether they conceive of the term as a factual description of a social formation, as an ideology or political goal, as an orientation of public policies, or as a mode of intercultural interaction. Concerned with the recognition and equal treatment of cultural diversity, "multiculturalism represents a kind of corrective to assimilationist approaches and policies surrounding the national incorporation of immigrants," anthropologist Steven Vertovec has claimed (Vertovec 2001). Theories and policies of multiculturalism advocate a kind of migrant incorporation that seeks to leave cultural diversity intact. Consequently, they rarely problematize the production of cultural differences and cultural change that takes place within a social formation, because the starting point of cultural pluralism appears to be the "adding-up" of more or less discrete, preexisting cultures that are spatially relocated and thrown together as a result of migration. This carries with it the danger of an "implicit essentialism," as Ralph D. Grillo has observed, which often haunts both multicultural theory and practice (Grillo 2003).[17]

The problems pointed out by multiculturalism's critics reveal many parallels with earlier debates in anthropology about the concept of ethnicity. In the 1970s, analysts of ethnicity tended to stress "substantive" qualities: like shared kinship ties, language, traditions, and other aspects of culture. But the notion that ethnic units were primarily discrete groups of people that had evolved in isolation from each other had already come under attack within the discipline. Frederik Barth (1956, 1970) had tried to explain the persistence of cultural difference among ethnic groups that share the same environment. He suggested that cultural differences and ethnic identification were not the result of isolation, but more often a product of the interaction between groups. Barth's approach shifted analytical attention from the "content" or "internal constitution" of separate groups to the maintenance of boundaries between them. With such a relational concept of ethnicity, ethno-cultural differences become much more problematic: one can no longer simply regard them as the result of a mixing of formerly isolated or at least unconnected cultures, but rather must consider the possibility of their mutual constitution in a "contact" situation.[18] If the insights of earlier debates in anthropology are taken on board, any analysis of ethno-cultural differences must consider the wider framework and system of classification through which ethnic units and cultural markers are differentially produced and interrelated.

The analysis of labor migration to (West) Germany is a case in point: migrants in the 1960s and 70s did not introduce their cultural particularities into an empty conceptual space. German public discourses concerning their cultural difference and "lack of culture" were rooted in the ideological climate of the postwar "economic miracle" (*Wirtschaftswunder*) that defined the standards of desirable individual comportment, the boundaries between public and private, as well as virtues and vices that were deemed to affect economic productivity, for example, with regard to time management. Fordist production regimes such as David Harvey has described them (Harvey 1990) rendered issues such as "Mediterranean idleness" or "fear of modern machinery" prime topics of discussion, carried out among state experts, employers, and social agencies, but also among the general public. Migrants entered a discursive space in which the category of "Southerner" (*Südländer*) or "Mediterranean" was already defined as culturally and socially different in specific ways: as requiring certain forms of sociability alien to German habits, as an exotic male sexual temptation luring German women, as lacking principles of hygiene, and so on. The cultural particularities introduced by migrants were thus already apprehended within a system of classification that rendered the perceived "differences" to a large extent inferior, morally suspect, and problematic.

More than three decades ago, anthropologist Joan Vincent drew attention to such systems of classification, when she criticized approaches to ethnic identity that defined it simply as multiple and context-bound. Her critique is still highly relevant today. Vincent argued that in order to explain why certain ethnic groups have more power over the definition of their identity than others, or do not appear as "ethnics" at all, it is necessary to pay attention to the conditions of "structured inequality" within the context of polities, and to how they are produced (Vincent 1974). Brackette Williams has more recently expanded upon Vincent's critique, noting that like situationalist and essentialist perspectives on ethnic identity, resource-competition models are unable to explain why 'ethnic" tends to appear as a label for subordinated groups in nonacademic usage (Williams 1989). Attention has to be paid to the question of how modes of competition and struggle between ethnic groups come to be structured, how the ideological riches of such pursuits come to be defined, and how states intervene in such processes.

It is useful to reexamine these critiques for contemporary analyses of multiculturalism, as they highlight problematic assumptions that tend to go unexamined in multiculturalist paradigms. Many conceptions of multiculturalism show parallels to these earlier and still widespread conceptions of ethnicity, particularly when ethnic groups are defined in terms of "essences" or apparently internal qualities such as shared traditions, kinship ties, and the like. The semantic blurring between culture and social group turns group boundaries into boundaries of culture, thus taking as a given that culture will become a basis of group formation and mobilization rather than inquiring about the conditions under which such forms of cultural membership can emerge.

In the case of migrant minorities, it seems to go without saying that differences separating immigrants from the native population are introduced from "outside."[19] As a consequence, the questions of how the standards against which difference is measured come to be developed, and of how ethno-cultural distinctions function in relation to forms of stratification in the "host country," cannot easily be posed. Most debates on multiculturalism in Western Europe focus on how to deal with differences arising as a result of international migration. Yet when ethno-cultural differences are analyzed in relation to the conflictual production of national culture, the "misplaced concreteness" that ethnic groups and nations tend to have in such debates stands revealed (Alonso 1994). Discovering the context of the nation-state as the terrain on which ethno-cultural differences come to be identified, classified, and ranked has allowed anthropologists to denaturalize the concept of ethnicity, and instead move toward an understanding of culture as conflictually produced and linked to power. The reciprocity that many scholars in the 1990s have come to see in constructions of ethnicity and nationalism has opened the way for addressing questions that earlier approaches toward ethnicity left unanswered, namely why "ethnic" often appears as a label for subordinated groups, and how to account for both as-criptive and self-claimed dimensions of ethno-cultural identity. Such a per-spective provides an important tool for criticizing the multicultural para-digms currently dominant in Germany. However, focused on the frame of a single nation-state alone, it fails to explain the transnational dimensions of migrant broadcasting practices.

Migrants represent a very particular kind of minority within nation-states: they are the only type of sociocultural group that originates, so to speak, outside the nation-state.[20] While this fact contributes to their being excluded symbolically (and practically in the case of naturalization laws) from the national community, it also points toward migrants' potential en-gagement with two different nation-states. Multiculturalist positions rarely take the border-crossing dimension of migrants' cultural, social, and eco-nomic ties into account, leaving the nation-state as a focus of common at-tachment unchallenged (Vertovec 2000). Even though immigration is re-garded as the root cause of cultural pluralism in most parts of Western Europe, immigrants are seen primarily as ethnic minorities within a single "society," usually meaning the nation-as-state.

In the (West) German context, the view that insisted on immigrants' belonging to the country of residence rather than to their countries of ori-gin was in fact politically rather progressive during the 1980s, brought forth by the left-of-center opposition against the conservative government's pol-icy of encouraging return migration. However, this perspective also en-couraged a misrecognition or deliberate denial of ongoing and newly forged ties that linked immigrants with the countries from which they had emi-grated. It was even less able to recognize the emergence of transnational and diasporic ties that migrants from Turkey had begun to establish across dif-ferent European nation-states. The former "guestworkers" had become eth-nic minorities, and the subsequent politics of integration explicitly encour-aged migrants' identification with their place of residence.

3

Foreign Voices—
Migrant Representation
on Radio MultiKulti

It is my fourth week of working as an intern for Radio MultiKulti, and one of the editors for the German-language programming has given me an assignment typically given to newcomers: I am to find out what young people have to say about the Loveparade in Berlin, an event that draws millions to dance on the street in a parade of techno music. My assignment is to go out and do a quick survey, asking "young ethnic Berliners" about the Loveparade and what it means to them. My piece is to be run as a trailer in the morning program, with the moderator giving more specific information about the parade. The voices in my trailer have to speak for themselves; no names or special context will be given that could indicate immigrant origin and the like. Get some foreign (*ausländische*) voices, the editor tells me.

I spend a hot summer day out on the streets with my microphone. First, I go to a neighborhood in Wedding, an inner-city district with a high percentage of Turkish residents. I walk up to young people on the street whom I identify as potentially "ethnic," of immigrant background based on their looks, and I ask in German: "What do you think of the Loveparade? Will you go?" Most are eager to answer, and have a lot to say. It is only after having talked to about five people that I come to realize my predicament: Who on earth will identify their authentic and appropriate "ethnic difference," given that almost all the answers have been produced in the local Berlin dialect? Second- and third-generation migrants do not, of course, speak German with a foreign accent. I decide to shelve the project for the day and talk it over with the editor. When I report back on my dilemma the following day, she does not respond immediately, just looks at me with an expression of slight annoyance and amusement. Then she offers a single piece of advice: "But you do know what it is that we're looking for, don't you? So just go get it." I am dismissed, and take to the streets once more.

I get lucky with a few people in front of a shopping center, though they are not particularly young. Opinions about the Loveparade are forthcoming in accented voices. Not enough, though. Eventually, I end up in front of the language instruction center in my own neighborhood, where a friend of mine is attending a "German for foreigners" course. During breaks, the students assemble to smoke in front of the building. No danger of not finding accents there, and my friend and her classmates are eager to help me out. The problem is, most of the students are here for summer courses only. They are tourists rather than immigrants, and thus not exactly the people the trailer is claiming to represent. But the trailer needs to get done, and so I collect a beautiful-sounding assortment of accents, and statements ranging from "I hate the whole thing" to "oh yes, I'll definitely go," just as the editor has requested, in the interest of "balanced objectivity." My friend wants to be included: after all, being young, Italian, and planning to stay in the city, she actually qualifies! I hand her the microphone and she rehearses a sentence she herself has come up with: "Oh no, I don't like the music at the Loveparade, I'd much rather listen to Radio MultiKulti!" Eventually, she has a laughing fit. In the afternoon, I return to the station and cut the trailer, including her statement and subsequent laughter at the very end. One-and-a-half minutes. I inform the editor of where it has been saved in the database, and expect to hear no more about it. The next day, though, I receive praise: the editors had really liked it, especially the laughter at the end.

Learning to produce contributions for the German-language programs of Radio MultiKulti involved internalizing a certain set of standards that makes MultiKulti both similar and different with regard to other public service stations under the common roof of the public service corporation Rundfunk Berlin-Brandenburg (RBB).[1] The ways in which an assignment is composed—how much interview material and sound to use, how to give background information, choose the right statements, and come to a particular conclusion—are quite similar across different stations. In fact, Radio MultiKulti enters its own productions into a database shared by all public service stations in Germany, and productions are often picked up and rebroadcast by other stations. The difference lies, obviously, in the "multicultural" orientation of the station, the very reason and justification for its existence.

"We Speak with an Accent"

Radio programming entails quite distinctive challenges for the production of identifiably "multicultural" broadcasts. As an audio medium, radio cannot rely on visual appearances that are usually central to processes of categorization along ethnic and racial stereotypes. There are no images that could function as indicators of ethnic belonging in the context of radio broadcasting, and so language has to play a central role in signaling ethnic otherness. "We speak with an accent" is a prominent slogan that Radio MultiKulti uses in its promotional material (Vertovec 2000).

The station not only wants to represent immigrants in the sense of broadcasting *about* them, it also claims to give immigrants a voice by involving them directly in production. And it unquestionably does so as far as the foreign-language programs are concerned: the editorial and journalistic staffs of the various foreign-language programs are entirely composed of immigrants. However, these programs target only specific immigrant groups in the city, and are not directly tied into the second mission of the station, which is to contribute to intercultural understanding among *all* inhabitants of the city. German is the *lingua franca* of the station, and necessarily so, given that MultiKulti wants to counter racist and xenophobic attitudes among the German nonimmigrant population. The potential to counter such attitudes was a central legitimizing factor in the political decision to establish the station in the first place, and has been continuously mobilized in the station's efforts to secure permanent funding.

It was after the racist murders in the cities of Solingen and Mölln in 1993 that the often-voiced demand for multicultural broadcasting finally found sufficient political support in the Berlin state parliament (Bünger 1995). A station that could serve as "a forum of integration and communication among ethnic minorities and Germans in the city" (Holler 1997, 15) was seen as an appropriate response to increasing anti-immigrant sentiments and racist violence. "Speaking with an accent" contains an important claim that pertains to the nature of such intercultural dialogue: At MultiKulti, immigrants are to present their own views on all kinds of topics, instead of just being the topic of discussion themselves. The first director of the station, Friedrich Voß, has highlighted the aim as a central aspect of MultiKulti's broadcasting philosophy:

> The magazine parts in the lingua franca German are dedicated to comprehensive information but also to the idea of integration. Above all, the program wants to let foreign moderators and commentators have their say, so that the programmatic stance of a "different viewing angle" is rendered audible as well. (Voß 1996, 6; author's translation from German)

"Speaking with an accent" thus denotes the entry of immigrants as active participants into the public domain. MultiKulti aims not only to reflect multicultural diversity in the city but also wants to act as a forum of intercultural dialogue. Challenging the widespread assumption that cultural differences are private or communal matters whereas public space should remain the domain of the majority culture (Rex 1991; also see Vertovec 1996a), MultiKulti wants to give immigrants a public voice on the airwaves. The "different viewing angle" suggests that the substance of what is focused on is similar to other public service stations: matters of common and public concern, but now seen and discussed from a different, "foreign" perspective.

Creating a shared public space in which different ethnic communities are able to interact, represent themselves, and engage in dialogue was a major concern of "progressive" Western European multiculturalist policies in the 1990s (Frachon and Vargaftig 1995). The public spheres created through public service broadcasting in Western European nation-states was always implicitly linked to "a whole way of life" (in Raymond Williams's [1971] term) in the sense of national majority cultures. Giving a voice to immigrants in public service broadcasts potentially "denaturalizes" the link between public space and this dominant "way of life." An article on Radio MultiKulti published in the German UNESCO journal describes the benefits for members of the dominant majority culture in Germany:

> Listeners should learn to relativize their own German standpoint, gain a foreign perspective on themselves and accept that their own attitudes and behavior have only limited importance. The German-language part is produced with the strong participation of foreign, German-speaking staff . . . . This leads to the questioning of judgments and prejudices, and to the acceptance of different perspectives. (N. N. 1995,177)

It is taken as a given that immigrants will provide a perspective that represents a different viewing angle or foreign view. At Radio MultiKulti, this is rendered audible through the accented voice that inevitably denotes foreignness, approaching the German language and majority culture from elsewhere. The accent—as opposed to making mistakes in the sense of grammatical errors, lacking vocabulary, and so on—is a subtle indication of ineradicable difference, one that has come as close to linguistic and cultural mastery as it can, but remains always a bit off the mark in its sentence melody and pronunciation of words. Ethnic minority moderators in the German-language programs of Radio MultiKulti tend to have an excellent command of German, but the preference is for immigrants whose German retains a "foreign flavor," so to speak.[2]

It is instructive to draw a parallel between "unmarked German," German spoken without accent, and the "unmarked ethnicity" that differentiates those who pass as Germans from stereotypical "foreigners" in everyday life contexts. Even though explicitly racialized categories have disappeared from mainstream public discourses since World War II, the general concepts of "foreigner" and, more recently, "migrant," as used in policy discourses and mainstream German media, implicitly produces and stabilizes a form of German whiteness.[3]

Whiteness has been brought forth as an analytical concept and object of study in order to investigate how structural positions of privilege and power among racialized groups are simultaneously constructed and masked (Frankenberg 1993). Noting that the study of race had been by and large focused on people of color, scholars have focused on the question of how whiteness could become an implicit norm against which racial "otherness" is represented (Dyer 1993, 1997). In the context of radio broadcasting, racial and ethnic differences cannot be seen, they must be heard. In the absence of visual markers, it is the accent that denotes marked ethnic and racial differences on Radio MultiKulti. However, as is to be expected in the course of immigration history, second- and third-generation immigrants are no longer speaking with an accent.[4] It is thus predominantly people who have indeed come from another country, first-generation immigrants, that are mobilized to represent the "multicultural normality" of the city in the broadcasts of MultiKulti.

One reason this is not much of an issue for the station might be that the term "foreigner" (*Ausländer*) is still widely used to describe immigrants and their descendants in Germany. The term, literally referring to people (from) outside the country, functions to exclude immigrants from symbolic belonging to the nation, and has increasingly become a racialized category (Mandel 1994; Räthzel 1990; Stolcke 1995). As such, the term now somewhat paradoxically also refers to descendants of particular immigrant groups who in the course of their lives might have never set foot outside Germany. While the descendants of certain immigrant groups become assimilated to the "unmarked" category of majority Germans, other groups remain outside this category. Prior histories of migration such as the incorporation of Eastern Europeans into Prussia and the early German nation-state have been erased from public memory. The fact that a considerable part of the German population has Polish and other Eastern European surnames (such as my own) has for a half-century not been taken as an indicator of ethnic difference or "foreignness."[5] The concept of being a foreigner veils the process of racialization that defines certain ethnic groups as inferior "others" and as people who cannot claim symbolic belonging, regardless of their length of residence in the country.

Radio MultiKulti's use of accents to denote a "foreign view" reinforces the problematic functioning of the foreigner concept instead of questioning it. The ethnic minority viewpoint is a view from outside, a "foreign perspective" that at the same time has to be represented as "normality." As the head of the German-language programming section has stated in an interview:

> Just to be here, we are changing minds. Just to be on air, just that German listeners are listening to people with an accent and are getting used to it. And they're seeing: hey, it's normal. (Wolfgang Holler quoted in Vertovec 2000, 22)

Getting used to people with an accent refers to the station's effort both to reflect the normality of multicultural life in the city, where German is spoken with manifold accents, and to normalize foreignness for German nonimmigrant listeners. But what is it exactly that ethnic majority listeners are getting used to? The performance of voices with an accent can emphasize that Germany is indeed a country of immigration, a fact that for a long time remained unacknowledged in the country's postwar history. But what it does not reveal is the fact that immigrant groups have been inserted into a racialized system of ethnic classification that is anything but foreign, but very much an indigenous classificatory process of "differential incorporation" (Smith 1969). To maintain that ethnic diversity can best be represented through "foreign voices" is to reinforce rather than interrogate the process of "othering" that turns all racialized ethnic minorities into people who have just crossed the border.

It is only with regard to the German-language productions that the slogan "We speak with an accent" makes sense. In the Turkish-language broadcasts of Radio MultiKulti, accents are in fact deemed completely inappropriate. But speaking with an accent does not imply editorial control over program contents. While about half of the moderators of the German-language programs have immigrant backgrounds, the reality in the editorial backrooms is radically different.

At the time of my research, five of the eight German-language moderators for the crucial time slot from early morning until early afternoon were of immigrant background. This period is most important for ratings, since radio cannot compete with television during late afternoons and evenings. Of the editorial staff, however, only one out of eleven fully employed staff members had an immigrant background. This ratio has important consequences, since moderators in fact have very little influence over what actually goes on in the course of a program. They present it, but they do not plan it. It is the editorial staff that has control over the contents. On the airwaves, however, moderators appear to be in charge of the program.

"Giving a voice" to ethnic minorities thus often means to merely perform contents that have been decided upon by nonethnic producers through an accented voice. The consequences for the much-acclaimed project of renegotiating the political culture of the public domain are evident. Represented as a different viewing angle, the accented voice conveys the illusion of participation and dialogue, but it does so only by capitalizing on a particular form of cultural essentialism that equates the accent with a "foreign view" and remains ignorant as to the actual production process of statements. It is tempting to draw a parallel: just as the MultiKulti accent does not challenge the dominant consensus of how German should be spoken—it combines "correct" German with a "foreign flavor"—what immigrant moderators say does not necessarily challenge the dominant political culture of the public domain. Accents can much more easily be normalized than substantively different perspectives that would denaturalize the dominant political culture, in the sense of revealing its link to a particular imagined national community (Anderson 1983) and thus marking—in the sense of rendering discernible—cultural "Germanness."

It has to be said that the lack of ethnic minority journalists (as opposed to moderators) was quite early on acknowledged as a problem to be rectified by the station.[6] Radio MultiKulti's management has lamented the lack of qualified journalists who could meet the high standards of public service broadcasting. The station therefore aims to train ethnic minority journalists, but due to budgetary constraints such training is very limited. There are two avenues through which training takes place: internships, which require no prior broadcasting experience; or a so-called *Volontariat,* during which a trainee will work with different departments and take on different responsibilities over the course of two years. This avenue is usually required for anyone wanting to move beyond freelance status and work as an editor. Interns stay with the station for six weeks, and the permanent staff is far too busy to provide more than superficial training for them. As an editor told me toward the beginning of my own internship, such efforts are not worth the investment—interns do not stay long enough for the station to reap the harvest of this training. As a consequence, interns have to "tough it out" and get a working knowledge of production practices without much guidance. If they manage to accomplish the small tasks given to them initially—such as producing surveys like the one described at the beginning of this chapter—they can move on to more demanding tasks such as producing small features. Interns have to show that they understand what kind of interview material is desired and go out and get it. They also have to meet production deadlines, master the technical aspects of recording and editing material, and show that they can produce features that meet the standards of public service broadcasting. If they seem capable, the editors will gladly work them as hard as they can, because their work is not paid per feature as is the case for the freelance staff and thus allows more flexibility with the budget.

The station prefers interns with an immigrant background, but first-generation immigrants tend to require more intensive supervision, which the notoriously overworked permanent staff cannot provide. At the level of the official training stage called *Volontariat,* it is more difficult for the station to influence who is assigned to them, since it is the public service corporation Rundfunk Berlin-Brandenburg (RBB) as a whole that potential *Volontäre* apply to, not a particular station. MultiKulti has managed, however, to cooperate with the Grimme-Institut, a state-funded institution dedicated to "quality in public service broadcasting," in the context of a project aimed at training female first-generation immigrants as journalists. The women were based at the Grimme-Institut, but also spent several months working for different public service broadcasting corporations in Germany. MultiKulti benefited from this, and several women journalists-in-training spent time at the station.[7]

Formal Standards

The difficulties of not being able to attract enough foreign colleagues, as the director of the station put it, seem closely related not simply to a lack of so-called foreign journalists in Germany, but also to the standards of public service broadcasting that the station is not willing to compromise. Newcomers have to quickly adapt to these standards; they cannot challenge them. The standards appear to be merely formal: knowing how to write a particular kind of prose for a feature, how to conduct interviews and select appropriate statements from it, how to structure a feature and make it "interesting to the audience," and how to record one's composition during the tightly allotted half-hour production time in the studio. Yet these formal requirements also function to regulate the "different viewing angles" that the station claims to introduce.

The nonaccented majority listeners who form the imagined audience of the German-language programs can not only count on "proper German," though spoken with an accent, they can also count on the features produced by immigrant journalists to comply with the very same standards guiding production in general. While the length of a feature and the balance between interview material and spoken text (within a span of three to three-and-a-half minutes, about half of it allotted to interview material and sounds) might still leave some room for "difference," things get more problematic when it comes to the particular "message" of a feature and how it is conveyed. Every manuscript has to pass the desk of an editor who discusses it with the author and suggests changes before the feature can be produced in the studio. Whether of immigrant background or not, the editor will ensure that the manuscript is turned into an appropriate product for a particular program and its audience. When it comes to particular concepts, expressions, and details, apparently formal issues directly affect the content of broadcasts.

The guiding principle in these decisions is that only one idea and main argument can be presented during a three-minute feature, in order not to create confusion. Judging the clarity and complexity of arguments, however, implies a firm understanding of who will be listening to a particular broadcast (nonimmigrant Germans), and how these listeners will make sense of it. These assumptions have grave consequences for what needs to be said and what cannot be said in a feature production.[8]

Berlin has a number of Turkish theater groups, and one exclusively Turkish theater, the Tiyatrom. Once a year, the Tiyatrom organizes a festival in which different groups participate, some of them invited from Turkey. The event is advertised locally in both Turkish-language and German-language media. In the fall of 1998, it included a panel discussion in German on the topic of "What kind of Turkish theatre does Berlin need?" Radio MultiKulti asked me to cover the event and produce a feature for the following morning. Late at night, I faxed the following manuscript to the editor:

Feature: What Kind of Turkish Theatre Does Berlin Need?

Intro for the moderator:

What kind of Turkish theatre does Berlin need? Last night, Turkish theatre producers and their guests debated this question at the Tiyatrom theatre in Kreuzberg. The panel discussion opened this year's Turkish theatre festival, which focuses on the Borderless-culture program between Berlin and Turkey. Does the city need more theatre imports from Turkey or rather Turkish-language theatre made in Berlin? The issue was hotly debated. Kira Kosnick was there.

Text:

One shouldn't argue like that in front of the Germans, a Turkish woman said to her partner after the event last night. There was general disappointment with the panel discussion, which was meant to debate new perspectives for a Turkish theatre in Berlin. But instead of new perspectives, the panel gave an insight into the conflicts among Turkish theatre groups in the city. About one hundred guests had found their way to the Tiyatrom. Many of them were themselves part of the Turkish theatre scene, and some did not miss the chance to criticize it severely.

Sound bite: (27 sec.)

"It is really important for me to have at least some kind of theatre here that we can call Turkish, but it needs to have its own voice. I want to state very clearly that we do not have such a theatre right now. That is a fact. This theatre [the

Tiyatrom] does not have its own voice. It also doesn't have any perspective."
(Tape 2, 4)

Text:

In the tumult that ensued, the speaker did not have a chance to elaborate on
what could be the voice of Turkish theatre in Berlin. The actor Ilse Scheer who
moderated the discussion announced a break for tempers to cool off. Other
panel participants included Barbara Esser from the Senate Administration, İs-
mail Koşan from the Green Party, and Joachim Preuss, theatre expert from the
SFB. The Turkish theatre world was represented by Metin Tekin, Yüksel Yolcu,
and Yalçın Baykul, directors of different theatre groups in the city. But the panel
did not have much to offer on the issue of voice. Instead, it was the audience
which tried to describe what kind of Turkish theatre is needed in Berlin.

Sound bite: (28 sec.)
"Turkish theatre and Turkish-language theatre, these are two completely different things. The second of course includes the first. But it is a lot more. Turkish-
language theatre is theatre in general. In the Turkish language. I want to be able
to also see Brecht in Turkish in Berlin. I don't want an ethno-theatre." (Tape 2, 2)

Text:

But what the needs of a Turkish audience in Berlin might actually be remained
an open question. Instead, professionalism and money was at issue in the debate. Many charged that the local Turkish theatre scene is dominated by ama-
teurs who have managed to monopolize much-coveted funding from the Berlin
Senate. Thus all of the local producers came under attack. Only one of the producers present was met with approval by the audience, and he was flown in from
Turkey. Müşfik Kenter will present his famous work on the poet Orhan Veli this
coming Friday and Saturday. Ethno-theatre yes or no, the Berlin audience needs
to have access to quality theatre productions from Turkey, this was the one fact
that everybody was able to agree upon.

Soundtrack from Müşfik Kenter's work, reciting Veli's most famous poem:
"Ben Orhan Veliyim."

For the moderator:
The Turkish theatre festival continues with German and Turkish contributions
until the first of October at different locations throughout the city.

The manuscript moves uneasily between the topic the MultiKulti editors had been interested in—the question of whether Turkish theater should
be ethno-theater—and the actual debate that had taken place. This debate
was also interesting, but it addressed a very different issue, namely the competition among different Turkish theater groups and their relationship to
German funding agencies and institutions. To a Turkish audience, this is an
issue of great importance, since the question of how public funds explicitly

designated for "ethnic" purposes can be mobilized for competing cultural and social projects is relevant to other realms as well. The discussion also revealed that the German funding structure was directly involved in shaping what kind of Turkish theater could and should exist in the city. But for the MultiKulti editor, the "infighting" of Turkish theater groups was not something that could be turned into anything close to the expected focus of the feature. As we talked on the phone late that night, after I had written the manuscript and faxed it, she decided to cancel the feature. The issue was too complex, presupposing too much knowledge of the lines of conflict in the Turkish theater world and its implicatedness in German funding schemes, leading away from the artistic question of what Turkish theater in Berlin should look like.

In a sense, the editor's conclusion was similar to what the Turkish woman, a friend of mine and herself an actor, had said to her partner after the debate: One should not argue like that in front of the Germans. Asked what she meant by that statement, she explained that the podium discussion had been an opportunity for Turkish theater groups to present themselves to a German audience in a positive light, given the presence of many journalists working for German media in the audience, and to voice shared concerns instead of revealing conflicts and saying bad things about each other. For the German editor of MultiKulti, there was simply nothing to report on: the expected discussion had not really taken place. People fighting over public funds was not what the audience expected and wanted to hear about with regard to Turkish theater in Berlin, she felt. To explain how and why the discussion had taken a different turn would have introduced too much "irrelevant" information.

Beyond the obvious editorial decision about what kinds of topics should be addressed in a feature, complexity and clarity function as standards that influence content in more subtle ways. Linked to the needs and interests of a particular imagined audience—which might not even know that Turkish theater exists in Berlin—these standards are more than formal ones, and all the more powerful because they are hardly ever contested. While freelance journalists can try to convince editors at MultiKulti to commission a feature on a particular topic, they have to "sell" it to the editor by appealing to the very same standards of what is interesting and "digestible," and they have to accept revisions of their manuscripts based upon formal criteria that implicitly invoke these standards and the imagined audience they are tied to.

The particular insights and points of view that ethnic minority journalists could bring to a topic are thus often in conflict with such standards, as the freelance journalist and second-generation immigrant Emine Gül describes. She criticizes the way in which Turkish cultural traditions are represented on Radio MultiKulti:

> The problem is that the foreigners are always objectified, and then the German audiences say to themselves, ok, this is how the Turks do it, wow, exciting! . . . Whatever, but it also annoys me that 99 percent of the editors are German. That just doesn't work. . . . For example, I did this live report on a religious holiday reporting from a Turkish family home, and there I explained . . . that people kiss each other's hands and such. And I talked about the family, and it was just so normal for me to celebrate Şeker Bayramı[9] with them there. And then the editor said to me: "But you've said nothing about the Şeker holiday! What do people do there?" You know, that is so normal for me, what am I to say about it, about the Sugar Holiday? Why don't [editors] take care of that themselves and have [someone] introduce my report like, this is what people do on the Sugar Holiday, and Emine Gül will tell us now what it is like to celebrate it with a Turkish family. But they can't. As I said, you have to approach a topic as a Turk, then you have to be German again, that is to look in from the outside, and then comment again as a Turk! I find that very difficult.[10]

"Approaching the topic as a Turk" refers to the fact that Emine is Muslim[11] and able to mobilize her personal connections to find a family willing to celebrate the holiday with a radio journalist. "Having to be German again" refers to what Emine experiences as a form of alienation, describing the event from and for the viewpoint of a (particular) outsider, to an audience completely unfamiliar with it. "Commenting again as a Turk" points to MultiKulti's simultaneous wish to provide an "insider's view," an immigrant journalist making an alien cultural and religious event intelligible to a German majority audience. The fact of Emine being Turkish and Muslim formally authenticates her representation of the event, yet the information that is demanded of her was at odds with that authenticity, she felt. Being Turkish and Muslim, her point of view was a horizon of familiarity that took the event as such for granted, so that it did not even occur to her to describe it in the terms requested by the editor.

The "foreign view" that MultiKulti is aiming for in its German-language programs has to explain "foreignness" in "indigenous" terms. Ethnic minority journalists have to be able to anticipate a certain cultural horizon of meaning within which the imagined audience will make sense of their statements. The "insider" perspective—sharing a particular background and horizon of meaning with the people one reports on—always has to be confronted with what counts as intelligible and interesting reporting for an audience of "outsiders," and reworked accordingly. The reverse process does not take place in the German-language programs. Such reversal could mean to anticipate the horizons of meaning shared by immigrant groups listening to Radio MultiKulti, and to actively question what might be called a German majority horizon of common sense and taken-for-granted understandings. But being German is not one ethnicity or culture among others, it is the implicit referent toward which German-language programs are geared. Even though the station wants to reflect the multicultural everyday reality of the city, Emine feels that the station broadcasts for an imagined German majority audience that appears to have no contact with immigrants. MultiKulti is thus implicitly assuming a state of affairs that it otherwise explicitly denies with its claims to represent the "normality" of intercultural dialogue and interaction in Berlin.

Happy Hybridity

The German-language programs of MultiKulti often reify cultural difference in their depiction of Berlin as a mosaic of different ethnic groups that live together. By forcing an ethnic angle on all issues, they work in fact to entrench ethnicity as a salient marker of cultural difference. Culture can as a consequence rarely emerge as anything but a marker of ethnic group identity, adding its share to the urban multicultural mosaic. Such essentialist conceptions of cultural diversity have of course been criticized across the social sciences over the past ten years (Hannerz 2000). The concept of hybridity, much celebrated in anthropology and various disciplines as an antidote to essentialisms and reifications of various kinds, seems more sensitive to grasping cultural processes that cross the boundaries of social groups. And with regard to second- and third-generation migrants, the German programs of Radio MultiKulti do indeed employ the notion. However, the way in which hybridity is conceived of in these programs does not necessarily free the culture concept from its essentialist baggage.

My friend İpek suggested that I interview her on her monthly deejay activities for a "queer oriental" night at a Kreuzberg nightclub, to increase attendance and to "get her name out." I offered the story to both a women's program on Kulturradio on Sender Freies Berlin (SFB) and to Radio MultiKulti. For the first feature, I interviewed two other female DJs, and produced a manuscript on the difficulties women were facing in the profession. It just so happened that two of them were of immigrant origin, one from New Zealand, the other (İpek) second-generation Turkish. For the MultiKulti production, I concentrated on İpek. What the editors wanted was an emphasis on İpek's Turkishness: how did it affect her work? I asked the obligatory question, and received a somewhat obligatory answer: yes, her musical mix was a reflection of having multiple cultural ties, a "double" or even "hybrid" identity. The following is an excerpt from the broadcast:

Text, Kira Kosnick:
Berlin's only female Turkish DJ İpek has almost as much fun at work as does her audience. However, she does not like to be called Turkish. Second-generation migrant from Turkey, that is a big difference, she thinks. Because migrants are at home in more than one culture. And that is also reflected in İpek's music.
Music Intro: Sezen Aksu with the song "Rakkas"
Voiceover İpek:
"Yes, that is who we are! We are double. We are not just Turkish, we are not just German, not just European, but lots of other things. And a lot more. And that is what I find really cool. I could never play just Turkish music, or Arabic music, Mezdeke, for five hours on end without also playing something Anglo-American in-between."

Not being at home in one culture alone is an almost programmatic statement for MultiKulti as a whole. İpek's queer-oriental clubnight emerged similarly as a "multicultural" event, with sexual orientation as another cultural dimension the radio station otherwise rarely acknowledges as 'culture":

Text:
For many young migrants it is difficult to be openly gay or lesbian within their families, İpek states. And in the context of the German gay-lesbian scene, on the other hand, there is little room for the differences of their culture of origin. At the Gayhane night, this is very different. Nobody is excluded here. German gays and lesbians can be found on the dance floor just like heterosexual relatives of the migrants. İpek's brother wouldn't want to miss a single Gayhane night.

The event emerges as a celebration of hybridity: the often problematic complexities of ethnic and sexual belonging appear to be suspended in the multicultural space of the nightclub, offering a refuge from the homophobic and racist landscapes outside. My manuscript does not mention the recurring problems with the occasional straight Turkish man entering the space and accosting women and transgendered guests ("all kinds of femininities," as the organizers of the nightclub and concert space SO36 like to put it), nor the occasional nonimmigrant German gay man wanting to find his exoticized temptation.

In the second piece, which compared the experiences of different female DJ's in the city, the emphasis was different. What was it that allowed these women to establish themselves in the male-dominated world of disk jockeys? The question gave room to a different aspect of İpek's experience, one that rendered the relation between her Turkishness and her music a lot more problematic:

Text, Kira Kosnick:
And, if desired, she can also play nothing but Disco. But not everybody thinks that she is capable of switching styles, and people's rigid categorizations make her angry. The label "Turkish female ethno-DJ" has already cost her the occasional job assignment.
Music Intro: Sezen Aksu with the song "Rakkas"
Voiceover İpek:
"That which at times restricts me is of course at the same time my particular niche, that what makes me special. I'm special because I play the kind of music that the others don't. On the other hand, if I had not had this Turkish background—apart from that, I have to say, not every Turkish woman likes Turkish music—I have no idea how I would have established myself."

İpek was much happier with the second piece, which interwove that aspect with her situation as a woman in a male-dominated field, and touched upon other aspects of her experience that she felt were more crucial. Her work was more than an expression of "happy hybridity":[12] it was also affected negatively by being categorized as someone restricted to "minority music." She therefore regarded her own position as an ambivalent one: while her ethnic identity allowed her to carve a particular niche for herself that kept her in business, it also became stifling when she tried to move beyond the boundaries of the ethno-cultural capital she was assumed to possess. As she points out in an aside, there is no necessary connection between her ethnic background on the one hand and her cultural competence and affinity with Turkish music on the other. While this background might arguably facilitate such affinity and competence, it should not restrict her and force her to focus on Turkish music only.

This problematic dimension of being limited by ethnic stereotypes does not surface in the feature production for Radio MultiKulti. Since İpek regarded the production as something that would promote the Gayhane club night, she accepted this omission: "happy hybridity" was the point that she wanted to get across for the sake of attracting a larger audience, and this was not an entirely strategic argument. For gays and lesbians who have Turkish, Persian, Arabic, or other "oriental" ethnic backgrounds, the Gayhane club night offers a rare social and cultural space in which crucial identity dimensions that often work to their disadvantage in public spaces are valued positively (Kosnick 2005). Furthermore, in the context of Gayhane, they become compatible. As İpek has stated, her ethnic background is often ignored or exoticized in Berlin's dominant queer life, whereas being openly gay or lesbian tends to be quite difficult in migrant contexts ranging from family life to public migrant spaces.

There is another dimension of identity which the emphasis on "happy hybridity" in the MultiKulti production does not allow to surface explicitly. To Turkish listeners, İpek's dislike of being called Turkish and her insistence on being a second-generation migrant from Turkey would have signaled much more than "being double," as İpek puts it. It would have sent a straightforward message as to her political positioning with regard to Turkish nationalism in Turkey. Ethnic minorities within Turkey, such as Kurds who are critical of the Turkish nation-building project, as well as left-leaning "Turks" who share that criticism of Turkey's ethno-nationalism, will refer to themselves as "stemming from Turkey" rather than as Turkish, as *Türkiyeliyim* (I am stemming from Turkey) rather than *Türküm* (I am Turkish). The insistence that "Turkey belongs to the Turks" (*Türkiye Türklerindir*) is a basic tenet of state-supported Turkish nationalism. Depending on whether İpek's statement is understood against a background of ethno-nationalism in Turkey or against a background of ethno-essentialism in Germany, two different messages surface. Both of them were in fact intended by İpek, but only one of them could be given deliberate attention in the context of broadcasting for the German-language program on Radio MultiKulti.

In three-and-a-half minutes, which was at the time the maximum length for a freelance feature production, there is no time to explore complexities. A good production at Radio MultiKulti has to get its point straight across without creating possible confusion, and it has to introduce its topic in a way that requires no prior familiarity. Of course, some background of understanding and knowledge is necessarily assumed in any kind of broadcasting, forming a baseline of taken-for-granted meanings that no longer appear as questionable or culturally specific. But, as has been shown above, what is assumed as self-evident or common knowledge in the German-language productions for Radio MultiKulti is geared toward a nonimmigrant German audience that has to be introduced to migrant issues in particular ways.

Essentializing Culture

Within the short span of three-and-a-half minutes, it is difficult to do more than what is already known (to a German nonimmigrant audience) and expected, making it particularly difficult to "unsettle" familiar points of view and to question stereotypes, as the station in principle would like to accomplish. Brainstorming in the weekly meetings with freelance reporters often took the form of identifying a particular migrant organization, or an event either staged by them or directed at them, which could then be reported on as a window on "ethnic community life" or "culture contact" in the city. Since it is usually the ethnic dimension of any particular event, problem, or activity that is focused on in MultiKulti's programming, it becomes difficult to explore the areas of cultural activity in which people of different ethnic backgrounds engage without ethnicity or cultural difference being an issue. Freelance journalist Emine criticized another assignment she was given by the German-language editors:

> For example, this church group. I was so totally annoyed, because, those children, my God, they're seven or six or nine, they don't care if their parents come from I don't know where. They just go there and get church instruction, and here we go again: what do these kids bring along from their culture? Not a damn thing, I think! That is just so idiotic, that one should insist, they just have to bring something from Mozambique! They probably didn't, I figure.[13]

In his analysis of the station, anthropologist Steven Vertovec claims that Radio MultiKulti moves back and forth between two kinds of multiculturalism: one pluralist, one cosmopolitan. Following David Hollinger, he terms pluralist the kind of approach that reinscribes the boundaries of ethnic groups in an essentialist manner, while the cosmopolitan type of multiculturalism "represents an emphasis on individual, multiple affiliations" (Vertovec 2000, 22). This distinction is similar to the one introduced by Gerd Baumann in his study *The Multicultural Riddle,* where he insists:

> What needs to be recognized . . . is not one reified culture as opposed to another one. Rather, it is the dialogical nature of all identities and, consequently, that different cultural identifications can and will, in a multicultural society, cut across each other's reified boundaries. (Baumann 1999,119)

In Baumann's study of Southall, a district of London, the reified "culture as essence" appears as an argumentative tool applied by communities and individuals in the context of particular discursive strategies, while the actualities of everyday life point toward flexible, hybrid identities and "culture as process." Baumann terms this a "double discursive competence," and states that "People know when to reify one of their identities, and they know when to question their own reifications" (Baumann 1999, 139).[14]

At MultiKulti, though, it is not so easy to distinguish between strategic essentialism and cosmopolitan hybridity, as the example of the Gayhane feature shows. The issue of "speaking with an accent" presents problems as well: while Vertovec interprets it as an instance of "cosmopolitanism as practice," I have shown how the accented voice is used to construct representations of "foreign views" that are controlled and circumscribed within the actual practices of program production at the station. Undoubtedly, the station wants to project an image of letting immigrants present their views on air and "expose the public to difference," as Vertovec claims (Vertovec 2000, 23). But it is only a certain kind of difference that is allowed for in its context, and thus the "facilitation of cosmopolitan dispositions—open to gaining familiarity and ease with that which is different" (23) is a very limited and problematic one, mostly erasing forms of difference that would sit uncomfortably with the implicit majority identity against which "ethnics" are depicted.

Very different representational aims inform the work of the foreign-language editors at Radio MultiKulti. After 5 P.M. on weekdays, it is specific immigrant groups that form the targeted audience of the station, which reaches out to seventeen different linguistic groups each week. The frequency and scope of programs mirrors the size of the respective immigrant groups in the city. A daily program produced by an immigrant staff with considerable editorial independence, the station's *Türkçe Programı* (*Turkish Program*) has a different take on multicultural broadcasting and the particular needs and expectations of its audience.

Pure Turkish

Berlinliyim, çok kültürlüyüm, her gün Radio MultiKulti'yi dinliyorum.

"I am a Berliner, I am multicultural, I listen to Radio MultiKulti every day."

This jingle appears regularly during the daily hour of Turkish broadcasting on Radio MultiKulti, and it conveniently describes its self-understanding as well as its desired audience. Given the number of Turkish-speaking residents in Berlin, Turkish plays an important role at the station, with a daily hour of programming every afternoon. However, Turkish-language broadcasting is not a new development at Berlin's public service broadcasting corporation. The Turkish program, produced by the same group of editors, has existed for more than twenty-five years, dating back to the early days of labor migration. But its mission has changed: the focus of the program nowadays is on life in Berlin, no longer as an orientation for newcomers, but rather as a service for an ethnic group that is firmly established in the city. A typical daily program might include a report from the Berlin Film Festival, a review of the main stories in Berlin newspapers, news items such as an exhibition against racism opening in a Berlin youth center, a report on the latest matches of local Turkish soccer clubs, and the local weather forecast. Turkey's first-division soccer results are not omitted, but generally the emphasis is clearly on events in Berlin.

As shown above, an audibly accented German is an essential element of claiming and expressing multicultural diversity in the German-language productions of Radio MultiKulti. Turkish-language programming at Radio MultiKulti has followed rules that are quite different from the German programming's use of "foreign" accents. One significant difference concerns the way in which voices qualify as appropriate for broadcasting. Whereas the German-language programming uses accents to authenticate its multicultural qualities, anything but "pure Turkish" used to be unacceptable for the Turkish program. A younger member of the staff, Cem Dalaman, now chief editor, told me about the situation up until the mid-1990s when the program was still directed by the "old guard":

> Back then in the generation of Mr. Özgüç we were very adamant that the Turkish language should be broadcast in its pure, I don't know, perfect form. I think that is very nice, but it does not correspond to reality. For example, I remember that from my own productions, whenever some young people would mix some German words into their statements or interviews, that would be cut out immediately. You can't do that! And there are also people, they just speak German! And one has to keep it like that. We leave it like that now. Yesterday, there was a feature . . . a young guy was asked a question and he answered back in German. It stays like that. If he can't do anything else, still he is a Turkish person! One who speaks German now.[15]

Passing on the Turkish language in its "pure" form: this educative aim was and is in certain aspects still central to the Turkish program of MultiKulti, as it is for other Turkish broadcasting projects in the city. In the first instance, it could rather innocently be regarded as part of the general mission of foreign-language productions at MultiKulti, namely to facilitate the maintenance of cultural identity. In light of the changes the Turkish population in Germany is undergoing at present, with a relative decline in the use of Turkish and certainly in its proficiency among younger generations, maintaining high standards of Turkish was seen as a growing necessity by the older editorial staff. In fact, the more "pure Turkish" was in decline among the program's audience, the more urgent it seemed to provide this audience with such Turkish as a corrective in the context of broadcasting. As a result, however, the program had to increasingly modify the voices of Turkish Berliners to render them appropriate for representation in the broadcasts.

The task of preserving cultural identity, which in the Turkish case is particularly closely related to the issue of language, was seen as a priority. As far as the older editors were concerned, the objective cultural needs of Turkish migrants in Germany were mirrored in the decline of "pure Turkish" among the migrant population. Meeting those needs thus meant to produce programs that did not reflect this decline, but would rather stem the tide by featuring "pure Turkish" in an effort to educate the listeners. The state politics of language transformation in Turkey have similarly sought to enforce *öztürkçe*, "pure Turkish," as a homogenizing tool in order to produce a new subject population in line with the modernist-nationalist agenda.

As is evident in the development of the Turkish-language program at Berlin's public service broadcasting corporation and in the conflicts among its staff, there is a tension between the desire to "preserve" identity based on an essentialized notion of immigrant culture that fits quite well with certain multiculturalist frameworks, and the desire to reflect the obvious transformation of immigrant life and identities and to respond to new needs. The current chief editor wants the program to reflect the changing realities of what it means to be Turkish in Berlin today, and has in fact begun to introduce significant changes.

But the interview material is just one part of the language dilemma in the Turkish program at Radio MultiKulti. Another part pertains to the journalists themselves. Whereas the German-language programs see the somewhat imperfect German of their moderators and commentators as an asset, this is not at all the case in the context of the Turkish-language program. The program might now tolerate linguistic diversions in the interview material that is broadcast, but "high Turkish" still sets the standard that its journalists are expected to meet. This affects the very composition of the staff. Among young Turkish people born and raised in Germany, it is extremely difficult to find anyone whose Turkish will live up to this expectation. This is linked not only to a creolization process in which German and Turkish are interwoven in everyday conversations, but also to the variants of Turkish spoken among the parent generation. The majority of migrants had only limited schooling in Turkey, and many of them have come from regions in which different dialects or in fact other languages such as Kurmanci, Zazaci, or Arabic are spoken. The Turkish that is defined as "correct Turkish" by the editorial staff of Radio MultiKulti's Turkish program is the language molded and imposed upon the population by the Turkish state. It reflects the modernization of Turkish enforced by the Turkish Language Commission after the birth of the Turkish Republic, a commission that would continuously decide upon words to be expelled from the standard vocabulary and replace them with new ones.[16] "Correct Turkish" has changed so much that schoolchildren in Turkey today have to use a dictionary to read and understand the speeches of the very person responsible for this course of action, the founder of the Turkish Republic, Mustafa Kemal Atatürk. Migrants were considered to be "culturally lacking" even before their migration, and are now deemed to be at risk of losing the little ethno-national cultural capital they possess.

Most of the staff members of the Turkish MultiKulti team, including those working on a freelance basis, have been raised and educated in Turkey. The second-generation freelance journalist Emine, born and raised in Berlin, tried to work for the Turkish program, but was eventually told that her Turkish simply was not good enough. She now works occasionally for the German-language programs. In a conversation with me, having lunch at the cafeteria, Emine reflected upon her Turkish-language abilities:

> At home we have always spoken Turkish. My parents always took care that we did. So, I don't know, I didn't see any problems in terms of my pronunciation . . . I am pretty convinced that I can actually speak Turkish quite well. . . . But for some things it is not enough. I have to think harder when I have for example political discussions in Turkish and such. Or I have to watch out, because if people mix German and Turkish when talking to me, in my answer I do the same.

Such problems do not arise for her colleagues who have had schooling in Turkey. Comparing herself to another young woman who works for the Turkish program, she said:

> For example, she did this live broadcast, and I would have tripped about three thousand times. That happens to me sometimes in German, too, but she is really more fluent in Turkish. She just begins to rattle off, doesn't fear the microphone at all. With me, when I do it in Turkish, I think, Oh my God, now I have to be perfect, and then I have a blackout. So I am not that sad that I can't work for the Turkish program.[17]

Emine 's parents were able—and took great care—to teach their children "pure" Turkish in the migration context, yet even for educated families it is difficult to live up to the standard of perfection demanded by the MultiKulti staff. The obvious consequence is that despite the claim to produce a program "made by Berlin Turks for Berlin Turks," most the members of the staff have spent an important part of their lives in Turkey. The Turkish program of Radio MultiKulti presents at first sight a paradoxical case in which a particular "local" agenda—maintaining a linguistic identity—sets in motion a staff recruitment process that necessarily has a transnational dimension.[18] The program is emphatically not transnationally oriented, but nevertheless relies on "imported" cultural capital in order to push its local agenda. With regard to the maintenance of linguistic identity, it defends "pure Turkish" against the widespread syncretic forms that mix Turkish and

German, but it can do so only with people who have acquired skills and knowledge in both Turkey and Germany. Staff members are thus required to have transnational competences, in the sense that they have to have both a command of "high Turkish" and a familiarity with Berlin life. The former can only be acquired in Turkey, whereas the latter can be acquired somewhat more easily after some years of residence in the city.[19]

At the same time, the "Turkey connection" is deliberately disavowed as far as program contents and listeners are concerned. It is the local life of migrants in Berlin that constitutes the major focus of the program, in line with the integrative mission that Turkish editors embrace. Cem Dalaman explained to me:

> We want listeners who identify with Berlin . . . who see themselves as Berlin Turks. . . . We want to reach people who see themselves as part of this society, not as part of the society in Turkey.[20]

For Dalaman, seeing oneself as part of this society means to identify as a Berlin Turk, not as a Turk from Turkey but also, significantly, not as a German Turk. "Living here" refers to the city rather than to Germany as a whole, and this is in keeping with the local orientation of MultiKulti's programs. Multiculturalist campaigns in Germany often emphasize the local in the sense of a community of residence as the place where ethnically and culturally different kinds of people can belong. The second important aspect of Dalaman's statement pertains to his categorization of Turkish immigrants into "those who live here" and "those who live in Turkey," referring not to an actual place of residence but rather to people's interests and identifications. Different from other Turkish-language broadcasts available to immigrants, MultiKulti is for those who identify with life in Berlin. For Dalaman, this is a question of "either-or," and programs that report on Turkey for him are "backward-oriented." Maintaining ties with Turkey and identifying as a Turk from Turkey appears as a residue, something that characterized the early period of immigration but should no longer dominate people's identifications. The appearance of satellite media imports from Turkey is therefore seen as problematic by most of the Turkish staff members of MultiKulti. Atife Öztürk, one of the former editors of the Turkish-language program on Radio MultiKulti who witnessed its very beginnings agrees with this general assessment of satellite imports, but does not regard this turn as quite that dramatic.

> The negative aspects, integration has taken a step back, in my opinion. People are more oriented towards Turkey. But there isn't much to be found on these channels . . . . They are all soap operas. Most people follow them, and then some

go to their coffee-shop and . . . then the talk focuses on Turkey rather than on their own surroundings here. [But] . . . from many I hear, now it's enough. . . . I switch between five channels, they all tell the same story, nothing is happening. I've seen enough now, they say, and then they re-enter life here. How long does that take? That depends on the generation. The new generations will automatically separate themselves from this, and with the migration of a people, thirty-five, forty years are nothing. At this point one is fully half here, half there. And sometimes only there.[21]

In Atife Öztürk's opinion, the advent of satellite television does not represent a development that has the potential to alter the migratory experience and process. While it does have an impact on the first generation (it is mainly men of the first generation who frequent the coffee shops), this is due to a particular moment of the general migratory process at which the migrant is "split"—half in one place, half in the other. This view converges with dominant migration paradigms: migration is a process of slowly changing identifications that go along with an initial uprooting, movement, and eventual 'growing of roots" in the destination locality. Accordingly, watching satellite television from Turkey constitutes one way of "being there," of not engaging with life in Berlin but identifying as "part of the society in Turkey," as Cem Dalaman has put it. "Either you live here, we think, or in Turkey," he has stated, and just as a person could not actually physically be in two locations at once without experiencing a possibly harmful split, so the entry onto the mass-mediated imaginary territory of Turkey seems to require leaving Berlin. Eventually, "they re-enter life here" is Öztürk's expectation, meaning that the engagement with satellite television has taken viewers on a journey that is very much unrelated to their daily lives in Berlin.

Öztürk and Dalaman articulate a basic assumption that underlies much thinking about the integration of migrant populations in different parts of the world. Whether integration is thought of in terms of assimilation, ethnic pluralism, or segmented insertion, the dominant expectation and desire has been that migration processes end with the cutting of ties to the former country of origin, and the growing of local "roots" (Malkki 1992, 1995). This perspective has been challenged since the 1990s from a variety of academic disciplines, noting the continued importance of affiliations that link migrants in different ways to countries of origin or other diasporic locations.

However, while the concepts of transnationalism, diasporas, and transmigrants currently exert a strong influence upon academic thinking, the integration policy discourses and initiatives aimed at migrants show few traces of such influence. This is certainly the case for the German politics of migrant broadcasting in Berlin. "Turning migrants into locals" continues to be the dominant strategy that informs integration efforts in the arena of broadcasting, and in this regard the German- and Turkish-language programs of Radio MultiKulti converge. The station as a whole exemplifies this strategy, addressing people "who identify with the life here in Berlin" and deliberately encouraging such identifications. Cultural diversity is represented as a quality of the city, an ethnic mosaic of immigrant groups. Its representations of migrant life in the city for the most part inscribe ethnicity as a salient marker, turning it into a lens through which migrant life can be understood. The emphasis is on local affairs, both in the German-language program that represents ethnic minorities to the majority population and in the Turkish-language program that sees itself as broadcasting for Turkish Berliners, not just Turks in Berlin. The space allotted to reporting on events from the "home country" in the Turkish-language program is carefully circumscribed. It is only when these events become newsworthy across a range of German mainstream media that more space is given to them in reporting, for example, the last major earthquake in Turkey or the capture of PKK leader Abdullah Öcalan.

The emphasis on local life is in keeping with an understanding of multiculturalism that is defined in terms of ethnic pluralism within the country of immigration, or, more narrowly, within a particular city of residence. Migrant organizations, events, and initiatives that appear to further integration at the place of residence are given more space in reporting than those that appear hostile to it, such as Islamic and nationalist groups. This orientation separates the "Good Guys" from the 'Bad Guys" in other institutional contexts of Turkish migrant broadcasting in the city. However, the Turkish program's parallel mission of cultural maintenance forces it to breach its strictly local orientation and import the cultural capital required for this mission from Turkey.

Subaltern Voices

Despite the different representational aims of editorial teams at Radio MultiKulti, the station as a whole claims to give a "voice" to immigrant minorities, and to thereby contribute to minority empowerment. There is a strong consensus across European policy discourses and academic studies of ethnic and indigenous media that access to mass media will allow disadvantaged minorities to "speak for themselves."[22] As a consequence, Radio MultiKulti has received applause from both academic researchers and political institutions such as UNESCO, without a serious investigation into how "foreign voices" actually come to be constructed at the station. For many analysts, the very presence of immigrant voices in the media seems to guarantee minority representation and participation. Subaltern ethnic groups are assumed to "speak," if given the chance, and what is voiced, particularly in a native tongue to the members of the native group, has to consequently be an authentic expression of minority culture. It is this assumption that informs statements such as that by German academic Jörg Becker, who describes the emergence of a Turkish media sphere in Germany as an "ethnicization process":

> Ethnicization of media means, from a cultural perspective, the primacy of including that which is one's own over the exclusion of that which is not. Ethnicization of media allows the members of one's own group to see themselves, one's own fates, one's own problems, one's own bodies. Ethnicization of media enables finding oneself, determining one's own fate and cultural identity. (Becker 2001, 16; translated from German)

In the contrast between ethnic minority and majority society, the possible heterogeneity of the ethnic minority population is effaced. Media produced by migrants for migrants appear to by necessity reflect that "which is one's own" (*das Eigene*) and represent "themselves."

In such an understanding of ethnic minority media, two basic meanings of the concept of representation are collapsed: representation in the sense of *darstellen,* as a form of subject-predication where the community is invoked as a given entity, and representation in the sense of *vertreten,* as a form of "speaking-for" as in political representation. In her influential essay "Can the Subaltern Speak?" Gayatri Spivak has argued for the importance of keeping the two meanings conceptually distinct. To collapse them, she challenges, means to (re-)introduce a constitutive subject of the oppressed who can unproblematically "know and speak for themselves" (Spivak 1988). Both dimensions of representation are problematic when it comes to media invocations of the Turkish immigrant community: the stipulation that such community can be represented as an objectively existing entity, and the further assumption that members of this community will "voice" its innermost interests.

While respect for diversity as *ethnische Vielfalt* (ethnic diversity) is a basic premise of multicultural policies and projects such as Radio Multi-Kulti, the enthusiasm for difference comes to a sudden halt when the "internal" composition of ethnic groups is concerned. In the conceptual slide that turns immigrants from Turkey into the equivalent of a Turkish community, the possible heterogeneity of Turkish life in Germany is effaced. The concept of community signals a homogeneous, clearly delineated entity, with definite criteria for membership and belonging (Amit and Rapport 2002). The relative sameness that is attributed to its members becomes an implicit precondition for migrant media representations to not only depict or "talk about: migrants (in the sense of *darstellen*), but to simultaneously "speak for" them (in the sense of *vertreten*). Appearing to speak from the inside of a community, migrant voices are thus imbued with an inescapable authority that could also be described as a representational burden: rarely challenged with regard to the authority of their representational claims, but simultaneously forced to represent the ethno-cultural Other. The huge success of Turkish German author Necla Kelek and her bestseller *Die fremde Braut* (The Foreign Bride) hinges both upon her representational authority as someone with Turkish background and upon the promise given in the book's subtitle: to reveal shocking facts in a report from the "inside of Turkish life in Germany" (Kelek 2005). When the German mainstream media celebrate Kelek's revelations regarding the oppression of women in certain Turkish Islamist circles, they rarely foreground her academic authority as a sociologist. It is her own migrant background and personal story of growing up in a Turkish migrant family that render her account authoritative. In turn, it is highly unlikely that Kelek will ever be considered an authoritative source on anything other than Turkish migrant integration and gender oppression among Muslims in Germany.

It is precisely in the difficult ideological space between representation as *darstellen* and representation as *vertreten* that the central problematic of this book unfolds. What kinds of voices are constructed in the Turkish-language media programs produced by and for migrants in Berlin? How do they speak about different kinds of community, and how can they claim to be their voice? In what language do they articulate community concerns, and how does this language relate to other, dominant discourses of national and ethnic identity?

To regard migrant media as a form of collective self-representation is to accept their claims to represent the community in this double sense, of being authorized not just to speak or produce images of it, but to also be its political voice. Radio MultiKulti receives praise on the widespread assumption that its foreign voices can represent immigrant groups in this second sense of the term. Many among Berlin's Turkish migrant broadcasters would beg to differ. Yet almost all of them similarly claim to speak for migrants and represent their true qualities and concerns. Needing to legitimate their own productions within a German framework of multiculturalism that tends to reduce culture to a marker of ethnic group identity, many migrant producers take recourse to arguments of ethno-cultural membership to authorize their work. It is not necessarily Turkish culture as such that is posited as constituting the arena of membership, but often German-Turkish culture that serves as the cultural and ethnic territory to which producers claim to have an organic link.

The anthropologist Ayhan Kaya, for example, has used Gramsci's concept of 'organic intellectual' to describe the German-Turkish Hip Hop stars
that claim to articulate the experience of young German-Turks in Berlin
(Kaya 2002a). Similarly, the producers of Berlin's Turkish radio station
Metropol FM claim that having grown up German-Turkish in Berlin constitutes proof of sharing the same *Lebenswirklichkeit,* the same life-world as
the audience that one is both addressing and representing in the double
sense of positing as subject and speaking for (Duyar and Çalağan 2001).
What characterizes organic intellectuals is that they are brought forth by social groups as their own, and their function is ideally in turn to elaborate
and make coherent "the principles and the problems raised by the masses
[the social groups of which they form part] in their practical activity, thus
constituting a cultural and social bloc" (Gramsci 1971, 330). The unity between "intellectuals" and "the simple" should be the same as that between
theory and practice, with intellectuals providing the social group with "an
awareness of its own function" (5).

However, in Gramsci's analysis the background of an intellectual does
not guarantee that she or he will in fact theorize that function and bring the
group to awareness.[23] Disregarding for the moment the problematic separation implicit here between objective fact—the function of a class or social
group within economic, social, and political fields—and its truthful articulation/theorization, an assumption that plagues Gramsci as well as many
other Marxist theorists who subscribe to a base-superstructure distinction,
it is only in a context of ethno-cultural essentialism that claiming membership of a social group can serve as evidence of being able to authoritatively
articulate its practices and function.[24] Even a cursory look at Turkish-language broadcasts produced by and for migrants in Berlin reveals instead the
conflicting heterogeneity of positions articulated as authoritative representations of migrant life.

But what are the factors that render some representations of migrant life
more authoritative than others, and for whom? This is not simply a question of particular audiences that will differ in terms of how they engage with
such positions and interpret, contest, or accept them. It is also a question of
the wider social and cultural fields within which these audiences and the
producers of programs are situated and that shape the frames of reference
they employ. The authority of a position depends on the extent to which it
builds upon meanings that are accepted as common sense in those fields,
and thus aligns itself with hegemonic articulations. Representation can
never be mere *Darstellung:* The predication of a subject is always caught up

in the ideological, as common sense is not that which is naturally evident, but has been established as evident (Bourdieu 1977; Hall 1982). The Russian linguist Voloshinov insisted, "The sign may not be divorced from the concrete forms of social intercourse," in which different "classes" use one and the same language as part of a sign community (Voloshinov 1973, 21). As a consequence of the conflictual character of this intercourse, the ideological sign is "multiaccentual," carrying within it the refractions of social conflict. Voloshinov suggests that the sign becomes an arena of class struggle, with the ruling class seeking to " impart a supraclass, eternal character to the ideological sign, to extinguish or drive inward the struggle between social value judgments which occurs in it, to make the sign uniaccentual" (23).

The political project of making signs uniaccentual becomes all the more problematic when the different "accents" active in the sign originate from within different sign communities in which migrants are simultaneously situated. While the nation-state continues to be a crucial political entity that shapes and contains the boundaries of sign communities, current globalization phenomena encourage the transnational formation of such communities, and also enable people, particularly migrants, to participate in more than one at a time. Turkish migrant broadcasters in Berlin actively partake in multiple sign communities. Multiaccentuality acquires a much greater complexity when thought of not just in terms of the politics of cultural struggle within one social formation,[25] but when the articulatory practices of migrants draw upon and intervene in different national fields of cultural struggle. The contested meanings of Turkishness in both Turkey and Germany are a case in point. Migrants who deliberately call themselves "Anatolian" in Turkey or in Turkish migrant circles can at the same time endorse the label "Turkish" in debates about minority rights in Germany. Pace Radio MultiKulti's Turkish editors, such multiple orientations are anything but a sign of backwardness. Instead, they indicate the complexities of strategically representing transnational minority interests in intersecting, yet distinct fields of cultural struggle.

4

The Gap between Culture and Cultures

Radio MultiKulti's particular take on culture is best understood against the background of the larger cultural policy context and broadcasting environment in which it operates. In Berlin, Radio MultiKulti coexists with Kulturradio, a radio station that also forms part of the public service broadcasting corporation RBB. Kulturradio focuses on Western classical music, theatre, opera, and all forms of fine arts and performing arts conventionally associated with German *Hochkultur* (high culture). Non-Western art forms and immigrant artists are rarely featured on its programs, since they appear primarily as signifiers of ethno-cultural differences that are deemed to be the domain of Radio MultiKulti instead.

The coexistence of culture as a domain of the arts and culture as a marker of ethnic group identity produces peculiar dilemmas for immigrant cultural production in the city. The influence of multiculturalist paradigms on cultural policy is felt not just by media producers, but also by immigrant artists ranging from musicians and theater activists to writers and dancers. Berlin's non-Western immigrant and postmigrant artists regularly lament that they find it difficult to overcome the symbolic, institutional, and financial constraints of cultural policy domains within which their creative work is always seen to protect or hybridize ethno-cultural minority traditions. The gap between *Kulturen* in the plural—as building blocks of ethno-cultural diversity—and *Kultur* in the singular—as culture in the sense of performative and fine arts—goes almost unnoticed in Germany, since the latter is implicitly deemed a Western affair, whereas the former concept tends to be used with reference to ethno-national groups outside the Western world. Condemned to signifying ethno-cultural difference, non-Western immigrant and postmigrant artists are used to implicitly stabilize and naturalize what might be called the "whiteness" of Berlin's cultural establishment. Given that they are primarily seen as ethno-cultural "others," their absence from the mainstream of "high cultural" life in the city is hardly ever noted.[1]

In the late summer of 2003, a new poster began to appear on street corners and along the sidewalks of Kreuzberg and Neukölln, Berlin's neighborhoods with the highest percentage of Turkish residents. Pasted next to or on top of countless other Turkish-language posters announcing concerts, political gatherings, and nightclub events, this one advertised the release of a new CD by Turkey's most famous female pop star, Sezen Aksu. Rather than simply enticing passersby to go and buy it, however, the poster featured another important announcement: this CD would be available in large-chain German music stores only. Unlike the myriad of imported CDs and cassette tapes that are sold in small Turkish stores all over the city, often together with other goods in import-export shops, Sezen Aksu's CD would try to break into the market and distribution networks that sell the bulk of audio consumer products in Germany. For immigrant consumers, this was anything but good news. Used to paying about eight Euros for CDs imported from Turkey, they would now have to pay twice that amount to buy Aksu's *Yaz Bitmeden* (Before the Summer Ends) in German mainstream music stores. The reasons were patently commercial: apart from commanding a higher price, the CD could reach German nonimmigrant consumers who were unlikely to buy their music in small import-export venues. What is more, using mainstream distribution networks, the sale of CDs would for the first time be entered in the German charts, and thus offer new advertising possibilities as video clips were played on music channels, radio playlists, and the like.

Another Turkish pop star soon followed suit: Mustafa Sandal's song "Aya Benzer" (She's Like the Moon), already well known in Turkey, was re-released by the German label Polydor in a spiced-up version. The new version targeting the German market featured a heavy beat and a guest appearance by young and attractive Gülcan Karahanci, known to television audiences as the moderator on the music channel Viva, Germany's equivalent of MTV. The channel had also heavily promoted the video of Eurovision Song Contest winner Sertab Erener, well-established as a singer in Turkey, but new to non-Turkish European audiences. German newspapers took note, announcing Turkish pop music to be the latest wave of global pop exoticism making it big in Germany. Local promoters of the artists in Berlin had high hopes: it was only the lack of a viable distribution and sales network that had kept Turkey's pop music from gaining mass appeal in Germany, they felt. While confident about the appeal of this music to nonimmigrant consumers, they were also quite convinced, however, that Turkish immigrant audiences would hardly accept higher prices. The latter could always resort to picking up the CDs at much lower cost during their next holiday trip to Turkey.

Their hopes seemed well founded. One might expect the Turkish presence in Germany to make itself felt in the cultural sector as well, and to introduce Turkish influences into the mainstream world of arts and entertainment. Turkey is also becoming an increasingly important tourist destination for Germans, a factor that has already helped a number of Italian artists to break into the German charts after summer vacation periods, given the popularity of Italy as a tourist destination for Germans. Yet, Turkish cultural influences nevertheless still play almost no role in German cultural life, even though interest in world music and non-Western art forms has been growing steadily over the past decades (Greve 2003). In the heyday of labor migration to West Germany, most of the recruitment countries found entry into the most notorious of German pop musical genres, the *Deutscher Schlager*. Hugely popular, references to Spain, Greece, Portugal, and Yugoslavia were pervasive in lyrics performed by German-born artists, and were embodied by foreign nationals such as Costa Cordalis and Vicky Leandros (Greece), Bata Illic (Yugoslavia), Milva (Italy), or Roberto Blanco (Cuba).[2] Turkey and Turkish-born artists did not feature in this German genre until 1999, when the Turkish German group Sürpriz won second place in the German Eurovision Song Contest qualifiers, and was sent to represent Germany because the winner was disqualified. Put together by the notorious *Schlager*-producer Ralf Siegel with the aim of capitalizing on the song's message of interethnic peace and understanding, the group reached third place in the final competition only to be immediately forgotten. While their song included a few Turkish lines, most of the text was in English and German and did not contain any overt references to Turkey or the "Orient."

The acknowledgment of Germany as a multicultural society obviously does not answer the question of how exactly the cultural contributions associated with different immigrant groups are to be recognized and valued in national public arenas. Nor does an apparent increase in transnational flows of cultural commodities and musical production between Turkey and Germany necessarily mean that immigrant and postmigrant artists find it easier to achieve public recognition and establish an artistic "voice" in German cultural arenas. The reasons for this do not have to do with commercial distribution networks alone; cultural policy plays an important role in structuring the fields within which artists with immigrant backgrounds are trying to make their mark. An entrenched conceptual divide between culture as *Hochkultur* (high art) and culture as a representation of the ethno-cultural diversity of ways of life traps immigrant and postmigrant cultural production in Germany within separate funding-schemes, institutional structures, and discourses.

BERLIN AS A CULTURAL CAPITAL

Both federal and state government efforts have concentrated over the past decade on bolstering Berlin's image as a "world-open" (*weltoffene*) capital city composed of diverse groups, fast-changing and in synchronicity with global cultural flows (Vertovec 1996a). The city has managed to attract and promote a range of cultural industries since reunification, and increasingly markets itself as Germany's cultural capital. While Berlin's economic importance does not allow it to claim the status of a "global" city (Krätke 2001), it nevertheless represents Germany's image to the world, and in the national context figures as the place where Germany is most strongly caught up in global cultural developments (Hoffmann and Schneider 2002). To reinforce this image, city representatives point to the ethnic diversity of Berlin's population as well as to the range and quality of cultural institutions and artistic scenes. Two different concepts of culture are intermeshed in the representations of Berlin as a "happening" capital city: culture as a marker of ethnic groups, characterizing traditions, values and a particular way of life; and culture as a limited domain of artistic activities and institutions, associated with theaters, museums, opera houses, and the like. The characterization of Berlin as a world-open city hinges upon both its multicultural composition and its creative-artistic vibrancy. These are ideal conditions, one might assume, for immigrant and postmigrant artists who can lay claim to making cultural contributions in this double sense.

Yet, unlike other world cities that tout their cosmopolitan qualities, Berlin does not have a particular reputation for launching the careers of immigrant or postmigrant artists. And despite the recent crossover attempts of Turkish pop music into German mainstream markets, these artists are based in Turkey, not in Germany. There is no Turkish equivalent in Germany to the success stories of French Rai or British Bhangra music, both of which have been significantly shaped by artists with immigrant backgrounds, even though Turkish pop has been similarly described as a synthesis of "Oriental" and "Western" elements.[3] Different histories of migration might account partly for this lack. But taking into account the popularity of Turkish music among immigrants and postmigrants, as witnessed by music sales as well as the nightclubs that have emerged in many German cities in the 1990s, it seems curious that Turkish pop stars should not also emerge from within the migrant population. In fact, they have, but the German music business has scarcely taken note. Like Turkey's most famous male pop star Tarkan, several well-known singers were born or spent parts of their childhood in Germany, but launched their musical careers in Turkey (Bax 1999, 2003). As Martin Greve has described in his detailed study of Turkish musical life in Germany, aspiring migrant musicians of all musical genres hope to gain fame in Turkey, as the context that provides the true yardstick for both musical quality and audience appeal (Greve 2003).

Ten years ago, the relatively brief success of rap and hip-hop artists from Berlin was an exception. In the mid-1990s, groups like Cartel and singers like Aziza-A were heralded by German music publications as the representatives of authentic ghetto voices, doing for postmigrant youths what American rap stars had done for African-Americans in the United States (Cheesman 1998; Rose 1994). However, they had only moderate commercial success in Germany. Cartel enjoyed a brief period of notoriety in Turkey, heralded as defending Turkish culture abroad. A decade later, scientific interest appears to have exceeded musical and commercial interest in migrant hip-hop artists, judging by the number of recent academic publications (Burul 2003; Kaya 2001; Soysal 1999, 2002). None of the Berlin hopefuls has been able to make a lasting name for themselves.[4] But hip-hop remains the one musical domain in which artists with a Turkish background have been able to make at least a small dent in German cultural life.

Soziokultur and High Culture

Ayşe Çağlar has pointed out that the phenomenon of German-Turkish rap might be ironically described as a "prescribed rebellion" (Çağlar 1998). As a musical genre that relies on its street credibility, rap has in fact been explicitly promoted to postmigrant youths in Berlin as a mode of expression and activity deemed appropriate and beneficial by social workers and youth center institutions, with public funds going into the creation of performance spaces, workshops, and public contests. "Keeping it real" is a much-invoked motto of representational authenticity in hip-hop that operates not just as a promise of commercially successful artists to stay true to their minority roots (McLeod 1999). In the German social work and cultural policy environment, it also articulates the expectation that hip-hop is in fact the most appropriate medium for minority youths to make sense of their own marginalized experiences. Though often presented as spontaneous "organic intellectuals" who articulate the plight of postmigrant youths in opposition to a dominant system that excludes them (Kaya 2002a, 2002b), German-Turkish hip-hop artists have been actively encouraged and were able to substantially benefit from cultural policy measures in the city.

Like other cultural activities supported by public institutions concerned with social issues at the city or district level, the main aim behind such promotion has not been to create artists, but rather to get kids off the streets and out of "trouble." In neighborhood associations, youth centers and *Volkshochschulen* (publicly subsidized schools that offer training courses in everything from arts and languages to vocational courses for a small fee), culture is firmly linked to social goals. German-Turkish rap is valued by policymakers for its alleged integrative potential and expected social benefits, not as an art form. It thus falls into a domain of cultural policy that has been termed *Soziokultur*, or socioculture.

The notion of *Soziokultur* dates back to the 1970s in the Federal Republic, when as part of a general social revolt against traditions, *Kultur* was redefined as a good to be enjoyed and practiced by all parts of the population (Heinrichs 1997). Rather than promoting what was seen as an elitist and conservative cultural establishment restricted to the middle and upper classes, cultural policy was to promote widened access to both cultural consumption and production. Particularly on a communal level, different forms of culture were as a result "discovered" for cultural policymaking, such as folk music, photography, and cultural activities formerly labeled as "hobbies." The focus thereby shifted from performative, public-oriented forms of cultural production toward the recognition of cultural production as a form of self-realization and social participation, not geared toward a public audience but toward the transformation of its participants. The concept of *Soziokultur* emphasized the importance of creative activities for personal growth and social cohesion, and sought to radically democratize cultural landscapes, particularly at the grassroots level of the communes (Deutscher Städtetag 1992).

The new institutions and initiatives that were to implement these goals did not replace the established landscape of theaters, opera houses, and concert halls that were associated with the concept of *Kultur* as "high art" and "national traditions." In times of relative affluence, federal states and communes could afford to simply add to what was already there. The result has been a dual structure of *Soziokultur* and *Hochkultur*, in which different meanings of culture and different aims associated with those meanings have been institutionalized in different arenas. *Soziokultur* tends to be the concern of low-level public bodies and institutions, with city districts and communal governments allocating funds that serve different purposes of cultural education and social integration. *Hochkultur*, on the other hand, falls within the domain of higher-level policymaking. It is Berlin's state senate that provides the budget for established theaters, museums, and orchestras in the city.[5] In matters deemed to be of particular representational relevance, the federal government has been stepping in. Cultural institutions in the capital city whose image is deemed to reflect upon the entire country receive funding from the federal government, as stipulated in the *Hauptstadtkulturvertrag,* the Capital City Culture Contract signed between the city and the *Bund* (Regierung Online 2001).

Another distinction between *Soziokultur* and *Hochkultur* pertains to policymaking: Berlin's Senate Administration for Science, Research and Culture (*Senatsverwaltung für Wissenschaft, Forschung und Kultur*) finances and regulates primarily the arts-oriented domain of *Hochkultur*. However, other Senate Administrations also deal with cultural matters and engage in policymaking in cultural domains. The Senate Administration for Education, Youth and Sports as well as the Administration for City Development, for example, provide funding for cultural activities and initiatives that are deemed to further their respective policy goals. Thus, the task of managing disadvantaged neighborhoods (*Quartiersmanagement*) might entail engaging residents in cultural activities, and advertising the latest "family passport" (*Familienpass*) offering discount theater, movie, and concert tickets to families on the Senate's education web pages. The divide between *Soziokultur* and *Hochkultur,* the forms of its institutionalization, and its influence on cultural policymaking have significant consequences for immigrant and postmigrant cultural production.

Immigrant Culture(s)

Historically, it is important to note that the rise of sociocultural politics in the 1970s Federal Republic coincided with the peak of labor migration to West Germany. Civil society organizations (such as unions, the churches, and so on), employers, politicians, and the media intensively debated the distinctive cultural needs of labor migrants, and how these needs could be met in order to increase productivity and minimize social conflict (Kosnick 2003). Cultural difference had to be managed in the interest of social harmony. Up until the mid-1980s, it was preserving the connection with cultural traditions "back home" that formed the undisputed center of cultural policy concerns toward labor migrant populations. Significantly, most immigrant cultural activities took place in the very contexts and locations that also enabled *Soziokultur*: in youth centers, *Volkshochschulen,* neighborhood associations, and local cultural facilities linked to the smallest entities of cultural policymaking in Germany, the *Kommunen* or city districts.

The gradual political recognition in the 1980s that the guestworkers and their families were "here for good" (Castles 1984) prepared the ground for the eventual conceptualization of Germany as a multicultural society a decade later. Immigrant groups have since then been understood as culturally distinct groups whose "difference" is to be accommodated and protected. Yet, discourse and policy concerned with immigrant and postmigrant cultural production is still primarily tied to sociopolitical goals. The preservation of distinctive cultural traditions has remained high on the agenda, but is now linked to ethnic identity politics in a multicultural framework (Kolland 2003). In a society understood to be composed of multiple ethnic groups that are carriers of distinct cultural traditions and qualities, immigrant cultural production can demand public support, both to preserve identity and to publicly represent its traditions as a contribution to multicultural life and diversity in Germany. It is important to note, though, that the *Kulturen* to be supported are approached as cultures in the plural, as markers of ethnic group identity, and not primarily as *Kultur* in the sense of the creative arts.

When artists from immigrant backgrounds seek recognition in this second domain of cultural production, both meanings of culture are invoked. Their work provokes a confluence of different semantic contents of the culture concept, and mobilizes different policy contexts and modes of public intervention. This has profound consequences for immigrant and postmigrant cultural participation and expression in Berlin. Despite the recognition of immigrant cultural influences as an asset for the city and its cosmopolitan ambitions, this has not automatically opened the doors of "high culture" to immigrant and postmigrant cultural production as occupied by state theaters, opera houses, concert halls, and museums. Instead, this kind of production remains closely associated with socioculture, a link that becomes particularly visible in the institutional structures and practices that deal with non-Western cultural-artistic forms in the city.

The comparison of two major cultural institutions in Berlin that both focus on non-Western cultural traditions and developments in the arts can illustrate the exclusionary effects produced by the gap between *Kultur* and *Kulturen*. The first institution is the House of World Cultures (*Haus der Kulturen der Welt*, HKW). It receives its funds from the federal government, which signals its strategic importance in representing the new capital city. Its focus is on bringing cutting-edge work in performance and fine arts that has significant non-Western influences to Berlin, and initiating discussion of global cultural trends. The second institution, the Workshop of Cultures (*Werkstatt der Kulturen*), operates with a much smaller budget to support the work of immigrant artists actually residing in Berlin.

The House of World Cultures

The House of World Cultures has set itself the task of presenting cultures from outside Europe through their fine arts, theatre, music, literature, film and the media and engaging them in a public discourse with European cultures. The House of World Cultures' programme focuses on the contemporary arts and current developments in the cultures of Africa, Asia and Latin America as well as on the artistic and cultural consequences of globalisation. It gives priority to projects that explore the possibilities of both intercultural co-operation and its presentation.[6]

The House of World Cultures might be Berlin's strongest argument for taking seriously the artistic potential and relevance of non-Western cultural influences. The HKW is Berlin's most prestigious cultural institution focusing explicitly on the representation of artistic work from outside Europe and the "Western World." Significantly, this includes artists and art forms that might be located in Europe or the West, but that are importantly influenced by cultural developments and traditions in the non-Western world. In terms of cultural policy in Berlin, the HKW plays an important role as a showcase institution for the city's artistic vibrancy—to both the rest of Germany and to the rest of the world. It was taken over as a cultural institution of national importance by the federal government in 2001, along with several other institutions likely to enhance Berlin's image as a capital city. For artists, to perform at the HKW is tantamount to confirmation that one has reached the highest level of artistic development as an "international" artist, and (at times *or*) that one's work is cutting-edge. Just what is considered cutting-edge can be learned from its online mission statement published on the internet.

The House of World Cultures' programme work reflects changing global conditions and creates a basis for new forms of interdisciplinary artistic co-operation. . . . Migration, international networks, encounters with other traditions and other modernities have transformed cultural conditions throughout the world and created new conditions for art. National cultures, even where they are still experienced as homogeneous by many people, no longer ensure binding cultural affiliation. . . . All over the world, artists, authors and scientists are relating to these changes in their works. In co-operation with them, the House of World Cultures seeks to develop a programme presenting responses and artistic models that reflect these international conditions in terms of what they mean for the individual and for human beings living together in a global world.[7]

The prominence of issues such as migration, international networks, and new living conditions in a global world is an indication that the HKW is not content to put "foreign cultures" on display, in the tradition of out-of-date anthropologies that saw culture as firmly rooted in (preferably national) territories. Instead, global transformations and interconnections form the central artistic interest of the institution, reflected in programs and festivals that stress cultural hybridity and flow: yearly events such as the festival for new music, TranSonic, the performance festival In Transit, and the open-air music festival popdeurope—migrating sounds in and out of Europe.

Migrants are key in one sense for the House of Cultures and the fluid concept of culture it tries to promote. The cross-border movement of people complicates the relationship between culture and place, and migrants seem particularly likely to have multiple and complex cultural affiliations. The House prides itself in promoting and participating in the cutting-edge analysis of cultural flows, taking on board the work of leading contemporary cultural theorists. The HKW's then Secretary-General Hans Georg Knopp liked to quote Homi Bhabha when reflecting upon approaches that adequately capture the cultural state of the current world. As for Bhabha, the migrant is a key figure for the HKW in an abstract sense, insofar as this figure epitomizes shifting forms of identification and challenges to notions of cultural homogeneity. Hybridity and mobility, key terms associated with migration, appear as frequent *Leitkategorien,* leading concepts in much of the House's promotional material and exhibition catalogues. In a more concrete sense, however, migrants enjoy far less representation at the House of World Cultures. Immigrants and postmigrants living in the city of Berlin are not particularly targeted as an audience for HKW events, and no special effort is made to recruit them as performing artists. When describing the pedagogical mission of the House of World Cultures, Knopp painted a telling picture of its audience:

> It is something of a pedagogical mission, one could say, but one that is filled with art, to make people realize that there are other values, be it social or aesthetic ones, that there are other modes of expression, which carry the *same* value as that which I know, that which represents *my* culture.[8]

While cultural hybridity and global flows are very much at issue in the contents of what the HKW tries to offer Berlin, these processes seem not to have transformed the city itself—at least not that part of the population that Knopp imagined to be the HKW's audience. Despite claims that national cultures can no longer ensure binding affiliations, this targeted audience seems to be in firm possession of one particular culture, against which the equality of non-European cultures needs to be asserted. Thus, implicitly, cultural difference still comes from elsewhere. Berlin needs to be taught about the cultural dimensions of globalization; it does not seem to participate in them.

As much as cultural hybridity, migration, and globalization are addressed as topics in the work of artists and thinkers presented by the HKW, they are almost always brought in from "outside" the city, and rarely represent the cultural complexity and dynamics of Berlin itself. Even the popdeurope festival, claiming to present the diversity of popular music cultures that the children of immigrants have created in European metropolises, does not involve the city's musicians. The 2003 concert series offering "migrating sounds in and out of Europe" featured musicians from cities such as Lisbon, Marseille, Budapest, and London, but none from Berlin. Turkish musical influences were represented by the artist Mercan Dede, who moves between Istanbul and Toronto, and fuses religious Sufi music with electro beats. Local Turkish DJs were invited to spin tunes for the crowd before and after the concert, but no Berlin artist was featured in the concert line-up. Such selective practices are indicative of the institution's relationship with "local" immigrant and postmigrant artists.

When asked why the House of World Cultures does not seek to cooperate more with Berlin's immigrant population, Knopp referred to the particularities of the city's migration history: "Berlin has a different migration history. Berlin has labor migration. I am not quite certain, but I think most of the Turks who came here came from Eastern Anatolia." They have little understanding of contemporary developments in the arts, he claimed. Lacking intellectuals, Berlin's immigrants are less likely to produce, let alone appreciate, artistic work of the kind the HKW seeks to present, which is "high quality" work of an internationally competitive kind. To Knopp, immigrant and postmigrant artists are nevertheless not disadvantaged through the HKW's policies.

> I still think that an artist is either good or he isn't. No matter where he comes from, no matter in which milieu he is working, he is either good or not. And I don't give someone credit because of their background, not in an art project. Neither positive nor negative.

Knopp saw no conflict between this assertion of absolute standards regarding artistic quality and the HKW's mission to assert the equality of non-European modes of expression. But the precise nature of his standards of judgment when it comes to "good art" remains unclear. If artistic quality will automatically assert itself and rise to the top, one would indeed have to infer from the international line-up at the House of World Cultures that such quality is lacking among immigrant and postmigrant artists in the city.

Yet, it is difficult to see how such quality could even be discovered, given the selective orientation of the House of World Cultures. Knopp delegates responsibility for "local" immigrant and postmigrant artists to another institution: while the HKW has a decidedly international orientation, another institution in the city that is concerned with non-European culture focuses on work emerging from within the city: the *Werkstatt der Kulturen* (Workshop of Cultures).

The Workshop of Cultures

> With their culture, religion and language, with their aesthetic notions and their art, almost half a million people from more than 190 nations, among them many artists and intellectuals, make up the international atmosphere of Berlin— a world city in transformation. In this context, the *Werkstatt der Kulturen* presents itself as a place of intercultural art and communication, as a platform for the impulses of new social and cultural movements emerging from the urban milieus shaped by migration.[9]

While the HKW has its home within a stone's throw of the German Chancellor's office in the geographical and geopolitical center of Berlin, the Workshop of Cultures (WdK) is in the district of Neukölln, one of Berlin's poorest neighborhoods with a high percentage of immigrant residents. Conceptualized as a "workshop for integration in a new Berlin" in 1993, the WdK seeks to play an active role in facilitating intercultural encounter, exchange, and transformation among and across different ethnic, cultural, and religious groups in the city. The former Commissioner for Foreigner Affairs Barbara John (*Ausländerbeauftragte des Senats,* today renamed Commissioner for Integration), who coined the term "workshop for integration" (*Integrationswerkstatt*), was a driving force behind its inception, and her office continues to provide the basic financial support for the WdK. At present, the Workshop has a guaranteed budget of no more than 625,000 Euros per year—just enough to cover basic maintenance costs. Financial support for the WdK's different projects has to be obtained from other sources of funding, and thus the WdK staff each year enters the application race for grants from institutions like the *Hauptstadtkulturfonds* (Capital City Culture Fund), the *Klassenlotterie* (public lottery money), the Sociocultural Fund of the *Kulturpolitische Gesellschaft,* and others.

Presenting intercultural art is only one of the aims of the WdK, as part of a wider conception of intercultural exchange and development in the city to which the Workshop seeks to contribute. Calling itself a "forum for the multicultural civil society," the WdK foregrounds not so much artistic as social criteria and goals, but aims to be "a place of active citizenship and

FIGURE 3. 2004 poster advertising Berlin's yearly Carnival of
Cultures. *Photo by Raymond Augdes for* Karneval der Kulturen,
design by Ständige Vertretung Design und Kommunikations GmbH.

self-determined engagement with the legal and political processes of the democratic society," as the institution states on its Web page. The presentation of immigrant and postmigrant artists consequently aims at showing
the diversity of lifestyles and aesthetic orientations as a cultural resource and
development potential of the city, with the hope of promoting dialogue and
social change in the urban environment.

Significantly, it is the House of World Cultures and not the Workshop
of Cultures that has been taken on by the federal government as a showcase
institution for the new capital Berlin. What is more, the WdK's budget is
not part of Berlin's official Culture Budget (*Kulturhaushalt*), but it comes
from the Office of the Commissioner for Integration (formerly the Commissioner for Foreigners). It is thus culture in the plural, particularly immigrant cultures deemed to form part of a multicultural Berlin, which are key
at the Workshop of Cultures, not culture as a singular domain of aesthetic
production. While both the House of World Cultures and the Workshop of
Cultures speak of cultures in the plural, it is culture in the singular, with reference to an implicit universal standard of artistic quality, which dominates
the work at the HKW. The Workshop of Cultures is best-known in the city
for its yearly Carnival of Cultures (*Karneval der Kulturen*), with four days of
street festivities and a large parade to which a wide range of immigrant

groups in the city contribute. Figure 3 shows the poster used for its advertising campaign in 2004.

Over the past eight years, the Carnival has been growing steadily in size, with around 1.5 million visitors per year and around 5,000 active participants. The parade is advertised as a demonstration of Berlin's cultural diversity, put on display by "participants from more than eighty nations living in Berlin" (as stated on the institution's Web page), and is an important tourist magnet. The cultural diversity of urban life in Berlin is strongly tied to ethnic groups that are mobilized to represent their cultural distinctiveness. It is thus difficult for the Carnival to avoid accusations of staging a form of "picturesque multiculturalism" (Frei 2003), which glosses over the social inequalities and conflicts that characterize everyday life in Berlin. Though participants are encouraged by the organizers to represent intercultural projects and groups in the city, the overall impression of culture as a marker of ethnic or national identity remains central to the Carnival's choreography and public reception.

The WdK's managerial staff does not subscribe to this vision of urban multiculturalism at all, and actually works politically to challenge the boundaries of publicly financed culture in the singular.[10] Yet, given its main sources of funding, its public mission, and its representational practices in the city, the Workshop of Cultures has little choice but to operate as a firmly sociocultural institution, rather than an arts-oriented one. The House of World Cultures, on the other hand, strongly rejects sociocultural projects as part of its own agenda. It also rejects any particular responsibility for showing the work of immigrant or postmigrant artists, or targeting immigrants as part of its audience, deeming this the task of the Workshop of Cultures.

Importantly, then, a correlation can be detected between immigrant and postmigrant cultural production and the domain of socioculture, with institutional structures and public funding schemes favoring the recognition and evaluation of such production in integrationist terms. Just as importantly, there is significantly less public funding and support available for work with an intercultural agenda that draws upon local experience, as the director of the Workshop of Cultures Andreas Freudenberg explained succinctly in a debate at Berlin's House of Representatives (*Abgeordnetenhaus Berlin*):

> There is a big difference between international art and international arts exchange and what is developing in terms of intercultural work in urban milieus. The difference is that in one area, impulses are brought in from outside, while the other area brings in and integrates the substance available here, thus taking on and culturally working through experiences that take place here in the urban milieus. It is important to clearly mark this difference . . . . International cultural

Table 1. Culture Budget for the City of Berlin 2005.

Budget Area	Amount for 2005 (in 1,000 €)
Total City Budget	21,109,162,2
Total Culture Budget	377,295.3
Theaters	206,349.0
Museums	53,654.0
Music, Orchestras	30,638.7
Libraries	25,614.4
Sociocultural	2,836.0
Support for Foreigners	343.0

Source: Senatsverwaltung für Wissenschaft, Forschung und Kultur, *Kulturhaushalt 2005,* found online at http://www.berlin.de/sen/wfk/, accessed December 20, 2004. Table has been adapted from source in a condensed form.

work receives support, the urban, intercultural scene does not receive such support. (Ausschuss für Kulturelle Angelegenheiten 2003, 15)

Despite such statements, public spending on culture has over the last decade exacerbated rather than alleviated this situation.

The "Whiteness" of Cultural Policy

The Cultural Budget of the city serves as a stark reminder of what kind of culture is deemed most worthy of state support. Table 1 shows both how different domains of cultural production are separated out as categories, and how they are ranked in terms of their importance and financial needs.[11]

The table shows the primacy of "high culture" institutions as a matter of municipal concern, with sociocultural and immigrant cultural activities ranking lowest on the scale of financial support. What the figures reveal is firstly that *Soziokultur* is anything but a priority in the overall budget allocation. Secondly, "foreigners"—a term meaning in fact immigrants living in the city[12]—have to make do with a very small and ever-decreasing slice of this sociocultural budget. Public funding for sociocultural activities in general and for immigrant and postmigrant artistic expression tends to be made available in other policy contexts as well, such as the Senate Administration for City Development or the Office of the Commissioner for Integration. But it is worth taking a look at the ways in which immigrants and postmigrants are considered within the public sector of *Kultur* proper, the domain of culture in the singular.

The fund "Project Support in the Area of Cultural Activities of Citizens of Foreign Descent" (*Projektförderung im Bereich der kulturellen Aktivitäten von Bürgerinnen/Bürgern ausländischer Herkunft*), which administers the "support for foreigners" budget, offers competitive grants for which eligible groups and individuals can apply once a year. In the informational material distributed by the Senate Administration, the criteria for funding are described as follows:

> Support is given to artistic and socio-cultural projects of citizens of foreign descent living in Berlin, at the center of which stands the maintenance and development of cultural identity, and/or the encouragement of intercultural dialogue.[13]

The concept of culture employed in this context clearly refers to cultures in the plural, linking them to ethno-national groups as their representatives. Even though the funds are to be made available for projects, not for institutional support, more than half of the budget is regularly reserved for Berlin's Turkish-language theater Tiyatrom, founded in 1984. Representatives of the theater have so far failed in their efforts to be recategorized as a "regular" theater and receive part of the institutional support the Senate provides for the city's nonethnic theater landscape. What is more, within German-Turkish circles there is a heated and ongoing debate as to the lack of quality productions at the Tiyatrom, and the exclusive reign of some theater producers to the disadvantage of other groups and individuals producing Turkish or German-Turkish theater in the city (Türkoğlu 2003). Reflecting on the history of Turkish-language theater production in Berlin, dramatic advisor Hülya Karcı has pointed out the connection between the current miserable state of this theater scene and its "exotic" status in academic and cultural policy contexts: "To be interesting/exotic at the same time carries within it the notion of being foreign. But it is impossible to create culture as a foreigner."[14] Tracing back the efforts to establish a viable Turkish theater scene in the city, she admonishes that many immigrant producers have become complacent and made their peace with support structures that keep the Turkish scene marginal. Fighting over their share of an increasingly diminishing funding source, they have failed to direct their attention toward the ways in which general theater funding is allocated in the city.

The fund for "citizens of foreign descent" has ironically contributed to this marginality. Intended as a kind of affirmative action tool to increase participation of immigrant and postmigrant artists, the fund has become something of a trap, keeping artists out of other funding circuits that offer considerably more money and/or institutional continuity. A Senate Administration representative for the fund told me in a personal interview that the advisory council that makes funding decisions in the area of noninstitutionalized theater projects regularly turns away Turkish applicants, advising that they should rather submit an application to the "foreign descent" fund. Instead of being just an additional source of funding complementing those opportunities that are open to everyone, the fund now hinders immigrant participation in "mainstream" categories of cultural production, effectively keeping out people and issues deemed to represent culture(s) in the plural.[15] What is more, the fund's resources have also been more than halved over the past ten years. In this sense, it is possible to speak of the "whiteness" of cultural policies in Berlin. It is precisely the lack of an obvious racial bias within seemingly neutral institutional practices and discourses that characterizes white privilege and establishes whiteness as an unmarked, normative position (Hartigan 1997). It is the racial or ethnic Others that carry the burden of race as a category of difference and deviance from the norm. As Richard Dyer has remarked, "Whites must be seen to be white, yet whiteness as race resides in invisible properties and whiteness as power is maintained by being unseen" (Dyer 1997, 45).

It is obviously not only the concept of race that is stabilized by the normative invisibility of dominant categories. Along similar lines, the obsession with publicly identifying gay, lesbian, and transgender individuals has been analyzed as the implicit construction of binary gender categories and of heterosexuality, stable as categories and norms only in the context of labeling its Other (Halberstam 2005; Warner 1993). In exploring the "whiteness" of cultural policy in Berlin, I thus do not want to claim that policymakers in the city operate with racial categories. Instead, I use the concept of whiteness to analyze how the difference between "culture" and "cultures" similarly inscribes immigrant and postmigrant cultural production as Other, denoting the primacy of ethno-cultural difference over artistic ambition. Forcing immigrant artists to represent multicultural difference first, rather than artistic excellence, the terrain of culture in the singular becomes the preserve of nonimmigrant artists. The burden to signify migrant Turkishness can rarely be shed, and often requires acts of dissimulation. Famous dance music producer Mousse T., based in Hannover, has chosen his alias with care, and has managed to achieve success in an Anglo-American music industry that does not operate with the ethnic categories dominant in Germany.[16] Sticking to his Turkish name "Mustafa Gündoğdu" might have made it much more difficult to "make a name for himself" outside the categorical confines of a racialized Turkish community.

"Whiteness" in this sense is at issue when Berlin actor Nursel Köşe finds it difficult to obtain film roles that do not replicate her performance as a

Turkish cleaning woman in the film *Anam,* when filmmaker Yüksel Yavuz
has problems obtaining funds for projects that have nothing to do with migration issues, or when the fact that Aziza-A., the rap musician, gives concerts at feminist and gay/lesbian/transgender events is completely ignored
in German mainstream media reporting. It is at issue when the Bavarian
film company representing shooting star Fatih Akın's new film *Gegen die
Wand* (Head On) at the 2004 Berlin Film Festival seeks an interpreter for
press interviews who knows Turkish as well as German and English, even
though all the German-Turkish actors involved are unsurprisingly in perfect command of German.[17] It is at issue when a music editor at Radio MultiKulti sends an e-mail to the host of one of their weekly radio programs,
Erci E., stating that an academic would like to interview him about Turkish
identity, even though I had said that I wanted to talk to Erci about his career as a rap musician.

It comes as no surprise that hip-hop and rap have been the artistic genres in which the contributions of musicians from Turkish backgrounds have
achieved the strongest public recognition—it is these genres of cultural production that seem to be the "natural" preserve of young postmigrants. Yet,
instead of assuming that young people with migrant backgrounds are simply naturally drawn to these genres because they best express their authentic marginalized urban experiences, it is worth asking to what extent such
assumptions come to structure cultural policies, market opportunities, and
media interest, thus making rap and hip-hop the only sensible choices for
young aspiring artists aiming for public and commercial success.

The "whiteness" of the *Kultur* establishment in Germany is stabilized by
deep-seated expectations that immigrant and postmigrant cultural contributions will be either concerned with maintaining ethno-cultural traditions
or with expressing cultural hybridity, always invoking culture as a marker of
group identity. Even though *Ausländer* has gradually become less acceptable
as a term for immigrants and their descendents in German political discourses, the cultural contributions of immigrant and postmigrant artists are
expected to be statements about cultural difference and Otherness.

Transnational Culture

It is in light of these circumstances that the transnational circuits of cultural
production and exchange between Germany and Turkey have to be considered. Turkey's pop stars and other famous musicians are regularly brought
to Germany on concert tours, performing in front of almost exclusively immigrant and postmigrant audiences. Since Germany's economic recession
has hit these population groups to a disproportionate extent, concert orga-

nizers are even less likely to risk failure by presenting little-known artists from Berlin on stage. The latter might appear as background musicians, but will not take center stage for fear of not filling concert halls. Stars from Turkey, well known in Germany partly through the ubiquitous presence of satellite television, promise greater crowds. If audiences are to spend between 30 and 60 Euros for a concert ticket, they will do so only for an act that has proven star-quality, as organizers had to find out.

In the European editions of Turkey's daily newspapers, one can find regular advertisements announcing the European concert tours of well-known artists, listing the different cities that are still available for turning a profit. Local organizers are invited to carry the financial risk, paying an agreed sum to the artist and his/her management, renting a location, and providing security, all in the hope that enough tickets will be sold to recoup the costs. It is often commercially ambitious individuals with little experience who take this financial risk—and subsequently crash. Among the small circle of successful organizers in Berlin, stories of financial ruin are legend. In this climate, promoting the careers of local artists seems like a positively foolish gamble, even though performers from Turkey have become increasingly expensive in the wake of an increasing commercialization and consolidation of Turkey's music industry.

When the twenty-four-hour Turkish-language radio station Metropol FM went on air in Berlin in 1999, a new opportunity seemed to open up for representing the variety of local Turkish life in the city, and for offering a platform to local musicians. But given the station's difficulties in becoming commercially viable with a relatively small and economically weak target group of listeners, every effort has been made not to alienate any part of its potential audience. As a result, the Turkish music that is featured in its programs must have already proven its chart potential and thus audience appeal—which up till then has only been able to prove in Turkey. Certain musical genres, such as rap and hip-hop, are considered by the station's management to be too narrow in their appeal, and too disruptive, to be played on air. This was a lesson that had to be learned quickly by the station's young Turkish-German staff members as Metropol FM went on air. The German station manager Werner Felten was annoyed by their initial views on what kinds of music Metropol FM should play.

> I said, there's got to be something equivalent here in Turkish, as there is in German, where music is simply nice to listen to. The worst thing that can happen to a radio station is when listeners are saying, hey guys, you play great music! That is just as bad as people saying, your music is awful. Music you listen to on the radio has to be nice. If you want to attract the broad masses, it has to be nice. It can't irritate people either way.[18]

Felten is proud to be intervening in the station's playlists himself, sifting regularly through stacks of freshly imported CDs, on the lookout for tracks that indicate radio play format—just over three minutes in length. The logic of commercial radio success is the same for migrant and nonmigrant audiences, he claims. It is positively dangerous, he thinks, when members of the staff start playing the tracks that they like, or tracks that their friends are requesting. Metropol FM has to provide audiences with pleasant background music, not actively engage them, in order to survive in Berlin's highly competitive radio market. Radio MultiKulti does not face the same kind of competition, and obviously makes a much more deliberate effort to "irritate" in its daily hour of Turkish-language programming. Its funding secure, its editors can afford to ignore mainstream tastes and present topics as well as music that are not as broadly appealing. But since the Turkish program has lost its onetime monopoly on Turkish-language broadcasting with the influx of satellite imports and the emergence of Metropol FM, few listeners still make the effort to tune in.

The local company responsible for the poster campaigns in the streets of Kreuzberg, advertising the release of Sezen Aksu's latest CD, once used to produce the work of local artists like Aziza-A. and Cartel. Ünal Yüksel's company Ypsilon Musix tried out a range of innovative marketing ideas, such as selling a döner-shaped CD with the work of local Turkish-German musicians at döner-kebap shops. None of these strategies proved successful. While the company still produces a few German-rapping hip-hop artists from Berlin, the focus of its business has now shifted toward promoting the work of pop stars from Turkey, in cooperation with larger international labels. Despite the intensification of "cultural flows" bringing music and musicians from Turkey to Germany, and despite the expansion of a Turkish media landscape in the city and beyond, the situation for immigrant artists has thus anything but improved.

Given a situation in which Turkish cultural life in Germany can rely on public financial and institutional support only in the preserves of multiculturalist policy, commercial reasoning has out of necessity taken center stage, allowing little room for the nurturing of local talent. The current economic crisis in Germany has dealt another blow to the feeble cultural scene that has been able to emerge on the commercial terrain. Infighting, fierce competition, and even legal battles between Turkish cultural organizations, groups, and individuals are a well-known constant of Turkish cultural life in Berlin.[19] As Martin Greve concludes:

> The central problem is that after decades of exclusion from German institutions and from public funding, German-Turkish musical life is in a condition of advanced atomization, in which almost all musicians have learnt to fend for them-

selves only, and in which institutions promising continuity seem like new and daring experiments. (Greve 2002,17)

In light of these findings, an increasing orientation of immigrants and postmigrant artists toward Turkey and its cultural life as well as its cultural industries seems like a logical and rather sensible turn. Aziza-A. has moved to Istanbul-based Doublemoon Records for her second CD release. Young singer Bekir Karaoğlan performs Turkish "wedding music" at events such as Radio MultiKulti's 2003 birthday party, but prefers to sing vocals for the "Oriental crossover" band Orientation, which has similarly released on Doublemoon. Former member of the hip-hop band Cartel, Erci E., moderates a weekly Turkish pop music show on Radio MultiKulti, but he released his last solo album *Sohbet* in Turkey with the Turkish media giant Raks Müzik, also based in Istanbul. Many young singers such as pop star Rafet El-Roman leave Germany altogether, preferring to pursue their careers in Turkey.

Such orientations have been facilitated by changes in the Turkish music industry. As Martin Stokes has described, the targeting of cassette piracy and enforcement of new copyright legislation in the 1990s has promised greater financial returns for recording companies, and the arrival of transnational corporate actors such as PolyGram and others has made commercial music a much more lucrative business (Stokes 1999). Sales of CDs and cassette tapes as well as copyright fees that can now be collected from the myriad of Turkey's radio stations promise not just fame but also wealth for artists who succeed in it. And the industry's relentless promotion and fabrication of new stars holds out hope even for those aspiring young migrant musicians who are neither well connected nor already established in Turkey. This is particularly the case for the genre of Turkish pop music, with its high turnover of stars and the huge advertising effort that goes into their promotion. Turkish music channels such as Kral, and countless television programs and paparazzi magazines that focus on the private escapades of these stars, reach migrant youths via satellite and German newspaper stands. Travel to Istanbul is cheap, and producing a demo tape at one of the city's many recording studios is financially not out of reach for those with a job in Germany. Yet, as much as the famous three "T's" of television, travel, and telecommunications might facilitate the growth of transnational affiliations and encourage young migrant musicians to turn toward Turkey, it also needs to be asked what the alternatives to such affiliations could be at their place of residence in Germany.

Political scientist Thomas Faist has problematized the link between multiculturalism and migrants' emphasis on ethno-cultural distinctiveness (Faist 2000). Ethnic minorities' insistence on collective status has long been understood as resulting from a denial of cultural recognition within the majority society, as Max Weber argued in the 1920s. Faist claims instead that the multicultural politics of recognition in liberal democracies can in fact promote the retention and development of transnational ties. Refraining from cultural assimilation, "tolerant" integration paradigms in countries such as Germany open up possibilities for transstate networking and resource mobilization. The transnational ties of migrants are thus not simply a result of repressive political measures, but might on the contrary be accelerated in their development by multicultural rights and policies granted in immigration countries. This suggests a somewhat different link between multicultural politics and transnational affiliations: policies and institutions that are designed to acknowledge ethno-cultural distinctiveness promote transnational activities not simply by leaving space for them, or offering resources. They also construct "multicultural traps" that make it difficult for immigrant cultural producers to gain recognition for cultural work that is unrelated to their status as an ethnic minority that forms part of the multicultural mix.

A divide runs through cultural politics, institutions, and artistic work in Berlin: between a domain of culture in the singular (*Hochkultur*) that aims for "artistic quality" and is governed by standards that are rarely questioned as to their implicit and sometimes explicit nonimmigrant bias, and a domain of "socioculture" that has sociopolitical aims and targets those at the bottom of economic and ethnic hierarchies. This latter domain seeks to emphasize cultures in the plural, namely the distinctiveness of "cultures of origin" that immigrants are assumed to have brought with them. As with Radio MultiKulti, Berlin appears as a patchwork of cultures that are tied to social groups as their representatives. The cultural production of immigrant and postmigrant artists is evaluated mainly with regard to its integrative-political potential. Though established in the seventies with emancipatory aims, the domain of socioculture has in many ways become a prison-house for immigrant and postmigrant artists.

The case of Turkish artists in Berlin shows the all-but-liberal consequences of contemporary German multiculturalism in action, which in fact excludes them from funding opportunities and venues available to nonimmigrant and external artists. In the gap between *culture* and *cultures,* immigrant and postmigrant artists are bound to disappear. Instead of containing their alleged urge and desire to turn to Turkey, the politics of culture in Berlin often leave them little choice but to seek their fortunes abroad.

Returning to migrant broadcasters as cultural producers, there is a range of Turkish-language programs that address their audience not as an ethno-cultural minority within Berlin but as expatriates whose primary identification is and should be with their country of origin and/or national belonging. Several locally and transnationally produced programs focus on the so-called home country and on migrants' relationship with the Turkish state and national community. It is not enough to consider German multiculturalism and its workings in policymaking and institutions. To understand the complexity of transnational orientations within migrant cultural production, it is important to consider a second nation-state context—that of Turkey.

5

Bringing the Nation Back In: Media Nationalism between Local and Transnational Articulations

The prior chapters have focused on the German institutional and discursive context within which broadcasting for migrants is embedded. However, Turkey and the cultural politics emerging from the Turkish national context form a second important frame of reference for the discourses of belonging and difference that construct migrants in Berlin as particular kinds of cultural and ethno-national subjects. It is therefore essential to outline those aspects of Turkey's cultural politics and particularly its nation-building project that significantly shape migrants' cultural practices and understandings abroad.

While some broadcasting initiatives in Berlin seek to encourage migrants' identification with the Turkish state and its nation-building agenda, others actively contest this agenda and challenge it, most often targeting its policies of secularism and of ethno-nationalism. As will be seen, the Turkish state itself is using broadcasting as a tool to reach out to migrants abroad, following the recognition that "Euro-Turks" in particular constitute both a political and an economic force that Turkey has to reckon with. Most migrant producers are acutely aware of these efforts, which together with commercial television imports from Turkey form the implicit or explicit background against which migrant broadcasting takes place. Thus, in order to understand the complexity of frames of reference that many Turkish-language migrant broadcasters employ in their programs, it is crucial to address the relevant cultural and political constellations and conflicts that have their origin in Turkey, as well as the transnationalization of these conflicts.

Migration as well as new forms of mass media and communication technologies have played a central role in de-territorializing Turkey's most volatile cultural and political conflicts. As will be shown, broadcasting, particularly television broadcasting, is used by the Turkish state and by anti-state forces to intervene in the politics of cultural struggle in but also outside of Turkey's territory. Satellite television technology and changing mass media regulations and infrastructures across Europe have dramatically changed conditions of access to mass media production and the potential of its reach. Migrants from Turkey have taken up these new opportunities, often to counter state-controlled narratives of nationhood and to develop alternative visions of community.

Kurdish nationalist broadcasting, discussed in the second half of this chapter, is a case in point and offers a fascinating example of how local activism is linked to diasporic politics, made possible by media technologies that continuously evade the control of nation-states. The examination of Kurdish nationalist production efforts in Berlin will reveal how migrant television broadcasting ties into these new forms of cultural struggle on both local and transnational scales.

Music across Borders: Cartel

In the summer of 1995, a Turkish hip-hop group from Germany created quite a stir in Turkey. The group, Cartel, consisted of seven young Turkish second-generation *delikanlı*,[1] a nonimmigrant German, and a Cuban. Announced as the voice of the second generation from Europe, the group raced to the top of the Turkish pop charts with their angry lyrics asking Turks to unite against a racist society. The Turkish weekly news magazine *Nokta* claimed:

> A Cartel-storm is blowing in Turkey. The hip-hop and rap culture which emerged initially in American ghettos has made its entry into Turkish territory. Meanwhile, there are voices that accuse Cartel of promoting Turkish chauvinism. "Turk, Kurd, Laz, Çerkez / if we divide / we will all be lost," Cartel is singing, currently making rap on slippery political ground.[2]

Upon their arrival at the airport in Istanbul, the group members were surprised to be greeted by a crowd of young male fans affiliated with the MHP, Turkey's extreme right-wing nationalist party. This scene was repeated during numerous concerts all over the country: their audience cheered them on with a nationalist greeting well known and often feared in Turkey.[3] This greeting consists of the right arm stretched out and upward, index and little finger pointing straight, symbolizing the ears of the wolf, which is the symbol of Turkey's right-wing nationalists. The "Grey Wolves," the youth organization of the MHP, terrorized the country in the years before the military coup of 1980, murdering and assassinating hundreds from the "leftist" political camp in the bloody confrontations of the late seventies, often with the clandestine support of Turkey's police forces and secret service.[4]

In press interviews, members of the group expressed shock over the apparent "misunderstanding" their songs had caused: their calls for Turks to unite were directed toward a diverse group of people affected by racism in Germany and Western Europe, not against ethnically self-conscious minorities in Turkey, they claimed. In an interview with the daily newspaper *Türkiye,* they proclaimed themselves to be "culture nationalists" instead:

> We live in a foreign place and we defend our own culture so that we don't lose our national identity. We are not nationalists in the sense it is understood in Turkey. Ours is a cultural nationalism. We are a group who defend our Turkishness, our individuality, and at the same time we give shape to our own lives.[5]

In the media debates on how Cartel's message should be understood, Turkish migration to Germany and the contemporary situation of the former "guestworkers" eventually became the core issue. The hype surrounding Cartel's concert tour in Turkey provided an opportunity for the mass media to paint a new picture of the young Turkish generation growing up abroad, under adverse circumstances. Once-familiar notions of the Turkish plight in Germany could be concretized and partially modified, now representing Turkish youths, who had been depicted in Turkey mainly as a "lost generation," as a force of Turkish rebellion. "The revolt against oppression has led to the birth of Cartel," the daily newspaper *Sabah* claimed in a special report on the group. Turkish youths could be shown to reassert their cultural and national heritage and vacate the symbolic space of the victim that they—and labor migrants in general—had long occupied in the Turkish mainstream media. "The families who migrated to Germany fought not to lose their own identity in a new society," *Sabah* wrote. "They were silent and oppressed . . . but now there is a 'second generation' in Germany."[6]

Most members of Cartel had problems when trying to give interviews in Turkish. Their language did not conform to the standards of *öztürkçe* (high Turkish), but instead betrayed the rural origins of their parents as well as their having grown up in Germany. Yet, these facts were no longer interpreted by Turkish mass media as indicators of cultural lack, as used to be the rule. Instead, Cartel and the youths they represented were shown to defend their Turkish identity by way of mastering and combining different cultural and musical genres, combining American hip-hop rhythms with Turkish melodies and texts that asserted an aggressive superiority: "*Cartel, bir nu-*

MAP 2. Map of Turkey. *Courtesy of Jürgen Frohnmaier, www.yoyus.com.*

mara, en büyük, cehennemden çıkan çılgın Türk!" ("Cartel, number one, the greatest, the wild Turk coming from hell!"), as their most famous song pronounced. Turkey's media had given extensive coverage to the racist arson attacks in Germany that had targeted Turkish migrants a few years before, producing a huge outrage in Turkey. Cartel's call to arms was seen to be an adequate response.

The case of Cartel's reception in Turkey is instructive, because it focuses attention on the important transformations of the public imaginary in the so-called homeland as a result of large-scale migration. As is well known by now, it is not just migrants who undergo a shift in terms of how they imagine communities or social formations under current conditions of globalization, but also those who stay put. What Mayfair Mei-Hui Yang has termed the "increasing cosmopolitanism of the homeland" is often centrally mediated by mass media (Yang 1997).

The media debate surrounding Cartel suggests a transformation of the public imaginary in Turkey that had once regarded migrants solely as a culturally poor and dispossessed social group. The domain of music can in this respect be taken as indicative of how different social groups are represented as producers of culture, and of how cultural hierarchies have come to be asserted and transformed in the context of nation-building processes in Turkey (Stokes 1992). Associating migrants with hip-hop music represents a significant shift of the public imaginary, assigning them a new agency that had been lacking in earlier cultural imaginings. The figure of the migrant had once been closely associated with the musical culture of *arabesk,* a hybrid genre popular among the recent poor arrivals to Turkey's Western cities, who had come from the eastern countryside in search of a better life.

Arabesk Culture

The *gurbetçi* migrant, "the one who lives far from home," has for several decades been a symbol of cultural loss in Turkey, produced by the processes of modernization and urbanization that were seen to uproot individuals from tight-knit social and cultural contexts. The migrant as a lost figure stands at the center of *arabesk* culture, pervasive in Turkey as an oppositional discourse of popular protest particularly during the 1970s and 80s. The term *arabesk* was originally applied to forms of popular music that were heavily influenced by Egyptian music, which reached Turkey by way of Egyptian film and radio imports. While the Turkish state severely restricted the musical forms that were broadcast on state-controlled radio channels, it was unable to control the spillover that allowed the population in certain parts of the country to receive Egyptian radio signals. *Arabesk* genres were thus hybrid, combining Western instruments with Eastern monophonic forms, to the dismay of the Kemalist elites that aimed to purge the Turkish nation from such influences (Stokes 1999).

Arabesk music could not be heard on official state radio channels, but it became extremely popular in the urban centers to which rural migrants had flocked, readily available on black market cassette tapes and emanating from the *dolmuş* cars that compete with public buses to shuttle people to and from remote corners of the city. Turkish analysts concluded that *arabesk* was in fact more than just music, it was a way of life and attitude toward the world and toward Western modernity (Belge 1990). Turkey's *arabesk* culture mourned the fate of the country's internal migrants who had moved to the large cities in the west, in countless films and well-known songs by stars like Müslüm Gürses, Orhan Gencebay, and Ferdi Tayfur. Depicted as individuals cut off from their traditional cultural and social background, which had provided them with moral orientation and practical support, *arabesk* migrants were shown to fall prey to the temptations of Westernization. Such Westernization was linked to the promise of easy money and amoral city life into which both male and female migrants were drawn. For male protagonists, the story of decline often involved a woman with blond hair who in the end would leave them destitute both emotionally and financially.

Turkish state elites did not approve of these dark and fatalistic tales of modernization, and *arabesk* music was banned from the state-controlled airwaves up until the 1990s. However, the state's problem with *arabesk* was not so much that it represented migrants as individuals at cultural risk, but that it denied any viable and culturally appropriate path toward modernization. The role of the state as it came to be defined after the Turkish revolution was precisely to provide its subjects with the cultural resources that would render them compatible with the country's path toward modern, Westernized nationhood.

Affiliates of the country's leader Mustafa Kemal Atatürk, such as Ziya Gökalp, who has been called the "philosopher of the Atatürk revolution," regarded music as one cultural arena among others in which the larger project of combining "originally Turkic culture" with "Western civilization" had to be carried out. Turkish folk music began to be systematically collected since the 1920s in different regions of the country, with the *türkü* folk song as the symbol of national village culture. At the same time, Western classical music began to be taught in Turkey's musical conservatories, while Ottoman classical music, *sanat müziği,* was denounced as Eastern and non-Turkish (Coşkun 1995a–d). The kind of hybridity the Turkish state wanted to promote was a "marriage between folk and Western music" (Gökalp 1968, thereby shedding Turkey's oriental heritage. For Turkish elites, *arabesk* represented the wrong kind of marriage between different cultural traditions, as it articulated a critique of state-promoted modernization and mourned the loss of village culture.

The migrants with whom *arabesk* was associated similarly represented the wrong kind of combining Eastern with Western traits. When the large-scale rural to urban migration process set in during the 1950s, the orderly fusion of East and West envisioned in the nationalist project of modernization seemed threatened. Flocking to the cities in search of work, migrants represented in the eyes of political reformers and social scientists the most problematic aspect of Turkey's efforts to "catch up with the West." Rural village culture—the location of the *halk* (folk) and origin of *halk müziği* (folk music)—and urban civilization—where Western classical music was introduced—were to complement each other, with the urban center educating the rural peripheries. But the migrants living in Turkey's squatter neighborhoods, the so-called *gecekondus* (literally, "built overnight"), seemed to represent a problematic counter-tendency. With women in village clothing and chicken and goats invading the urban setting, it seemed to Turkey's reformers as though the East was invading the West, resulting in a combination of their most negative traits. The migrants' search for a better life in the city did not fit their visions of exemplary progress: village school education, the relegation of religion to the private domain, the shedding of values and beliefs deemed both premodern and Eastern. The dominant image of these "uprooted" people depicted their relationship to the nation as a precarious one: while statist ideology maintained the compatibility of modernization with a return to national roots, the "out-of-placeness" of migrants, no longer the "folk" but not appropriately urban either, could not be integrated into the projected history of national renewal.[7]

Labor migrants who had left the country for Western Europe were depicted in similar terms: cut off from the positive aspects of their rural origins—the communal village culture that had provided moral guidance and social control—they were seen to lack the resources that would have allowed them to benefit from their "Western" experience.[8] What is more, during the 1980s Turkish elites became increasingly concerned with the image of Turkey that these migrants were projecting abroad. State agencies were unable to intervene through cultural policies and censorship the way they did in Turkey, but funds were increasingly made available to establish Turkish cultural institutes abroad, and to send religious representatives and school teachers to labor migrant destinations in Western Europe.

When the Turkish state monopoly on broadcasting crumbled in 1990, it was not so much *arabesk* music that blossomed but a new hybrid musical form, Turkish pop music. Whereas *arabesk* was regarded as a failed synthesis in which Eastern elements dominated, Turkish pop has been seen as a success: a musical form associated with and appropriate for Turkey's young generation, singing about Western-style romantic love and relationships. Pop music has been more likely to promote the image of a young Turkey firmly located in the West, with Turkish musical elements complementing but not dominating the compositions. Significantly, many of the young stars of Turkish pop music have been "transfers" from Germany or other Western European countries, as the largest Turkish daily *Hürriyet* calls them. Presenting a new pop star who has grown up in Germany, the paper quotes him as saying that the "oriental mediocracy in Turkish pop has to finally disappear.[9] Turkish pop has been celebrated as a "spontaneous East-West synthesis" in which European Turks have played an important role.[10]

The fact that the descendents of labor migrants play such a prominent role in Turkish pop music indicates the steep ascent of migrants in the cultural hierarchies articulated by dominant public discourses in Turkey. The latter still operate with an East-West dichotomy in which the East is—in the most positive reading—associated with Turkish tradition, in the worst with "oriental backwardness." But migrants are now no longer represented as country bumpkins who have lost the little cultural capital they possessed in a hostile foreign environment, but as modern hybrids who successfully fight to maintain their identity as Turks while incorporating Western cultural elements.[11] This transformation was aided by Turkey's "media revolution" of the 1990s, which fundamentally changed the conditions for the mass-mediated articulation and representation of culture, and cultures in the plural.

Turkey's Media Revolution

Even though Turkey's 1972 constitution for the first time declared the formal separation and independence of broadcasting from party politics, the Turkish Radio and Television Corporation (TRT) continued to function under rigid state control until the 1990s. Broadcasting played an important role as an instrument in the creation of a sense of national unity, promoting national folklore, nationalist narratives, and, most importantly, the standardization of an official Turkish language (Şahin and Aksoy 1993; Öncü 1995; Turam 1996). Successive governments made sure that they installed their representatives in important positions at TRT (Refiğ 1996). With the TRT restricting how the Turkish nation and Turkish national culture could be represented in the public sphere of radio and television, there was little room for dissenting representations that could address Turkey's cultural, political, and social conflicts. This situation changed dramatically in 1990, with the advent of new mass communication technologies that made it possible to challenge the state's monopoly on broadcasting from outside the country.

In May 1990, the private television corporation Magic Box began to broadcast its program via the Eutelsat F5 satellite from Germany into Turkey (Yengin 1994). While the constitution prohibited private broadcasting from Turkish soil to uphold the state's monopoly, no legislation existed to ban broadcasting from outside the country. The success of the Magic Box channel signaled an explosive proliferation of private television channels and radio stations. Local communities all over Turkey pressured their municipal governments into setting up local transmitters in order to make satellite programs widely available. The passive deregulation had devastating consequences for TRT: within a matter of months, it lost much of its audience and advertising income to private channels (Turam 1996). The advent of commercial broadcasting severely undercut the formerly unchallenged position of the TRT, forcing it to adopt features of its private rivals and to relax its tight regulations in order to remain competitive. By 1995, more than 500 television stations and 2,000 radio stations had begun broadcasting in Turkey on local, national, and international levels, in the absence of a regulatory framework. It is only since 1995 that a new state commission, the Supreme Board for Radio and Television (RTÜK), whose members are selected by the governing parties, has begun to control channels by planning legal frequencies and examining the content of programs on a national level. Current estimates put the number of private television channels at around 300, the number of private radio stations at more than 1,000.

The new commercial broadcast media have redefined the notion of a mass-mediated public sphere, formerly identified with the official voice of the state. Broadcast media now claim to reflect the voices of the "Turkish man or woman on the street," still linked to the hegemonic narrative of Turkish nationalism, but separate from the state (Şahin and Aksoy 1993). Almost all of the "cultural camps" that confront each other in Turkey's political arena—religious/secular, Sunni/Alevi, left/right, ethnic minority/majority—have now found some form of representation in the media. This was not an intentional development: most stations are guided by strictly commercial logic, competing as they are in an all-out free market situation in which broadcasting projects can be launched and disappear in a matter of months. New structures of ownership have emerged, with media conglomerates tending to own a range of newspapers, television stations, and radio stations that are primarily profit-oriented, but by no means politically neutral. Unchecked market concentration in the media sector has led to "cartels" of a kind very different from that discussed above, linking newspapers to broadcasting venues and dictating distribution prices (Sağnak 1996). More or less unfettered market mechanisms have thus provided a countertendency, narrowing the spectrum of opinions and positions articulated in the media.

What is more, Turkish analysts and scholars have also frequently lamented the problematic relationship between political parties and the media (Finkel 2000; Turam 1996; Sağnak 1996; Otan 1995). Evidence and rumors of party politicians attempting to directly influence media reporting abound. In 2002, the Uzan Group, one of Turkey's largest media conglomerates, even started its own political party, Genç Partisi (Party of Youth), which had considerable success in the 2002 November elections but fell short of entering parliament. The Uzan Group was implicated in the efforts to start Berlin's first Turkish radio station, Metropol FM, but withdrew its sponsorship just before it was scheduled to go on air.

Violence against journalists and media organizations in Turkey occurs with greatest frequency in relation to reporting on politically sensitive issues, such as that of Kurdish separatism and state actions against it. As Amnesty International reports, several journalists have been tortured in police custody or have "disappeared" (most likely been murdered) in the course of the 1990s. Most of them worked for Kurdish-oriented newspapers such as *Özgür Gündem* (Free Agenda), *Özgür Ülke* (Free Country), and *Yeni Politika* (New Politics), which were subsequently banned for alleged Kurdish-separatist sympathies (Amnesty International 1996). Human Rights Watch has noted that in subsequent years, even prominent journalists working for mainstream publications were imprisoned or had their work censored (Human Rights Watch 1999, 2004). Thus, despite the increased openness of the new public sphere that has emerged as a result of private broadcasting, there are still limits to what can be publicly voiced, printed, or shown on television.

This said, the new commercial media in Turkey have had significant impact on public opinion as well as public tastes, organizing meanings as "issues" and transforming the terrain of ideological discourse (Öncü 1995). Most analysts agree that the general liberalization of broadcasting has given new meanings to the concept of the mass-mediated public sphere in Turkey, diversifying the issues debated as well as the imagined national audience (Aksoy and Robins 1993). While foreign program imports continue to be dubbed in the voice of *öztürkçe,* the Turkish spoken by educated elites, the private commercial channels have given public articulation to other kinds of formerly marginalized voices, such as the "syncretic speech styles" of second-generation migrants and low-income metropolitan populations. The widening of the mass-mediated public sphere in Turkey has also given new visibility and recognition to the Islamist "counter-elites" whose emergence can be dated back to the post–1983 period, after Turkey's last military coup (Göle 1997b). Islamist groups have considerable funds to establish their own printing and broadcasting networks. Their television channels draw upon the older, "Ottoman" Turkish with Persian and Arabic expressions and concepts that had been deliberately abandoned by the Kemalist proponents of *öztürkçe.* Kanal 7 is affiliated with the former Refah party, the Nurcu movement operates the channel STV, and the oldest Islamic channel, TGRT, is affiliated with the Nakşibendi order (Öncü 2000).

But even for non-Islamist commercial channels, Ayşe Öncü has described how the "packaging of Islam" has shifted the grounds for political campaigning. Commercial television helped the Refah Party in 1991 to shed its image as a backward-oriented party of small-town shopkeepers. The central narrative on mainstream commercial television has remained secular, but within this core narrative, different "interpretive packages" compete with each other (Öncü 1995). One such interpretive package presents Islam as a global conspiracy of religious and financial interests. Rather than presented as "small-town" or linked to an invisible enemy within, television channels now present Islam in the context of Saudi finance capital, Iranian fundamentalism, and, increasingly, Muslim organizations in Western Europe. Noting that the secularist idea of Islam as global conspiracy resonates with broader cultural narratives of Turkish nationalism in which outside enemies are lurking to exploit Turkey's weak moments, Öncü describes a "packaging" of Islam that increasingly locates it as an outside threat, a threat in which migrants figure prominently.

As with the phenomenon of Turkish pop, Turkish migrant populations again appear as important cultural creators and political agents whose activities "feed back" into Turkey, but much more problematically so. The members of Cartel seemed to lend support to nationalist constructions of Turkish identity, claiming to protect it under adverse circumstances in the diaspora. The members of the "Islamist" Millî Görüş, the Kaplan Group, and also the Kurdish nationalists abroad present a danger to this identity, apparently mobilizing transnational support in order to gain political power in Turkey. In all of these cases, migrants have acquired a new public importance and relevance to Turkey's present and future development. They figure prominently in the new articulations of national identity presented on commercial, secular television that fuse consumerism with confident Turkishness in a globalizing world. But they also figure in the construction of an enemy who is at once "inside" and "outside," and thus needs to be combated through new strategies. The "television explosion," itself a reminder that the nation-state has decreasing control over what crosses its territorial boundaries, opened up new public arenas of ideological contestation and promoted alternative articulations of national, religious, and ethno-cultural identity.

The rapid development and expansion of commercial broadcasting also contributed to what Yael Navaro-Yashin has described as a commodification of the politics of culture in Turkey (Navaro-Yashin 2002).[12] The rise of consumerism was an important element and effect of the country's globalizing economy in the 1980s and 90s, and it involved the new Islamist elites just as much as the secularist establishment. Beginning with Turgut Özal in the mid-1980s, governments adopted neoliberal economic policies and further dismantled social welfare provisions. As a consequence, the gap between rich and poor in the country has increasingly widened. At the same time, styles of consumption have become prime indicators of cultural identities and political differences, as consumer items turned into "emblems of identity" (Navaro-Yashin 2002, 80). Private radio and television networks had an important role to play in this commodification of cultural politics, as they promoted an unprecedented expansion of advertising industries in the country.

Styles of consumption have been embedded in competing narratives of Turkish culture, in which both secularists and Islamists stake out their respective claims to represent the nation and its true cultural virtues. They are also heavily inflected by class-based strategies of distinction, even though this is rarely acknowledged in an explicit manner (Navaro-Yashin 2002; White 2002).[13] Attending to the complexities of social class and gender can reveal that there is no necessary correspondence between the "voices" that are represented in the new media and the subject positions that are inhabited by concrete groups of the population. Nor does the new media landscape offer conditions for an equal competition among the different "cultural camps" that surface in it. But the grounds for the public representation of culture, religion, and national identity in Turkey have decisively shifted, challenging media representations of national culture that were once exclusively state-defined.

Satellite Subversions

The beginnings of commercial broadcasting in Turkey had already revealed the limitations to state control over the mass-mediated articulation of opinions and positions coming from abroad. By way of satellite broadcasting, Turkey's laws and regulations could be circumvented, as the television channel Magic Box had shown. But soon after, other kinds of satellite broadcasts began to subvert Turkish laws and state policies in a much more challenging fashion.

In 1995, the Kurdish satellite television station MED-TV began to operate from Western Europe. With studios in Belgium, media expertise from different European countries, a license provided by the British Independent Television Commission ITC, and a transponder hired from France Telecom, MED-TV was conceived as a transnational project with a Kurdish nationalist agenda.[14] With broadcasting in Kurdish dialects forbidden in Turkey, and Kurdish nationalist positions being strictly banned from being articulated on radio and television in the country, as in other areas of Kurdish residence belonging to Iran, Iraq, and Syria, satellite broadcasting offered a way to simultaneously challenge state prohibitions in the territory claimed as Kurdistan and to reach Kurdish diaspora populations in the Mediterranean region as well as all over Western Europe. Thus MED-TV not only gave room to nationalist positions but also to groups that were actively fighting against governments in the region, most notably the PKK (Partiya Karkerên Kurdistan), the Workers' Party of Kurdistan.

Giving room to PKK positions meant to also at least passively accept violence, because the PKK had opened a guerilla war against the Turkish state,

Map 3. Kurdish Nationalist Map of Kurdistan. *Courtesy of Jürgen Frohnmaier, www.yoyus.com.*

and regarded the behavior of the latter toward the Kurdish population as a form of war, even if undeclared. The state of emergency (*sıkıyönetim*) declared by the Turkish military regime after the coup of 1980 for the entire country was continued for the Kurdish regions in the Southeast until 1987. It was abolished in these regions only to be replaced with a state of civil emergency (*olağanüstü hal*), which continued to give wide-ranging powers to the military and paramilitary organizations. Map 3 shows the residence patterns of Kurdish populations in Turkey and its neighboring nation-states, as claimed by Kurdish nationalist organizations.

In the mid-1970s, Kurdish-nationalist groups in Turkey had begun to struggle by violent means, not just against state forces but also against oppositional political groups and alleged "traitors" in a general climate of rising political violence in the country. The Turkish state responded with severity, mobilizing its military, police, and paramilitary as well as secret service forces to fight its opposition. Its means included systematic torture in police custody and prisons, assassinations, and the destruction of thousands of villages in the Southeast. The PKK in turn evolved more and more into a Stalinist-type organization that was centered around its leader Abdullah Öcalan. At times, it was fighting dissenters among its own ranks as ruthlessly as other oppositional groups and state forces, as a prominent founding member and later critic of the party has described (Çürükkaya 1977).

Given the difficulties of maintaining the organization in Turkey, Western Europe became an increasingly important hub of organizing activities for the PKK and other Kurdish-nationalist groups. Many labor migrants who reside in Western Europe originally stem from the Southeastern regions concerned, and the actions of Turkish state forces did much to create a climate of support for Kurdish nationalism not just in Turkey but also in the diaspora. The well-coordinated protests in Western Europe in the wake of the capture of PKK leader Öcalan in February 1999—he was abducted by Turkish secret service forces from Kenya and brought to Turkey to stand trial—manifested that the organization could count on structures across different countries to mobilize thousands of disciplined supporters in a matter of hours or even minutes.

It is estimated that up to one million ethnic Kurds have migrated as labor migrants and refugees to Europe since the 1960s. Their numbers are difficult to establish, since their countries of residence register them in terms of citizenship rather than ethnic background. But for many Kurds in Europe, national belonging and ethnicity form key issues of political mobilization. The emergence of a Kurdish diaspora and the drastic changes in communication technologies have produced a new form and practice of Kurdish nationalism. Satellite television and the Internet cannot be said to have produced this new nationalism in any determinate way, but as new technologies of mediation they have been crucial to communication and mobilization processes under diasporic conditions.

The Kurdish struggle in the diaspora context has focused on cultural unification and national sovereignty, and has done so in ways that differ from the bulk of Kurdish activism in the regions claimed as Kurdistan. Marked by varying tribal allegiances, linguistic differences, and diverging political interests, Kurds in those regions have often sought limited autonomy and toleration from the respective national governments in whose reach they reside. It is in the diaspora that the idea of a united and sovereign Kurdistan has been most strongly promoted. Thus, the main impetus for struggle toward a Kurdish nation-state was developed outside of the very territory that is now claimed as its appropriate location (Van Bruinessen 2000b). The very nation-states whose territorial integrity is threatened by Kurdish nationalism paradoxically promoted this development.

What seemed like a sensible strategy for governments dealing with sectarian struggle on their territory, namely sending Kurdish activists into exile, quite quickly turned against them: it is only in exile, and only under the conditions of much-facilitated long-distance communication and travel, that a unification of different Kurdish struggles has been possible.

As Van Bruinessen describes, Kurds in Syria, Iran, Iraq, and Turkey were initially fighting their own separate struggles against national governments (Van Bruinessen 2006). The first period of labor migration to Western Europe did not see an immediate upsurge in Kurdish activism. It was only with the mass expulsion of political activists in the 1980s, and with the transformation of media landscapes and communication technologies, that Kurdish nationalism in its present form became viable.

Although the Turkish state sought to solve the Kurdish issue by exiling its leaders, they found much better conditions for political organizing in Western Europe: a second generation ready to be politicized for the Kurdish cause, an educated elite that could build up infrastructures and represent in public, and new forms and technologies of telecommunication that allowed for a united, transnational Kurdish public to emerge. Thus, the Kurdish struggle has been deterritorialized, and at the same time unified in this very movement of deterritorialization. The emergence of the satellite television station MED-TV in 1995 was a crucial step in symbolically uniting dispersed Kurdish populations and addressing them as a national audience.

The station was a huge success among Kurds all over Europe and the Middle East. The sale of satellite dishes in Turkey's eastern provinces took a steep rise. One of the chief organizers behind MED-TV, Hikmet Tabak, described the reactions of Kurdish audiences when the station began to broadcast:

> MED-TV hit the airwaves spectacularly. . . . The word spread like wildfire and every Kurdish person was eager to get to a television screen. In the cities people rushed into cafes, in the villages everybody gathered at the houses of those with a satellite dish. . . . The Kurdish people were amazed at MED-TV, as if they had not seen television before. Kurds were singing in Kurdish. It was a revolution. Thousands cried with joy. I witnessed this at the Berlin Kurdish Association. They all chanted "Long live Kurdistan." . . . It is very difficult for non-Kurds to understand the significance of a television channel for a nation. (Tabak 2001, 160)

Tabak's presence at the Berlin Kurdish Association was probably no accident. The MED-TV station was built up with crucial help from Kurdish activists in Berlin, and it had close connections with migrant producers at Berlin's open access channel OKB (Offener Kanal Berlin).

Local Kurdish Television and Its Transnational Ties

My own introduction to Kurdish politics and media activism had begun with my efforts to learn Turkish while living in Berlin in the mid-1990s. After my relocation to the United States, studying the language had become more difficult, but I pursued it during my summer visits when I returned to the city. In the summer of 1994, I asked the owner of a newsstand in my neighborhood if I could put up a note in his store, offering German or English instruction in exchange for Turkish. He enthusiastically replied that there was no need for me to do so, since I could learn Turkish with him and his family. Deniz had two small sons, both in elementary school, and he wanted them to pick up some English so that they would get a head-start for their advanced schooling later in life. I was soon introduced to his wife Zerdi who worked with him in the store, and began to visit them there as they spent most of the daylight hours working.

That summer, we would often sit drinking tea in the backroom, where Deniz had installed a television set. It was turned on whenever Kurdish groups were broadcasting on Berlin's Open Channel, a cable television station that screens amateur productions made by Berlin residents. I soon learnt that he and his wife were avid supporters of the Kurdish separatist group PKK, and they would make special efforts not to miss any program that dealt with Kurdish issues. The Kurdish struggle in Turkey was a major concern in their lives, and the Open Channel offered at that point in time the only opportunity to have Kurdish nationalist positions directly represented on television. "These are our boys," Deniz would say and point toward the screen. I maintained a skeptical position with regard to the violent struggle of the PKK, and our contact eventually lessened that summer as the children were not too eager to pursue English—they had enough problems keeping up with German, since they spoke both Turkish and Kurmanci, the major Kurdish dialect, at home. But I remained fascinated with Open Channel programs, and with the range of programs that immigrants from Turkey were producing. When I returned to begin research in 1998, there were several Kurdish nationalist programs produced in Turkish on the OKB.

One of the most controversial regular Kurdish programs was called *Welat TV,* and it had predecessors dating back to 1988. Two earlier programs had been banned as a result of successful protests by the Turkish embassy and Turkish viewers for its alleged PKK endorsements. *Cudi* (Mountain) had been reporting on the actions of the Turkish state and military against the insurgency in the Southeast. When the OKB announced a three-month ban against its successor program *Barış* (Peace) in 1993, some of the producers decided to put together a new program that ran under the name of *Dersim* until it was also banned in 1994. They had received hate mail and bomb threats, one of the producers told me when I finally met him after lengthy efforts to arrange for an interview.

The location he chose for our meeting was an ice cream parlor in the southern district of Marienfelde, a middle-class residential neighborhood on the outskirts of Berlin with hardly any immigrant residents. I was to wait for him on the parlor's open terrace, which could be easily scanned from afar for potential threats. Mehmet Yüce[15] explained to me that he had to take precautions—the Turkish secret service MİT was operating in Berlin, he said, and his life was constantly at risk as a result of his broadcasting activities. The director of the Open Channel had suggested that they should do "apolitical" broadcasting to avoid conflict, Mehmet Yüce claimed, and told of several meetings with him and representatives of the State Media Council that had preceded the broadcasting bans. But the very idea of producing Kurdish television on the Open Channel was to counter Turkish-Islamic nationalism. The Turkish state was using mass media to influence both the population in Turkey and immigrants abroad, turning media into instruments of terror, Yüce said. He felt that he had a responsibility to use the Open Channel and the public forum it offered to tell the "actual truth" (*gerçek budur*). Welat occasionally broadcast live and allowed for viewers to call in, resulting in a huge number of incensed Turks to call in and swear at him. Yüce stated, quite contentedly: "For one thousand years they have silenced [*söz kesmek*] the Kurdish people, now it is me who cuts them off."

But Yüce was not just producing programs for the Open Channel, he was also contributing programs to MED-TV, he told me. In fact, he and another friend active at an Open Channel in another German city had gone to Brussels together in 1994 to train future staff for MED-TV, none of whom had prior broadcasting experience. It was the production of programs for the OKB that had taught him the necessary skills: "*Bizim için bir okul oldu*" ("it was an educational institution for us"), he stated. Now, he was regularly reporting on Kurdish events in Berlin for MED-TV, and they in turn provided him with material such as music videos to show in his program on the Open Channel.

Welat TV was not interested in the local life of Kurdish immigrants as a potential basis for new identifications and new forms of community—if events taking place in Berlin were reported on, it was their relation to the wider struggle for the Kurdish nation and for a Kurdish state that was stressed. Yet, Berlin as a locality did not completely disappear: it emerged as one place of activism among others where a dispersed Kurdish nation follows the command of its leadership, similar to other locations across Western Europe, Turkey, and the adjoining states with Kurdish minority populations. Yüce's connections to MED-TV reveal a more important role for local activism. The Open Channel Berlin provided a training ground that was crucial for the establishment of the satellite channel. Mehmet Yüce had no prior television experience, but the training provided to all so-called users by the technical support staff of the Open Channel and years of producing his own programs gave him sufficient skills to help set up MED-TV. Beyond production skills, Yüce also continued to contribute programs to MED-TV, as did other locally based producers in different locations in Western Europe.

Considering the issue of different articulations between global and local electronic mass media, then, local Kurdish broadcasting at the OKB was at once a response to national and transnational media from Turkey, and a crucial initiator of and contributor to a new transnational broadcasting project. The satellite station had great repercussions for Kurdish populations outside of Berlin: both nationally in Turkey and transnationally in Western Europe as well as in the regions of Kurdish settlement in the Middle East. On a transnational level, MED-TV played an important role in promoting a Pan-Kurdish identity, facilitating communication across different Kurdish dialects and promoting the standardization of Kurmanci as a shared national language (Wahlbeck 1998).

Hide and Seek

The Turkish state did everything in its power to prevent the satellite channel from being able to function. Turkish state representatives contacted telecommunication companies who lease transponders even before the MED-TV staff had spoken to them, warning the companies that the terrorist PKK organization was behind the channel. Such claims indeed could not easily be refuted. Though MED-TV always claimed political independence, it gave much room to PKK positions, often inviting PKK officials to explain their views, though not excluding rivaling Kurdish organizations. Turkish politicians also lobbied the respective Ministries of Foreign Affairs in the countries involved, which in turn applied pressure on different telecommunication ventures.

When MED-TV eventually did manage to lease a transponder from France Telecom and obtained a license from the British Independent Television Commission, the Turkish press initiated a protest campaign, denouncing the channel as a terrorist project. But it was protest at the highest political level that proved to be most effective. Tansu Çiller, prime minister at the time, went to visit her counterpart John Major in London to have the ITC license revoked. After the transponder lease was up, France Telecom did not renew the contract, and MED-TV was forced to lease from Portuguese Telecom, obtaining only a three-month contract. Turkey's president Süleyman Demirel went to Lisbon and publicly asked for the contract to be cancelled. It was not renewed, forcing MED-TV to start another search, ending with a contract with the Polish Telecommunications Agency PTS. Pressure from Turkey this time led to a straightforward cancellation of the contract. In the summer of 1996, MED-TV was off the air for 45 days before another contract could be signed with an American-based company. However, Belgian police raided the studios of the station and arrested staff members and guests, confiscating archives and computers. The station's bank accounts were temporarily frozen. The Turkish Interior Minister publicly claimed joint responsibility. Another problem arose when Turkish police and gendarmerie forces began to raid houses in Turkey that had their satellite dishes turned in the direction of the Intelsat signal that transmitted MED-TV.

> The police were trained to identify who was watching MED-TV. Turkish television viewers were pointing their antennas to Eutelsat at 10 Degrees East, or Turkish Sat at 45 Degrees East, and because Intelsat was at 18 Degrees West, our viewers were easily identified. They were arrested and their antennas shot at. Kurds begged us to change the satellite because of the risk using this transponder meant for our viewers. (Tabak 2001, 168)

Then MED-TV switched again, this time hiding behind another company that signed a contract with Slovak Telecom, allowing the station to have its programs transmitted again via the Eutelsat satellite. In July 1997, Turkey was able to jam MED-TV's satellite signal for twenty-three days. In September 1998, a Slovakian political delegation announced the cancellation of the contract during an official visit to Turkey, forcing the station to switch once more to an American satellite connection. But the final blow was dealt to MED-TV when the British ITC revoked its license on April 23, 1999. The ITC had repeatedly diagnosed violations of its regulations such as calls to violence and "hateful speech" during MED-TV's programs. Hikmet Tabak conceded that MED-TV did in fact violate ITC regulations, but put it in the perspective of an "information war" in which the Turkish state and its media had continuously the upper hand:

> To offer an alternative to this journalism, our emotional journalists felt they had to tell the story from their hearts. It was very difficult for them to be model jour-

nalists, because there was a very crucial war going on. Faced with this media empire of lies, it was impossible to be "impartial" in a universal journalistic sense. (Tabak 2001, 171)

Measured against Turkish laws, MED-TV was of course committing serious offenses, simply by promoting the idea of Kurdish cultural and political rights on Turkish territory. For the makers of MED-TV, however, broadcasting was a matter of both setting the record straight—countering what they saw as partial and misleading reporting in the Turkish media— and of mobilizing Kurdish people who were scattered over a wide range of different countries. They were involved in an information war, they felt. Given that MED-TV was a satellite television station made possible by different kinds of local knowledge and financial capital, by national broadcasting regulations in different states, and by transnational media infrastructures, it is not surprising to find that it was quickly replaced after its closure. After the station's license was revoked by the ITC, Medya TV began to broadcast from Paris with a similar agenda. In February 2004, the French authorities closed it down. Only one month later, a new satellite station, Roj TV, began broadcasting from Denmark, despite continued protestations from Turkish state representatives.

Media and the New Forms of Cultural Struggle in Turkey

The MED-TV station had a great impact on Turkey's cultural politics. Turkish state forces eventually came to realize that they could not stop the production of Kurdish-nationalist television abroad, and neither could they effectively prohibit and control the reception of such programs via satellite dishes in Turkey.[16] As a result, the Turkish state began to change its stance on the public use of Kurdish languages, formerly strictly prohibited in all public contexts including schools and the media.

In the context of the debate on how to gain membership in the EU— which had encouraged Turkey to grant cultural rights to Kurds—the government began to discuss radical policy changes. On November 15, 2000, the *Turkish Daily News* quoted then deputy prime minister Mesut Yılmaz of the center-right Motherland Party (ANAP) as saying that the unity and integrity of Turkey had to be preserved, but that

the real threat to the unity of the nation is the broadcast brainwashing of millions of our citizens by separatist organizations. Unfortunately, we cannot prevent this by imposing fines and bans because of advances in technology. The state should use its head and see that we have no other way of preserving our values.[17]

A few days later, even representatives of the Turkish secret service echoed this view. On November 28, 2000, Turkey's largest-selling daily *Hürriyet*—which next to its name sports the Turkish flag, a picture of Atatürk, and a text stating *"Türkiye Türklerindir"* ("Turkey belongs to the Turks") on its front page—came out with the following headline: *"MİT'ten 2 mesaj"* ("two messages from the secret service"). The two heads of the Turkish secret service had given an interview to Turkey's main daily newspapers in which they made astonishing recommendations to the government regarding Kurdish media: *"Kürtçe TV yayını serbest bırakılsın"* ("television programs in Kurdish should be tolerated"). They explained their position as follows:

> Everybody watches PKK TV—If you want to win the hearts and minds of citizens, you have to explain yourself to them. Medya TV, which follows the line of the PKK, is telling lots of lies. And everybody watches it via satellite. So how are you get the truth to people?[18]

It was suggested that the government should recognize the realities on the ground in the predominantly Kurdish areas—the fact that quite a large part of the population is not able to speak or understand Turkish—and try to compete with Kurdish nationalists over the loyalties of the local population. "It is one thing," second-in-command Mikdat Alpay stated in the same article, "if a theatre group is putting on a Kurdish play to promote Kurdish nationalism (*Kürtçülük*), and quite another if the state uses Kurdish to reach an understanding with its citizens." The MİT official charged that the Turkish state had failed to reach out to the Kurdish-speaking population and communicate its positions.

The arguments emerging since then from government circles and state officials are in stark contrast to the policies enforced since the beginnings of the Republic that were to ensure cultural and linguistic homogeneity. To regard Kurdish spoken by a sizeable part of Turkey's population as simply a neutral fact rather than a problem to be rectified was a first step toward the recognition of ethno-cultural differences, right-wing politicians feared. The other deputy prime minister who represented the extreme-right MHP party, Devlet Bahçeli, stated: "It is impossible for Turkey to look favorably upon 'cultural' and 'ethnic rights' which will only serve to fan the flames of ethnic conflict and discrimination."[19] Nevertheless, in 2003, the Turkish government enacted legal reforms that paved the way toward greater cultural rights for Kurds, including the right to use Kurdish personal names, the right to broadcast in Kurdish and establish private Kurdish-language courses, linked to Turkey's bid to join the European Union. In practice, however, these legal reforms have yet to show much of an impact.

TRT-Int—Representing the Turkish State Abroad

Selectively opening TRT-channels to formerly shunned forms of music and entertainment, liberalizing policies on the use of Kurdish, and establishing new institutional structures of control were among the significant responses to satellite broadcasting that affected the population within Turkey's territorial boundaries. But apart from Kurdish nationalists and shrewd businessmen, Turkish state representatives themselves had recognized quite early the potential of satellite transmission technologies, and sought to widen their sphere of influence. The result was the television channel TRT-International, established in 1990 and aimed at speakers of Turkish in Western Europe, two years later also at the Turkic populations of Central Asia (TRT-*Avrasya*).

TRT-International has a local office in Berlin, reflecting its importance as the largest "Turkish city" outside of Turkey. Several hours of programming are produced in TRT's Berlin studio space, mostly current affairs programs that deal with events not just in Berlin but in all of Germany and also in neighboring countries. Since employment at the Berlin office requires perfect Turkish skills that meet TRT's standards as a state broadcasting service, all of the staff members have been educated though not necessarily trained in Turkey. Directors are appointed by Ankara and changed every three years, often having little knowledge of local or even wider German affairs. For other former staff members, the Berlin office has served as a point of entry into Germany's professional broadcasting environment. Several of the staff members currently working for Radio MultiKulti's Turkish team have once worked for TRT-International, including its current chief editor Cem Dalaman. Berlin's Turkish radio station Metropol FM similarly employs former TRT staff, thus forging further links between "local" and "transnational" broadcasting circuits.

TRT-International's programs can be watched in Turkey as well, and thus it not only represents the voice of the Turkish state abroad but also makes this voice echo back to residents of Turkey. It raises awareness both of Turks living abroad and of the state's efforts to reach out to them. In this sense, TRT-International is an indicator and promoter of the "increasing cosmopolitanism of the homeland" that has been referred to above (Yang 1997). When viewers from Germany call in to participate in live studio discussions broadcast by the channel, they thereby contribute to an awareness of a Turkish audience and a public that reaches beyond the territory of Turkey. However, this version of cosmopolitanism promotes a state-defined "cultural transnationalization" (Aksoy and Robins 2000, 346), expanding Turkish nationhood beyond territorial confines rather than giving room to a range of diasporic identities. The very raison-d'être for TRT-International is the attempt to widen Turkey's sphere of political influence and draw especially migrants in Western Europe back into the imagined community of nationals from which they threaten to become increasingly detached.

There are several reasons for the Turkish state's special interest in the former labor migrant population. On an economic level, the remittances of migrants still provide an important boost to the Turkish economy. In the year 2000, worker remittances constituted more than 2 percent of the total percentage of the gross domestic product (GDP) (Aydaş et al., n.d.). At the same time, encouraging continued affiliations with Turkey—whether in terms of investments, support of relatives who have stayed behind, or holiday trips—requires increasing state effort in order to mitigate the factor of generational distancing. With the "myth of return" declining, migrants have begun to buy real estate in Berlin rather than in Istanbul, and second- and third-generation migrants in Western Europe are increasingly spending their summer holidays in destinations other than Turkey.

At the level of politics, the extent to which political opponents who are silenced within Turkey have used Western Europe as a base for organizing has been a matter of growing concern to the Turkish state, as has been shown above in relation to Kurdish nationalism. Islamist activism has similarly been a concern. The Cologne-based İCCB group around Metin Kaplan, self-professed "Caliph" who has advocated the violent overthrow of the Turkish government to establish an Islamic state, was the target of intense negotiations between the Turkish and the German governments. It was only after the 2001 terror attacks in the United States that the organization was banned in Germany, and it took another four years to deport its leader to Turkey, where he received a life sentence for plotting an attack on members of the Turkish government.

TRT-International thus provides a convenient platform from which to outline the positions of the Turkish state, and to defend its vision of the national community not just against challenges from ethnic separatists, but also from Islamists and from the Left. What is more, the channel has been used to directly call upon migrants to support the Turkish state in the fight against its enemies. In 1995, TRT-International started a fundraising campaign to support the Turkish military in its fight against the PKK in Turkey's Southeast.

In mid-April of 1995, TRT-International broadcast a fifty-six-hour live program under the slogan of *Mehmetçik'le el ele* ("hand in hand with our soldiers"),[20] which allegedly produced more than 130 million German DM in donations from migrants in Germany. In the course of the program, journalists in military fatigues reported live from the Southeast, praising the activities of Turkish soldiers and pledging the undivided support of the entire country. Horrifying images of bloody and mutilated corpses, alleged victims of the PKK, were shown. Schoolchildren were interviewed and delivered statements that praised the army as the savior of the fatherland, while the audience in Turkey and abroad was invited to call studio hotlines and pledge donations (Greiff 1995). Bank account numbers regularly flashed across the screen. A five-year-old girl was shown to donate her pocket money to the military, a scene that particularly incensed the critics of the program, who filed complaints and took legal action against TRT-INT in Germany.

The Media Agency for Human Rights (*Medienagentur für Menschenrechte, mfm*), based in the federal state of North Rhine–Westphalia, demanded that the state media council immediately revoke TRT-International's license. Several state media councils in Germany accused the TRT program of glorifying war, but the German courts decided that the channel had neither incited racial hatred nor "aided in the extermination of a people" (*Beihilfe zum Völkermord*), and thus could not be prosecuted under German law. However, the German press and public service broadcasters gave extensive coverage to the issue, prompting a closer look at media imports from Turkey in general and their potential effects upon migrants. The TRT-International scandal was seen as further evidence that the transnationalization of broadcasting might have adverse effects on migrant populations, tying their hearts and minds closer to the former countries of origin instead of "integrating" them at their place of residence.

Migration and the increased de-linking of mass media broadcasting from the nation-state are central factors that shape deterritorialized, transnational forms of cultural struggle. Despite such deterritorialization, however, the "classical" model of national statehood that links culture, territory, and political sovereignty is by no means a thing of the past. Ideologically, it is continuously mobilized in Kurdish nationalist visions of a once-pristine Kurdistan, visualized and articulated as historical fact on satellite television, Internet Web sites, and print publications that circulate across and beyond Europe. Likewise, the modernist project of Turkish nation-building that was begun by Mustafa Kemal Atatürk has not come to an end with the crumbling of the state monopoly on broadcasting and the growing importance of oppositional political projects and cultural visions that have transnational bases. Instead, the Turkish state has itself widened the definition of a Turkish national community to include people who do not reside within its territory, and makes use of new cross-border mass media technology to reach out to them.

Such incorporation efforts are ignored in policy discussions and academic approaches that treat nation-states as the taken-for-granted container of cultural politics and social transformations when discussing the impact of immigration on "society" (Castles 2003). The above discussion has shown that migrants are deeply implicated in the politics of cultural struggle in and across two different nation-states. In Germany, migrants from Turkey have come to symbolize the transformation of Germany into a multicultural society, but they also figure ideologically as a radically different ethnic "Other" that threatens to undermine integrationist projects. In Turkey, migrants are associated with external threats to unified nationhood, but are also seen as part of an extended national community that can promote Turkish state interests in the context of the European Union. These two national arenas are by no means unrelated. Apart from historical links that connect both countries at different levels, the transnationalization of broadcasting but also of political struggles has increasingly forged networks and relations that cross their borders.

Nevertheless, the power of nation-states to shape cultural politics has by no means waned. While cross-border flows of people and media representations present important challenges to territorial state politics, states can themselves widen their fields of activity: both internationally at the level of government politics and transnationally through a variety of means such as, for example, Turkey's TRT-International. The importance of the different national arenas of cultural politics will emerge also in the next two chapters, which discuss examples of locally produced Turkish-language broadcasting in Berlin. With their broadcasting efforts, migrants have themselves have entered the terrain of cultural politics. As will be shown, most migrant broadcasters as producers of subaltern media have to position themselves vis-à-vis the dominant discourses that shape hegemonic frames of reference in both Turkey and Germany. Far from simply speaking "for themselves" in autonomous voices, they are more likely to produce strategic interventions that are positioned at the intersections and in the interstices of dominant discourses.

6

Coping with "Extremism": Migrant Television Production on Berlin's Open Channel

The local context of media use and of production efforts has so far received rather short shrift in this book, with the exception of the public service radio station MultiKulti and its emphatically "local" agenda of integrative broadcasting for a multicultural Berlin. MultiKulti's emphasis on the local is not, however, an outcome of a "bottom-up" media initiative that aims to give voice to the city's diversity and distinctiveness. Rather, the local has been shown to be a highly charged ideological concept central to a wider integrative strategy of German policymaking vis-à-vis immigrant populations. In this context, the concept denotes commitment to a social context of residence with shared rules of engagement and a clearly delineated place for cultural differences—differences that can be contained within the communal space of the city. Radio MultiKulti thus qualifies more as a localizing than as a local broadcasting initiative: a program *for* the city, but not equally *of* the city. However, there is a multitude of other immigrant broadcasting efforts in Berlin that have a different local base.

A very different kind of "bottom-up" character can be found at a broadcasting institution in Berlin that describes its very purpose as giving media access to population groups otherwise marginalized in the media mainstream: Berlin's Open Channel (OKB). The institution, which receives its budget from the State Media Council, operates an open access radio and television channel that can be received via cable in the majority of city households. It is extremely popular among immigrants, with foreign-language programs at times reaching peaks of up to 40 percent of all programming on OKB's television channel. Immigrants from Turkey are particularly active, making use of the possibility to produce and broadcast live or recorded programs with minimal content restrictions. Producers may not engage in commercial or political advertising, programs must remain within the confines of Germany's constitution (*Grundgesetz*), and they must be self-produced.

Marginal in terms of commercial criteria, public respectability, and its very mission, Open Channel broadcasting occupies a peculiar place in the Turkish broadcasting landscape of Berlin, a place that reveals much about the complexities of local integration politics and transnational orientations in which this broadcasting is implicated. The OKB has attracted a large variety of Turkish-language amateur producers who put into practice their very divergent visions of television broadcasting. What unites them is the conviction that neither the media landscape in Germany nor the one available from Turkey represents the positions and issues that they seek to make public in their programs. Unfettered by commercial considerations or public service guidelines that would define the scope of what Turkish-language programming should express, Open Channel producers tend to articulate positions that are absent from the dominant broadcasting landscapes with which Turkish migrant audiences are confronted. Precisely for this reason, their broadcasting has become an issue of great political contention. The positions made public at the OKB have neither the financial nor the political backing they would need to be represented in the dominant, 'professional' arenas of television programming in Germany or Turkey.

These politically and economically marginalized positions and the debates that surround their public articulation illuminate more than just a marginal phenomenon. When we focus on the difficulties OKB producers face in getting across positions that run counter to the dominant cultural politics in one or both of the nation-states concerned, the power of dominant discourses and media landscapes is thrown into stark relief. What is more, these difficulties reveal not just the power of dominant cultural politics in two different nation-states, but also the challenges and possibilities that result from their intersection.

The Idea of Open Channels

In Germany's current media landscape, Open Channels form a counterpart to the two dominant pillars of German broadcasting, public service and private, commercial broadcasting. The fall of the West German public service monopoly and the parallel emergence of commercial broadcasting in the 1980s raised political concerns that ratings and profits would from now on come to determine mass media production. The role of broadcasting as a channel of communication for a public sphere as well as its openness for minority interests and opinions seemed at risk. The initiative to establish Open Channels sought to provide an answer to these concerns by using radio and television for the sole purpose of "democratic communication," excluding all commercial interest. Open Channels were to make radio and television accessible to every citizen, regardless of economic or educational background.

Open Channels in this sense put into practice theories of democracy and the public sphere that regard electronic mass media as the primary vehicles of political debate in complex societies, and thus as the place where opinions can become public and influence democratic decision-making processes. "The democratic process cannot function without the exchange of arguments, continuous public debate, and the struggle of opinions in the public sphere," Open Channel founders have argued (BOK 2000). No concern should be silenced, and no group excluded—the demands of critical theorists such as Jürgen Habermas and others (see Calhoun 1992; Fraser 1992; Negt and Kluge 1993; Robbins 1993; Warner 2002) are precisely the concerns of Open Channel advocates.

Central goals of Open Channel broadcasting in Germany are thus to promote local cultures of communication and to help underrepresented groups gain access to the public sphere. Open Channels are meant to turn passive consumers of mass media into active producers, and give a voice to those who do not find their interests, opinions, and identities reflected in the mainstream (Jarren et al. 1994; Medienwerkstatt Frankfurt 1998). Different from the dual broadcasting system of public service and commercial production where media representation is tied to different forms of economic and cultural capital, Open Channels are thus quite intentionally a place for the marginalized.

In order to facilitate participation, barriers to access are kept as low as possible. At the Open Channel Berlin, no fee is charged for the use of camera equipment, and producers or "users," as they are called, receive free technical assistance and training. In principle, channel representatives see the interest that the OKB has attracted among immigrants as a sign that their outreach work toward marginalized groups has been successful. When it comes to the content of programs, however, their enthusiasm is severely dampened: programs produced by immigrants often focus on Islam or on political agendas related to nationalist causes, and are often met with charges of extremism by viewers and the German political establishment alike.

Turkish-language programs take center stage among the foreign-language broadcasts at the OKB: in the late 90s, their share of overall broadcasting time averaged about 25 percent. This figure dropped after the attacks on the World Trade Center in September 2001 and the resulting backlash against political Islam and Muslims in Germany. The majority of Turkish-language programs still focus on Islam, but conditions for production have become increasingly difficult.

The groups and individuals engaged in Islamic broadcasting at the Open Channel form part of a religious spectrum that is united in opposing Turkey's state-condoned Islam. Whereas representatives of the Turkish Ministry for Religious Affairs (*Diyanet İşleri Başkanlığı*) have regular program slots on Berlin's commercial Turkish cable channel TD-1, the groups that make use of the Open Channel have no access to other radio and television venues in the city. They include several mystical Sufi groups; Shiite groups; and different *Nakşibendi*-derived organizations that are quite powerful in Turkey today, such as the Nurcus, the Süleymancıs, and Millî Görüş sympathizers.[1]

The second-largest Turkish-language group consists of a range of program producers that represent either right-wing Turkish nationalism or Kurdish nationalism. Apart from these, additional Turkish programs are produced by groups and individuals ranging from youth initiatives and soccer clubs to a retired journalist. But it is the first two groups of producers that constitute a major problem for the Open Channel.[2] Intended as a medium for local grassroots concerns of citizens that otherwise do not have easy access to the public sphere, the appearance of allegedly extremist groups whose political roots originate in Turkey or elsewhere seems to contradict the basic mission of Open Channels.

While Open Channels claim to make important contributions to a democratic culture of public debate, the actual broadcasts have little to offer, German media critics and others have charged. Instead of grassroots commitment, they have diagnosed egocentric banalities, or even worse, the voicing of fundamentalist and extremist positions. And it is above all the Islamic programs that evoke the charges of extremism, particularly since the September 11 attacks in the United States. The State Media Council Berlin-Brandenburg, responsible for supervising the Open Channel, receives complaints from television viewers on a regular basis. Often unable to understand what is actually being said, German audiences take particular styles of clothing, studio decoration, and iconography as indications of "undesirable" and "suspicious" program contents. The public spokesperson for the State Media Council told me long before September 11:

> Of course there are complaints about the foreign programs, because—well, there is some Mullah sitting there in his garb, or a woman with a headscarf who says something in a language that nobody understands, and you get the feeling, that can't possibly be anything good. Well, as a German viewer. And so we've often had people call and ask what is going on.[3]

Given the language of presentation in Islamic programs—most often Turkish, but also Arabic and different Kurdish dialects—it is difficult for German viewers to get a sense of program contents. But the public expression of Muslim religiosity in itself raises suspicion, given dominant perceptions of Islam within German society. Far from a grassroots discourse committed to the democratic ideals the Open Channel is supposed to stand for, the programs are suspected of trying to mobilize viewers against those very ideals, and thus of promoting authoritarian politics. In the case of German viewers and critics, this suspicion is obviously not linked to the close scrutiny of program contents but rather to a general perception of Islam as a dangerous political ideology, a perception that has become more widespread in recent years. However, this perception finds support in the complaints of Turkish-speaking viewers as well.

The State Media Council registers just as many complaints from Turkish-speaking as from German-speaking viewers about the Islamic and Kurdish nationalist programs.[4] They perceive the programs as antidemocratic, militant, and politically motivated. According to the State Media Council and the Open Channel management, it is not so much the concrete content of programs that is criticized, but the fact of "these people" being given a public voice. In Turkey, many callers argue, such programming would not be permitted. The criticism leveled against the political establishment in Turkey would certainly be deemed to promote *bölücülük*, separatist or divisive tendencies that threaten the unity of the Turkish state and nation, explicitly prohibited in Article 14 of the Turkish constitution,[5] or else they would be seen as a threat to the secularist foundations of the Republic.

The strength of the Turkish protest against Islamic broadcasts can indeed best be understood in the context of Turkish secularism. There is no other issue that polarizes public debates in Turkey as much as the (re-)appearance of political Islam in the country, with the exception of Kurdish separatism (Erzeren 1997; Van Bruinessen 2000a). According to dominant, state-identified public opinion, both issues seem to attack the very heart of the Kemalist Turkish state, which was founded on the sometimes violent separation of Islam from the state and the celebration of secularism as the guiding principle of public life. While movements like the Süleymancı and the Nurcu had operated as clandestine networks in Turkey since the 1930s, it was only in 1969 that an Islamic political party was founded which openly contested the state's secularist paradigm.

Several of the groups oriented towards a mystical Islam which produce programs on the Open Channel Berlin, for example, have faced violent persecution and legal bans in Turkey. Only the state-sanctioned Islamic organization DİTİB (*Diyanet İşleri Türk-İslam Birliği*), built in fact to channel the resurgence of Islam into state-defined and -controlled forms, is exempt from the accusation of fundamentalism and extremism, both from Turkish and German state affiliates (Ayata 1996, Heper 1997, Seufert 1999). DİTİB representatives, however, do not broadcast on Berlin's Open Channel since they have access to other mass media venues. Those Islamic groups and individuals who turn to the Open Channel are invariably critical of the Turkish state and the censorship of religious expression and organizing in Turkey. Not all of them have an agenda which is oriented towards political change, but many of them comment critically on developments in Turkey.

Germany has become a place where Turkish Islamic organizations can flourish, largely due to the different position of religion in the public sphere (Abdullah 1995, Amiraux 1997, Karakasoğlu 1996). Even though Islamic Turkish associations increasingly debate what it would mean to develop an identity as a religious minority in Germany (Jonker 2002, Schiffauer 1999, 2003), much critical attention remains focused on the Turkish state. The OKB allows Islamic TV producers to articulate positions and criticism that would be immediately censored in Turkey, as is often explicitly acknowledged in the programs themselves. Despite the increasing volume of Islamic programming which followed in the wake of privatization, and the recent success of moderate Islamist parties in Turkish elections, Turkey's state authorities keep a close watch on critical program contents.

As a consequence, Germany as well as other Western European countries have emerged as a place for politics-in-exile. A number of studies have underlined the importance of organizing efforts abroad for the flourishing of Turkish and Kurdish nationalist activities, or campaigns of the Islamist Welfare Party in Turkey during the 1990s (Arslan 2004, Karakasoğlu 1996, Mertens 2000, Metcalf 1996, Ogan 2001, Trautner 2000, Van Bruinessen 2000b, Wahlbeck 1998).[6] With regard to mass media, the case of MED TV, providing Kurdish-nationalist programming via satellite to Turkey but also to migrants in Western Europe, has already been discussed in the preceding chapter. But migrants in Berlin have also made use of their local opportunities to engage in political and religious media activism, as can be seen at the Open Channel.

At the OKB, some of the programs state their orientation quite clearly in their titles: *Islam TV* and *İslam Eğitim Televizyonu* (Islamic Education Television), *Ülkücü Gençlik diyor ki Türk Milleti mutlaka uyanacaktır* (The Idealist Youth Says That the Turkish Nation Will Definitely Awake), *Ben Kürdüm, Sen Kimsin?* (I Am a Kurd, Who Are You?), *Türk'ten Türk'e TV* (TV from Turk to Turk), *Kurden und Kurdistan* (Kurds and Kurdistan), and *Her şey Türk için Türk'e göre Türk tarafından* (Everything for the Turk, According to the Turk, by the Turk).[7]

Thus, many of the Turkish-language programs have their central—but not necessarily exclusive—focus of attention on Turkey and/or Turkish Kurdistan. Islamic producers also focus quite often on political events in Turkey, for example with regard to the issue of Islamic clothing at universities, Turkey's role in the Gulf Wars, or the status of *İmam Hatip*[8] schools. Several of the producers I interviewed were convinced that they would be imprisoned for their broadcasts in Turkey, and some thought that they were under surveillance by the Turkish Secret Service Organization (*MİT* (*Milli İstihbarat Teşkilatı*). Many of them have received threats of violence, a few have also been physically attacked by oppositional groups in Berlin.

It is not surprising, seen against this background, that a part of the Turkish audience feels motivated to protest against OKB programs and call for official intervention, particularly regarding Islamic and Kurdish programs. But the criteria of the Open Channel in the evaluation and censoring of programs are different. The director of the Open Channel Berlin feels that the viewers should learn to cope with positions that they oppose, unless these "cross the line," in the sense of violating constitutional rights:

> The social consensus is different. Well, there are these radical Islamic or nationalist groups, but what is surprising is that we have had their programs translated time and again. Okay, there are some things they say, where you can frown and say, well, that's not so nice. But it is very rare that there is reason to say, stop, you've crossed the line.[9]

After September 11, the OKB temporarily enforced a new rule for programs that focused on Islam. Producers had to provide a German-language summary of their broadcast in writing before it was screened, which effectively put an end to live broadcasts and led many to stop broadcasting altogether. Those that continued did not comment on the terrorist attacks, and the new rule was lifted again after several weeks. Despite the intense criticism of Islamic programs on the OKB, official scrutiny has in almost all cases concluded that producers have remained within the limits of what is protected as free speech in the German constitution.

This conclusion, however, does not remove the pressure the Open Channel is facing on a political level: the accusation of extremism can be mobilized whenever the use of scarce public funds for media projects is on the political agenda. The Open Channel depends on the goodwill of the Berlin and Brandenburg state parliaments, and budget cuts are a constant threat. "A nice idea, but one that does not work in practice" is the judgment of media specialists in Berlin's coalition government. Islamic programs are the first that parliamentary critics refer to when they claim that the Open Channel project has failed. Even before September 11, the programs were taken as an indication that the channel is a "playground for extremists"[10] rather than an example of lived, practical democracy.

The School of Democracy

> Open Channels are extreme by definition. Extremely freedom-oriented, extremely free of scissors in the head, free of censorship as they guarantee the constitutionally protected freedom of opinion.[11]

Extreme freedom—this postulate of a member of the Expert Group Open Channels turns the accusation of extremism into a principled avowal of free speech, to which the concrete contents of programs are secondary. In the case of the Open Channel Berlin, advocates and management rarely defend programs on the basis of their content. It is the form and process of production, not the content on which the OKB builds its defense, particularly in the case of immigrant programming.

In order to understand what Open Channels are actually all about, one has to focus on the production of programs rather than on the actual broadcasts, according to the director, Jürgen Linke. Linke claims that even the Turkish adherents of various political and religious faiths—often violently opposed in Turkey and the diaspora—come to meet and talk peacefully with each other in the context of daily production work. The shared use of the Open Channel facilities itself turns them into partners in a certain sense, he claims. For Linke, it is the "integrative effect" of using the Open Channel that is central, for both German and immigrant producers. All have to play by the rules that guarantee freedom of speech to everybody, regardless of political convictions and identities. It is the everyday activities of the most varied groups and individuals at the Open Channels that make for the practical experience of democratic values, Linke states:

> No matter how antidemocratic, radical or fundamentalist a program producer may be, if he crosses the threshold to the Open Channel Berlin, he is subjected to its rules and regulations. He accepts the fact that he is only allowed to transmit because and as far as the other is allowed to transmit, too. . . . By way of his activities in the Open Channel, he becomes part of a society that is based on the equality and freedom of all citizens. (Linke 1997)

Even if program contents do not directly reflect those values, the Open Channel aims to work as a kind of socializing agency that counteracts the antidemocratic potential of producers and teaches them the rules of democratic behavior. Open Channel broadcasts are thus defended not on the basis of their potential contribution to public debates, but by pointing to the merits of the production activity itself: It is the learning process that immigrant producers are thought to go through that is seen as valuable. Rather than giving extremists and fundamentalists a forum to indoctrinate viewers, allowing them to participate at the Open Channel is thus akin to taming the lion without telling him. Producers "spend their energies" and more or less unwittingly become transformed into partners and members of a democratic society. But it is difficult, Open Channel representatives admit, to convey this educative achievement to a public that judges the Open Channel by its broadcasts. The programs themselves seem to contradict it.

The problems with allegedly "extremist" programs and their reception point to a basic dilemma that the Open Channel has to face. Despite the postulated 'integrative effect" that engagement at the Open Channel is supposed to have, the producers rarely identify with the ideals that it wants to represent. The lack of interference and open access policy of the channel allows producers to introduce their own standards of what constitutes "good" broadcasting, and to articulate meanings that are relevant to their own particular life worlds, cultural horizons, and political agendas. In their practices of representation, Turkish-language immigrant producers undermine in different ways several of the core assumptions and ideals of Open Channel philosophy.

Türk'ten Türk'e

Given the strong links OKB producers have with groups and organizations that are either directly active in Turkey or affiliated with organizations there, it comes as little surprise that some of them subvert the Open Channel requirement of self-produced broadcasts. Program formats differ widely: while some producers simply sit down in front of the camera in the OKB studios and speak for an entire hour, others drop off prerecorded tapes. It is not always easy for the OKB to monitor whether or not producers have in fact produced the material themselves, such as when the makers of *Evrensel Din İslam* (Islam, the Universal Religion) show amateur recordings of the modern mystic and television preacher Ahmed Hulûsi addressing an audience in Turkey. Others, such as the producers of *Saadet TV,* make use of Internet Web cams to transport the Sheikh of their Sufi order, who is presently based in the United States, live into OKB television broadcasting. But sometimes OKB rules are overtly breached, and material taken from other television stations is shown.

Late in March of 1998, the makers of the program *Türk'ten Türk'e* (From Turk to Turk) were commemorating Alparslan Türkeş, leader of the right-wing MHP party in Turkey, who had died a year before. In their program, they were showing material taken from the local Berlin television station TD-1, who in turn had copied and rebroadcast a news program from Turkey's station TGRT, available in Germany via satellite. Thus, trickling down to the OKB via several media circuits, viewers could see the images of the masses who had gathered in front of the hospital in Ankara where Türkeş had died, shouting, "*Başbuğlar ölmez*" ("leaders are immortal"). This material was combined by the producers with pictures of Türkeş taken at different stages of his life, fixed to the studio walls of the OKB, and a soundtrack with *ülkücü* (idealist) political music celebrating the struggle of Turkish ultra-right-wing nationalists.

Apart from disagreeing with Turkish or Kurdish nationalist and Islamist politics, the Turkish producers at Radio MultiKulti and other critics will often describe such programming as "backward oriented," particularly with regard to Islamic programs. "Backward" here has a double meaning, referring firstly to the orientation of Open Channel producers toward Turkey instead of Germany, and thus taking "a step back" in the process of integration within a multicultural paradigm of migration. What is more, within the context of politics in Turkey, Islamist positions are often described as backward, since the trajectory of Kemalism has sought to reduce the allegedly "antimodern" influence of religion in public life and politics in Turkey. A part of the Turkish-nationalist spectrum is also described as backward by left or liberal secularists, because it stresses Turkish continuity with Ottoman times or Pan-Turkish roots dating back thousands of years.

However, it would be wrong to regard these activities simply as politics conducted abroad, oriented entirely toward Turkey and showing no interest in social, cultural, and political issues in the country (or city of residence). Kurdish-nationalist, Turkish-nationalist, and Islamist producers do not equally represent Germany as a place of exile. If this were the case, life in the country and city of residence would be addressed only—or at least mainly—in the context of "homeland" affairs. Kurdish-nationalist programs exhibit the strongest tendency to address their audience only as part of a Kurdish diaspora, geographically dispersed but united in its longing and struggle for Kurdistan, imagined as the homeland from which it has been exiled. Programs such as *Ben Kürdüm, Welat TV, Azadi TV,* and *Kurden und Kurdistan* at the Open Channel rarely take up issues unrelated to this political struggle, and Kurdish life in Berlin or Germany is usually shown in a context that feeds into it, such as a youth group learning Kurdish folk dancing at a local community center and other activities that represent forms of cultural nation-building. Interest in "local" affairs exists—as far as the programs are concerned—only insofar as they can be represented as evidence of the vitality, magnitude, and determination of the Kurdish diaspora.

The same does not hold true for other kinds of programs that have, to varying degrees, explicit political links and aspirations with regard to Turkey. The example of the program *Türk'ten Türk'e* can show how a right-wing nationalist agenda that has its political origins in Turkey is combined with and informs a "local" agenda that pertains to the life of Turkish migrants in Germany. The themes chosen for the monthly broadcasts vary. The main producer of the program is Abdullah Güneş, who came to Germany in 1980 at the age of sixteen. Readily identifying himself as a Turkish nationalist, his nationalism is primarily oriented toward defending Turkish culture in Germany, as he claims: "We want to enable a person, a Turkish child living in Berlin to say 'I am a Turk' when asked, without fear, without shame."[12]

In order to do so, Güneş feels the need to fight in two directions with his program: He has to make people aware of German political efforts to assimilate the Turks and erase their cultural identity, and he has to fight tendencies within the Turkish population to stress the differences that exist among them instead of standing united. With regard to the first point, he regularly translates articles printed in German newspapers on his television program that pertain to Turks and integration issues.

> In Berlin right now there is a politics of assimilation going on against foreigners, all in the name of integration. And nobody is aware of it. . . . [They want] the foreigners to assimilate! Because we already have a state of integration! I already respect the German laws. Integration is something else!

For Germany, Güneş defends a model of ethnic pluralism, in which people of different national cultures enjoy special minority rights to maintain their separate identities. The objective of the German state, however, is assimilation and the absorption of "foreigners" into a German majority culture, he suspects. For Turks in Berlin, it is thus vital to follow local and national politics in Germany, and Güneş surprisingly regards the effects of satellite television in much the same way as the editors of the Turkish program at Radio MultiKulti. Asked whether he has a satellite dish at home, he states:

> I make a point of not getting one, and do you know why? Because it distances people from what is happening here in Berlin. Some of the troubles in Turkey actually don't interest me that much! More the troubles that exist in the society I live in. Ok, I put up a satellite dish, I watch Star. Sports from Turkey. So ok, maybe it is a bit important to me, but what is going on in Berlin, in Germany, is more important.

Even though a Turkish nationalist identity seems to almost automatically imply a focus on the Turkish nation-state, Abdullah Güneş's understanding of himself as a "cultural nationalist" (*kültür milliyetçisi*) expands his focus of concern to include all locations where Turks are living or where he suspects any influence of Turkish culture. His identification with the Turkish state remains strong: when it comes to international relations and the position of Turkey with regard to Arab or European countries, he always speaks of a "we." But he does not long for a return, and does not see himself as exiled from the homeland, nor does he maintain that Turkish culture can only flourish in the context of a particular territory or state structure. Protecting Turkish identity might take the form of defending the integrity of the Turkish nation-state, but it might just as well consist of demanding minority rights in Germany. Whether it is "dividers" such as Kurdish nationalists in Turkey, among the Turkish community in Germany, or German politicians wanting to assimilate immigrants, the task is essentially the same in Turkey and abroad: to guard the unity of Turks and strengthen their identifications with Turkishness. Fighting the alleged enemies of such unity is a task that unites the *Türk'ten Türk'e* producers with their MHP allies and supporters in Turkey. Divisions are dangerous, says Güneş:

> I say, the Turkish nation is done in by this process of dividing it into smaller and smaller groups. They cut it up. But if the society is united, then you cannot ruin it. They call you rightist. They call you leftist, and the other one Alevi, Kurd, Sunni. . . . And then when they are separated into tiny groups it is easier to assimilate them or kill them! But if not, if they are united, they cannot do that. And that applies not only here, but also in Turkey.

Güneş links the conflicts that divide the population in Turkey to their situation in Germany: those who introduce divisions—by insisting on their identity as Kurds, as Alevis, or otherwise—not only weaken the Turkish state but also the Turkish nation outside of Turkey. German efforts to assimilate the Turks and turn them into Germans are aided by those who emphasize the divisions among immigrants from Turkey. If the Turks were united, those efforts would fail. It is thus not just Turkey that is under attack by those who allegedly want to split up the country, but also the Turkish nation abroad. Güneş sees an unholy alliance between German assimilationists and Turkish "divisionists," resulting in a joint onslaught against the Turkish nation as a national and cultural minority in Germany. The German state actively promotes conflict among the Turkish migrant population through its asylum policies, Güneş claims, and provides an example:

> There is a home for asylum-seekers over there. They come visit me here, those kids who have come from the Southeast of Turkey. "My son, why did you come

here?" "Well, ağabey,[13] you know about the conditions in Turkey. We've come for the money." "So what did you tell them, why did they accept you as refugees?" "We said we are Kurdish, that we are persecuted in Turkey. The Germans expect such an explanation anyway. They gave us asylum." "But weren't you ashamed when you said that? How can you claim something that doesn't exist?" "What can I do? . . . If I had said, my friend, there is no work for me in Turkey, that's why I came, they would have kicked me out."

The story confirms two central convictions for Güneş: firstly, the alleged persecution of Kurds and other minorities in Turkey does not actually exist, as the refugees themselves seem to admit. Secondly, the German state promotes separatist tendencies among the migrant population in order to push its own assimilationist agenda. I felt compelled to comment that the respect that he demands for Turkish culture in Germany as a minority within a multicultural society seems not warranted, in his mind, for the often quite similar demands that Kurds or Alevis make in Turkey. While in the German context, Güneş sees the current politics of integration as a form of assimilation and eradication, in Turkey the national identity has to override all differences, be they religious, ethnic, or even political.

However, the point I want to pursue here is not to reveal the points of contradiction in this Turkish nationalist line of arguing, but rather to look at the way in which Turkish nationalist positions become articulated for a minority rights agenda in the German context. Commemorating events such as the death of the right-wing nationalist leader Alparslan Türkeş in Turkey is perfectly compatible with such an agenda. The televised images of demonstrators grieving on the streets of Ankara and shouting, "*Başbuğlar ölmez*" ("leaders are immortal") are not shown to transport migrant viewers to Turkey, but rather to remind them of a collective endeavor. The task is an ongoing project of establishing and defending Turkish unity and strength, even under seemingly adversarial conditions such as those presented by the migration context. Güneş has no illusions regarding a possible return of the migrant population to Turkey, and even expects future generations to identify more strongly with Germany.

> Germany is our second mother country, really! Maybe in three, four years, ten years, fifty years our children will say, Germany is our first mother country. But they will say so as Turks!

While Güneş wants to retain his Turkish citizenship, he does not object to his brother and his entire family having obtained German passports. The passport does not change their culture, nor does it diminish the loyalty they feel toward the Turkish nation, he claims. Güneş does not elaborate on the possible consequences of naturalization, but his culturally essentialist understanding of Turkishness renders cultural assimilation a much greater threat than the change of citizenship. He is less interested in migrants' loyalty toward the Turkish nation-state than in their loyalty toward the Turkish *nation,* whose interests need to be defended on German ground as well. This orientation is also supported by the Pan-Turkism that has been a strong element in right-wing extremist politics in Turkey. Its most notorious leader, Alparslan Türkeş, stated already in the 1960s that the nationalist principle of idealism, *ülkücülük,* implied struggling for Turks everywhere, so that they could determine their own fate in various state contexts (Türkeş 1965; see also Landau 1995). Corresponding to this vision, the broadcasting rationale of *Türk'ten Türk'e* does not oppose the Turkish nationalist struggle to migrant interests in Berlin, but regards the two as closely interrelated. The program's local engagement represents part of wider Turkish-nationalist aspirations that extend to all countries in which Turks are thought to reside, yet as local efforts they are very much specific and respond to the particular sociopolitical environment that Berlin Turks live in.

Saadet TV

A second example of Open Channel migrant programming represents yet another approach to broadcasting that undermines the opposition between "life here" and "life in Turkey" as mutually exclusive orientations to which immigrants adhere. The term *saadet* can be translated roughly as well-being or happiness, and it is used also to refer to the era of the Prophet Muhammed. *Saadet TV* is an Islamic program that has been produced at the Open Channel since 1997. Even though the religious group that produces the program has its roots in Turkish Sufism, neither Turkey nor migrant life in Berlin or Germany form significant points of reference in *Saadet's* broadcasts.

Himmet Kabak, the producer, is a follower of the Sheikh Efendi Hazretleri İskender Ali Mihr, the founder and leader of the *tasawwuf* Mihr Foundation that has its center in Ankara. *Tasawwuf* denotes the "phenomenon of mysticism" in Islam (Hunwick 1998, 313), which goes back to the times of the Prophet. Very simply put, knowledge of the inner self and experiencing the love of God were to be achieved by special means, which could include poetry, music, and dance, among other exercises. Starting in the twelfth century, mystical Islam became increasingly organized in orders, which continue until the present day. Most of them put great emphasis on the relationship between teacher and student, marked by complete obedience as the only way to arrive at higher levels of religious knowledge. Different forms of mystical Islam existed in the Ottoman Empire and they have continued into the Turkish Republic, even though their religious orders were officially abolished in 1925. The Sheikh İskender Ali Mihr, who claims to be a descendant of the Prophet, started his Mihr Foundation 1989 in Ankara. It now also has official branches in Izmir, a large Turkish city south of Istanbul, in the United States, and in Germany.

Himmet Kabak and his family became attracted to the Sheikh's teachings in 1995, when they tried to permanently return to Turkey, but eventually returned to Berlin. The Mihr order has no more than a handful of members in the city, centered around Kabak's family, but they have close contacts with other members in Germany and of course with their Sheikh and his followers in Turkey and the United States. Kabak began Open Channel programming shortly after his return from Turkey, having seen other Muslim groups produce programs at the Open Channel. Apart from his group, which is responsible for *Saadet TV,* other Sufism-related organizations and practitioners rarely turn to the Open Channel for religious mediation. Most of them deem television broadcasting ill-suited for the particular, intimate interaction between teacher and student that the production of mystic experience and knowledge requires.

Saadet TV follows a simple format: the program usually starts with a musical introduction, with images of blossoming flowers, flowing rivers, and other things documenting the beauty of nature. Then, the Imam appears on screen, always seen from the same camera angle, speaking freely on particular subjects of Islamic instruction. Mostly, *Hadis Dersi* is given, instruction on the life of the Prophet. The program is produced exclusively in Turkish. Unlike other Islamic programs, on *Saadet TV* only the Sheikh or the Imam as his authorized representative ever appear on screen. His followers, who make up the entire production team, leave no trace apart from Kabak, whose name appears on screen as the person to contact about the broadcast. The visual absence of other members of the Mihr order from the broadcast is linked to their particular perception of religious authority and learning: it is only the authorized representative of the Sheikh or the Sheikh himself who can interpret and transmit religious truth. He aims to reach out directly to a general television audience, conceived as all interested people seeking the truth about Islam.

In 1998, the group was already making use of sophisticated communication technology for their internal communication. At home, the Kabak family used the Internet to hold video conferences with members in other German cities and Turkey. During a visit to their home, my main interview partner, the Imam based in another German city, was introduced to me on the television screen, with the same arrangement of camera, computer, and TV set-up on his end.

Given the dispersal of members across Turkey, Germany, and the United States, the Mihr community has been at the forefront of communication technologies in order to be able to communicate across vast distances. By the year 2000 they had introduced these new technologies into their program at the Open Channel as well. *Saadet TV* now provides a live Internet broadcast that is fed into the Berlin cable system—the first Islamic program to make use of Internet technology as an integral part of their broadcasts. Other programs announce e-mail addresses and Web sites as a means for further contact and information gathering, but *Saadet TV* has introduced the Internet directly into Open Channel programming. The program broadcasts somewhat halting pictures, with sound that is sometimes difficult to understand and is always lagging just a little bit behind the person talking on screen. But this typical Webcam format is still quite acceptable for *Saadet's* broadcasting purposes, given the general lack of different camera angles and complicated editing techniques. The technological production effort is still substantial: Himmet Kabak and his assistants have to arrive early at the Open Channel studios to set up the connection. During the entire broadcast and before, they talk on their mobile phones with their partners overseas, in order to give feedback on sounds and images and to solve any problems that might occur.

Introducing the Internet as a means of producing live programs gives an interesting twist to the aims of Open Channel officials: live programs are promoted at the OKB not just because they tend to be more interesting to audiences, but also in order to ensure that it is the so-called users of the channel themselves who appear in their programs and talk about issues of local interest, rather than dropping off tapes with broadcasts produced elsewhere. Live programs have priority when it comes to deciding broadcasting times. It was precisely the local dimension of broadcasting that the guidelines pertaining to live programming were to ensure. The Internet, however, allows programs to bring remote people and their messages live on air and into the local context of Open Channel production, without breaching the Open Channel rules. Immediacy of transmission is thus no longer tied to a physical presence in the studio. Despite the physical remoteness of the key presenter, the program nevertheless qualifies as a live broadcast, with all the benefits tied to live programs at the Open Channel. Instead of having to bring religious authorities to the studio space, any location in the world can be the point of origin, as long as Himmet Kabak and his team manage to establish the connection, even across national boundaries.

Saadet TV's subversive breach of Open Channel guidelines regarding locally produced program contents challenges the spatial dimensions of multicultural diversity as it tends to be understood in Germany today. By using Internet live streaming, the need for a physical presence of presenters in the OKB studio for live broadcasts is removed. Any spatial distance can be covered via the Internet in order to create the immediacy that prior to such technologies required face-to-camera interaction in the studio space. At first sight, introducing new spatiotemporal relations at the Open Channel does not appear as a particularly subversive step. But the OKB's policy to give preference to live programming formats is not just aimed at rendering its broadcasts more dialogical. It is also linked to its conception of "grassroots" broadcasting as a firmly local endeavor. As a liberal broadcasting institution designed to encourage pluralism in the public sphere, the Open Channel sees its role for migrants as an integrative one, tying migrants closer to local community life and allowing them to participate in public debates at their place of residence.

This preference to have migrant programs reflect the immediacy of locality (rather than of globality) also needs to be placed within the context of wider German diversity discourses and integration policies. Successful multicultural integration is measured by immigrants' involvement in issues that concern their city, region, or country of residence, thus rendering locality anything but an innocent concept denoting spatial presence. In light of the dominant German conceptions of national belonging that have until recently excluded ethnic minorities as "foreigners," regardless of citizenship status, the locality of urban spaces carries particular importance in German integration politics. Encouraging migrants' identification with the local constitutes a particular political project of regulation targeting low-status minorities, in stark contrast to the image campaigns of Berlin's government, which cast the capital as a "world-open" city and stress its connectedness with high-cultural global flows (Vertovec 2000).

Yet, *Saadet TV* aims to reach far beyond Berlin. The way in which the program addresses its imagined audience gives an indication of the "universal" conceptualization that underlies *Saadet's* transmission of religious truth: no reference at all is made in the programs to the particular circumstances of life—political, social, or otherwise—in specific regions, states, or localities. Different from many Islamic programs on the Open Channel that criticize political life in Turkey and debate the particular challenges of being Muslim in Germany, the teachings of *Saadet TV* claim universal applicability, appropriate to any local context the program reaches. The geographic dispersal of Mihr members is not addressed. The truth of Islam is the same for everyone, the program suggests, and local or national particularities are simply challenges to be overcome.

The Internet pages of the Mihr Foundation (http://www.mihr.com, accessed August 23, 1998) similarly support the conception of a universal, nonterritorial religious truth that can be transmitted to any location around the globe without modification or adaptation. A "virtual university" has been set up on the Internet (http://www.universityofallah.org, accessed August 23, 1998), with a four-year program to which one can apply online in English, German, or Turkish. The courses consist of the very same lectures that are broadcast on *Saadet* television.

The television program of the Mihr community broadcast on Berlin's Open Channel thus emerges as part of a wider network of communication that is organized along a strict hierarchy, with lessons being transmitted via different media to an ideally unrestricted audience. The community of Muslim believers is defined only by its relationship to the prime religious authority, the Sheikh, from whom it receives the truth of Islam. New communication technologies are put in the service of this relationship, helping to establish and support the bind between Sheikh and student by transmitting his teachings directly, without further human intermediaries. Religious instruction and technological mediation are co-constitutive here: Sufi teaching practices themselves constitute a form of mediation, and *Saadet's* producers have found the combination of Internet and television technology to both enhance and widen their possibilities for immediate communication.

Other Islamic producers show much greater concern for sociopolitical questions than the producers of *Saadet TV*, framing religious belief in different ways as situated, and as politically and culturally transformative. Many try to actively intervene through their programs in the politics of cultural struggle that they see themselves and their audiences implicated in. Devising their own strategies of mass-mediated representation, immigrant producers are thus forced to grapple with the dominant cultural frames and institutionalized discourses that relegate their public interventions to the subaltern fringes of national and transnational media landscapes. This can be seen in the broadcasting efforts of a Turkish migrant producer who is unaffiliated with any particular Islamic organization or group, and whose main interest is to free individual engagement with Islam from religious authorities.

Halimiz, Ahvalımız

And I say, this is what is happening among our people. The camel was asked, do you prefer to walk up the alley, or do you prefer to walk down? And the camel said, is there no alternative, no plain ground? Why is it that you want me to decide whether to walk up or walk down the alley? Unfortunately, a certain attitude has taken root in our society that holds, either you surrender like a disciple to a group or to a person, or else you will be regarded as an enemy. . . . But I am saying, it is not a question of enemies, why should someone who points out our mistakes not also be our friend?[14]

This contemplation on the state of conflict among Turkish migrants was offered by another OKB producer named Ramazan Ekici during one of his live programs in 2000. He has been producing his own television show *Halimiz, Ahvalımız,* which can be translated as "The State and Condition We Are In," on the Open Channel since 1996. Ekici fits the profile of the "average" immigrant producer of programs at the OKB: first-generation immigrant, male, and from a lower-class socioeconomic background. Ekici is in his early sixties, and has spent more than half of his life in Germany. He came as a labor migrant, with only five years of schooling in Turkey, and worked in different factories before opening a second-hand shop in his neighborhood. On weekdays, Ekici sells used furniture and trinkets in his small shop in Moabit, a poor inner-city district of Berlin with a large Turkish immigrant population. Once a week, he goes to the Open Channel buildings to produce his live program.

Helped only by a studio technician who adjusts the camera before the start of the program, Ekici sits at a small table carrying his papers and a telephone; behind him are the gray, unadorned walls of the small studio space. His program is divided into three parts: during the first, he reads from the Koran in Turkish; during the second, he presents his views on a chosen topic; and during the third, he invites viewers to call in and debate with him. The phone never stops ringing.

Unlike other Islamic producers at the Open Channel, Ekici makes no claims to be especially qualified to present the Koran to his viewers. Whereas other producers explicitly state or otherwise signal their religious learning, their piousness, the social context, and the particular Islamic tradition within which their authority is recognized, Ekici on the contrary stresses his lack of such potentially legitimizing qualifications. The main point of his program is in fact his insistence that every human being is able to and should approach the Koran him- or herself, without the intervention of religious authorities. Reading from and interpreting the Koran in his live program himself, Ekici aims to set an example of how even "an uneducated man" (his own words) can read and understand the word of God, and discuss it with others. He explained to me:

It is possible to read and understand the Koran without having had religious instruction, it is even necessary to do so, because Islam is no profession. And the biggest betrayal of Islam has been committed by the group of religious authorities.[15]

Thus, the major points of contention that are debated time and again in his program are the questions of whether someone like Ekici himself, with no particular authority and religious schooling, is authorized to interpret the Koran, and secondly, whether the Koran can be read in Turkish. Ramazan Ekici maintains that people should read the Koran in the language they understand best, and that this is a far better way of getting to know Islam than through the words of religious authorities and scholars.

While Islam does not have a structural edifice that corresponds, for example, to the Christian churches, questions of religious leadership and its legitimation have of course loomed large in the history of Islam as well. Ekici's radical approach is quite scandalous to most of the other Islamic producers at the Open Channel. For them, questions of religious learning and the authority attached to it are essential, and many maintain that knowledge of Arabic is a prerequisite for developing an adequate understanding of the Koran. As stated, Ekici wants to set an example in his program: if he can read the Koran and learn from it, so can anyone. This is a direct challenge to other Islamic programs such as *Saadet TV,* which take a very different approach to religious knowledge. These approaches entail, for example, setting up their program as an instruction session rather than a dialogue, thereby implying that viewers have less competence and authority to speak on a particular subject. They can also entail quoting from the Koran in Arabic and thus displaying their learning, or invoking great Muslim figures such as the Mystic Said Nursi—all elements conducive to legitimizing one's religious broadcasting activities.

The following presents a brief excerpt from one of Ekici's programs broadcast early in the year 2000, taken from the third part of his program. After having commented on the verses of the Koran he has read, he is ready to take calls from viewers.

"We are waiting for your opinion. Now you can have your say. . . . We ask our fellow countrymen [vatandaşlar] who call in to give their name, make use of their three minutes and say a few things. It can also be a question that they want to raise." The phone rings, he picks up the receiver. "Hello—[in German:] Yes, thank you, nothing else can be expected from your mouth. [Continues in Turkish] Yes, he just told me in German that I look really awful. And I have said to him: 'Nothing else can be expected from your mouth anyway.'" The phone rings again, he picks up. Listens quietly for a moment, then puts down the phone. "Yes, this was apparently someone from Mars, could be. But the language of this program is Turkish. Turkish on the phone." The phone rings. "Hello, good evening, can I take down your name? Your last name. Yes. I put you on the speakers now." Caller: "Sir, you've said something at the beginning of your program. Everybody should read the Holy Koran, analyze and study it in their own mother tongue, in the language they can understand. Those are *the principles of Islam, aren't they?"* Ramazan Ekici: *"I believe that it has to be that way."* Caller: *"Now, I don't want to drag you into political discussions . . ."* R. E.: *"Go ahead, your opinion."* Caller: *^""As you have said, with the forms of beauty given to the community of believers, today in Eastern Turkey there are a whole range of nations, of peoples. Those people are Muslims. They have Islamic roots. And their races are separate. Today, because of the pain and pressure inflicted by the Turkish Republic, these people can neither speak in their own mother tongue, nor pray or see images of themselves. So in your opinion, what should be said about this? What do you think, is there such pressure affecting the community of believers or not?"* R. E.: *"I don't know, I have stated my opinion. If you had listened to me earlier, this question probably— Well, I also feel uncomfortable about these things, I am saying, people should not pressure other people, they shouldn't hurt others or betray them."* Caller: *"Ramazan Bey, I agree, you've said very nice things. So ok, but isn't there this falseness, if we call ourselves Muslim, why don't we concede that others are Muslim too? . . . So are there wrongdoings or not? . . . You can give me a definite answer, yes or no?"* R. E.: *"Brother, . . . I have already given a definite answer in my talk, I am saying, there is nothing more important than the life of a human being."*[16]

The caller of course refers implicitly to the issue of Kurdish languages being banned in Turkey, and finds an interesting way to introduce Kurdish issues into a Turkish-Islamic program, which generally refrain from commenting on the "Kurdish question." Ekici himself struggles not to have to take a stand with regard to the issue, trying to maintain a general position rather than judging the policies of the Turkish state in this regard. But what is interesting here is that such a situation can arise during his program in the first place. Ekici's program is only one among a number of Turkish-Islamic programs that offer viewers the chance to call in and ask questions, or even debate with producers. While most of the other producers screen their calls in the backroom of the studio, and put on air only those that "fit" the desired concept of the program, Ekici and a few other producers take viewers' calls directly, in front of the live camera. Ekici does not immediately put callers audibly on air, but checks briefly whether or not he is dealing with a prank call, or deliberate insults. However, as long as the caller is willing to engage in a reasonably polite conversation, Ekici turns on the loudspeaker so that he (and much more rarely she) can be heard by the television audience. Ekici also tells viewers that he can be reached via phone for another half-hour after the end of his program, and also offers to meet with callers in person outside the studio space. He told me of a number of occasions when he was called in as a mediator, for example, when a young Sunni woman and a young Alevi man wanted to get married despite their families' objections. Most importantly, maybe, he is a regular guest at different mosques in the city, and has participated in a number of other OKB programs with and without Islamic orientation.

When I discussed Ekici's program with other Islamic producers, many were incensed by his activities and positions. In fact, other Islamic producers and representatives of different mosques in the city often call up during his program to criticize him.[17] Ekici told me that he has been repeatedly contacted and invited by different groups in the city who have tried to persuade him to discontinue his program and/or join their own circle, an invitation that he has always declined:

> If I don't stay independent, I can't think freely. If I form a group with you, and if you are my boss, what will I do? . . . If I am not independent, I will take care of our own group and attack the others, no? This is why I want to stay independent, so that the truth shall persevere.[18]

While Ekici deplores the political-religious divisions that he claims turn other Muslim groups into enemies, he is quite willing to enter into conversations with them. While some Islamic producers told me that they would rather not lend further legitimacy to his program by debating with him in public, a few have also begun to invite him into their own programs in order to have a discussion. Most notably maybe, Ekici—himself a Sunni Muslim—has appeared in Alevi programs and thus bridged a gap that is rarely bridged in Muslim religious life in the city, and beyond. Ekici wants to reach a German-speaking audience as well, and so in the year 2000 he began to produce the second half of his program in German, despite his rather shaky command of the language. But he thinks that Germans need to get a better idea of what Islam is really about, he told me. He said:

> You see, this is multicultural. . . . We affect each other. I love this Multikulti. It is no use just to talk about it, we have to live it. You have to give it a real chance. And there are definitely things that we can learn from the Germans and things they can learn from us. That's how the different parts come together, you know.

The opportunity to raise all kinds of issues, and to state one's opinion freely, is what Ekici values most about the Open Channel, and he sees this in direct contrast to the limited opportunities in Turkey, where freedom of speech is restricted. Like many other Islamic producers, he is convinced that in Turkey, he would be imprisoned by now for criticizing the secularist policies of the Turkish state. But he feels that open discussion also needs to take place among different Muslim groups, and with other faiths.

Among the Turkish producers at the Open Channel, he has brought about a lively debate on Islam. There has in fact been no other area of programming at the Open Channel that displays the same degree of dialogue among producers and their audiences. Even though Islamic producers reach out to specific audiences through choice of language, modes of address, and so on, they cannot know or control who watches, unlike in face-to-face settings like mosques and meeting spaces where visitors have to cross a physical threshold and give up anonymity. Producers are aware both of the multiplicity of Islamic broadcasts at the channel and of the wide range of potential reactions to their programs among viewers. In the context of live call-in shows at the OKB, migrant broadcasters are confronted with a complexity of dissenting views, ranging from verbal abuse to erudite statements, which they would be unlikely to face in non-mass-mediated settings.

What is more, in the context of broadcasting at the Open Channel, Islamic producers have also confronted each other, both face-to-face in the studio space and by watching and sometimes calling in to each other's programs. Different debates across Islamic religious orientations have thus been engendered, and have sometimes been carried out on as well as off the screen—conversations that, as broadcasters reported, do not usually take place among the diverse groups in the context of religious life in the city. The viewers of the OKB have been able to witness such debates in live programs, and even enter these debates themselves, since producers offer call-in opportunities and/or provide contact numbers and addresses at the end of their broadcasts. Confronted with a range of different and sometimes openly rivaling Islamic orientations, viewers have become aware of alternative approaches and the heterogeneity of forms and practices of belief. The threshold for engagement has thus been much lower than it would be if viewers had to leave the relative privacy of their homes in order to engage with them.

The opportunities at the OKB have also lowered thresholds of public articulation for producers themselves. In principle (and within the limit of the new restrictions imposed at the channel), anyone can speak about and for a particular Islamic perspective, taking the stage in the context of a mediated public forum, regardless of the extent to which the claim to representation is legitimized by an organization or community of believers. Gerdien Jonker has observed that young, second-generation men especially have made use of this opportunity structure and have articulated their visions in the context of OKB programming, while they tend to have much less of a chance to do so in the contexts of particular mosques and organizations where older religious authorities dominate (Jonker 2000). Ramazan Ekici is the only producer, however, who has explicitly called for a break with any kind of religious authority, calling for an open discussion of Islam based on direct study of the Koran.

As should have become evident, Ramazan Ekici's positions fit actually quite nicely with the basic tenets of Open Channel philosophy: encouraging discussion as a vital part of a democratic public sphere that is accessible to all, and admitting all kinds of positions as long as they are not insulting or threatening. Far from being a threat to the Open Channel philosophy, Ramazan Ekici's program can actually claim to have realized elements of this philosophy in exemplary ways. Yet, his program cannot escape the negative reputation that Islamic programs at the OKB have acquired.

Forms of Diversity

When I asked the director of the OKB to compare the Turkish-language programs produced at the Open Channel Berlin with the city's radio station Radio MultiKulti, he stated half-jokingly, "They have the good guys, we have the bad guys." The director's statement is an ironic, but nevertheless insightful comment on the dominant standards by which ethnic minority contributions to the mass-mediated public sphere of a multicultural Germany are measured. What is more, the statement also points to the peculiar pattern of dispersal that Turkish-language ethnic minority "voices" exhibit in relation to the mainstream of German broadcasting. Not all positions articulated by minority producers are equally welcome to enter mass-mediated circulation. Yet, the different political and institutional provisions for ensuring "diversity" in German broadcasting provide marginalized positions with access opportunities, albeit in "fringe" areas such as open access television. While German state representatives have only limited powers to curb the circulation and reach of transnational broadcasting based outside of Germany, federal state institutions and public councils are responsible for regulating locally based radio and television transmission in the different domains of public service, commercial, and open access broadcasting. Different concepts of desirable diversity in each of these domains, coupled with divergent regulative rules and practices, favor and help produce different migrant media "voices." These "voices," weak and strong, are themselves backed up by different forms and degrees of political and financial capital.

In the domain of commercial media, diversity is defined as a wide variety of program offerings with regard to category and content, and this variety is guarded by the German State Media Councils also responsible for licensing. It is thus mainly diversity of genres and orientations that guides licensing decisions, not the aim to service different ethnic groups or marginalized minorities in the country. Yet, when the Media Council Berlin-Brandenburg released a press statement late in 1998 announcing the licensing of a new Turkish-language radio station with its headquarters in Berlin, it expressed its hopes that a locally produced program would focus on local affairs and lure Turkish Berliners away from satellite media imports. Beyond an interest in genre diversity, the council came close to explicitly endorsing the widespread political argument that links migrant integration to their interest in local affairs. Such an explicit endorsement, however, would have imbued the licensing decision with an overt sociopolitical intent. Pressed on the issue, the council's press office did not admit to any intervention attempts apart from its mission to ensure "diversity" in the sense described above.

Quite strategically, though commercial and purely entertainment-oriented, Metropol FM had placed a strong emphasis on promoting local identifications and serving integration purposes in the license application materials it had submitted to the State Media Council. In its actual daily broadcasting routines, the station offers little spoken-word content, and limits itself to weather, news. and traffic—standard fare for the multitude of commercial competitors in the city, who differ mainly in terms of musical "color." The license stipulations force the station to offer news broadcasts in German, which are bought from a news company based in Munich. The staff in Berlin broadcasts almost exclusively in Turkish, as it is difficult to find staff members who are fully bilingual. As the German nonimmigrant manager of the station asserted in an interview with me, their intention is to make money, not to engage in politics or social work.[19] Nevertheless, when the then mayor of Berlin, Eberhardt Diepgen, attended the opening ceremony at Metropol FM's studio space in 1999, he emphasized his hopes that the station would one day broadcast to promote immigrant integration, and station representatives nodded politely. They knew well that they owed their license to an integrationist political agenda that supported the station as a tool for enhancing local identifications among immigrants from Turkey, and they were able to pay tribute to this agenda when necessary.

The strongest power of intervention exists within the public service domain of broadcasting. In the context of Radio MultiKulti, German broadcasting officials and public service management staff can narrowly prescribe and construct the kinds of "foreign voices" that fit into their vision of a multicultural Berlin. Defined by their distinct ethnic belonging, their notion of "diversity" is contained within a local cultural mosaic of the city that Radio MultiKulti seeks to both represent and address. In its German-language programs, geared implicitly toward a nonimmigrant audience of listeners, the slightly accented voice of presenters mirrors and reinforces the limits of acceptability within which "foreignness" can emerge. It offers a mode of enunciation that indicates its nondomestic origin, yet just as much denotes its educated high-cultural civility, and positions that carefully remain within the dominant horizons of meaning that a nonimmigrant, "world-open" audience is imagined to inhabit.

While the staff members of foreign-language programs at Radio Multi-Kulti have greater editorial independence, they similarly have to subscribe to a vision of their respective audience as a local group of ethnic minority residents. "I am a Berliner, I am multicultural, I listen to Radio MultiKulti every day"—this slogan of MultiKulti's Turkish-language program neatly encapsulates what "good" immigrant guys, or "good" immigrant women, for that matter, are expected to live and embody in the hegemonic version of German multiculturalism. The team that produces Turkish-language broadcasts at Radio MultiKulti does not have to be actively monitored by the station's management to adhere to this vision. Adamant that they broadcast only for those Turkish-language speakers who identify with the city, transnational orientations toward Turkey are denounced as "backward-oriented." Well-trained and university educated, the staff members report not only on Turkish affairs in the city but also on cultural highlights and issues of political contention that they deem relevant to all city residents, including its Turkish minority. They by and large stay clear of precisely those issues that incite heated debates on the Open Channel Berlin: Islam and secularism, the Sunni-Alevi divide, Kurdish struggles for autonomy and recognition. Beyond insisting on the irrelevance of such issues for migrant life in Berlin, engagement with these issues would also immediately polarize their audience in ways that would alienate many listeners.

Yet, despite their avoidance of such issues in MultiKulti's programming, they are nevertheless judged in these terms among migrant circles. In conversations with me the *MultiKulti* team was alternatively deemed secularist with a disdain for Islam, radically leftist with a disdain for the Turkish state, probably Alevi-controlled, implicitly Turkish nationalist because of its silence on Kurdish issues, or simply elitist and out of touch with the actual needs and expectations of its target audience. While some of these descriptions are mutually incompatible and clearly depended on the relative position of the speaker, the broad picture that emerges is one of secularists with somewhat left-leaning sympathies and high-cultural inclinations. As German public service broadcasting officials confirmed in conversations with me, they tend to think of migrant opinions on Turkish topics as almost inevitably partisan, and rarely informed by the standards of disinterested objectivity they claim for themselves as public service broadcasters. Yet, the general picture painted of the Turkish *MultiKulti* team among Berlin's Turkish population is one that the station can live with, as it is very much compatible with Radio MultiKulti's general orientation and unlikely to alienate their target audience of "integrated" Turkish Berliners.

Different from public service projects such as Radio MultiKulti, the Open Channel Berlin cannot ensure that migrant producers adhere to its vision of appropriately multiculturalist representations of immigrant life. Made possible by the rule of noninterference with program contents, the Open Channel offers the rare example of a disjuncture between the culture of a broadcasting institution and the actual programs that are produced and broadcast in this institutional context.

In the professional realms of television and radio production in Germany, the staff generally consists of trained experts who apply their professional knowledge and specialist practices in their daily work. Their training and experience marks them as "insiders" who are familiar with the standards used to evaluate their work at their respective broadcasting institution. These standards form part of the "cultural logic" of the institution, which its employees have to submit to. In the course of their training, they have to develop a practical sense of what constitutes "good programming." If they do not develop this sense or even object to the standards applied, they will most likely stop working before long. When I started as an intern at Radio MultiKulti, the chief editor of the German-language division pointed out to me that nobody would have time to train me: I would have to "fit in" and find out what was expected of me by emulating my colleagues and studying examples of successfully broadcast material. "Some pick it up, some don't," she said, and those interns deemed not to have succeeded were not invited to continue as freelance contributors after their internship had ended.

Contents and forms of representation are thus generally structured by the cultural logic of broadcasting institutions (Dornfeld 1998). Open Channels function quite differently, since they refrain in principle from imposing guidelines concerning contents and forms of representation. It is this policy of letting the "users" decide that enables OKB programs to differ at all from the ideals that the founders of Open Channels endorse. At the Open Channel, restrictions or guidelines regarding permissible orientations exist only to a limited degree. Immigrant producers can address whatever issues seem relevant to them, and present them in their programs as they see fit. The channel is thus the ideal "outlet" for positions that are not represented in other realms of broadcasting, be it that their orientation is not acceptable in these other realms, that they are articulated by a minority within the minority, or both.

The Open Channel's concept of diversity is not ethnically driven, but derives instead from a political conviction that mass media need to be kept accessible to all, particularly to those who do not have the political and economic power to set the standards for "mainstream" media production. Diversity here is key to the functioning of mass media as public spheres, in the interest of a democratic process of public debate to which all members of the public should have access and should ideally be involved in. Going beyond liberal versions of broadcasting pluralism, Open Channels in Germany actively seek to represent the "voices" of subaltern groups and are critical of both free market and state forces in broadcasting. Within this left-leaning liberal perspective on diversity, immigrants are encouraged as much as women, gays and lesbians, young people, and other members of social movements or neighborhood associations that "speak for" the disadvantaged. However, the majority of Turkish-language immigrants who avail themselves of the broadcasting opportunities at the channel hardly empathize with this perspective. The standards that the producers apply to their own work often differ radically from the cultural logic and democratic ideals of the OKB. What they consider to be "good programming" tends instead to be tied to the cultural, social, and political circles they move in outside the OKB as an institution.

Challenging Multiculturalism

As discussed above, the realities of Turkish-language immigrant engagement at the OKB thus not just disappoint but actively trouble channel officials and advocates, because they reflect in their overwhelming majority anything but left-leaning, liberal views. Instead, nationalist and Islamist agendas predominate, often right-wing and certainly not liberal in their orientation. While these appear as rather problematic contributions to the "grassroots" public spheres that Open Channels want to support, the objective of "giving voice" to marginal positions is nevertheless quite impressively realized, as was pointed out with regard to debates on Islam. The OKB has become a mass media outlet for all those Turkish, Islamic, and Kurdish migrant positions that do not have any other representation within the German broadcasting landscape. They lack both the financial capital to establish private, commercial radio, or television ventures,[20] and the political acceptance to gain entry into the public service domain or obtain a commercial broadcasting license.

Yet, the support for such broadcasting diversity is difficult to defend in public, particularly since the September 11 events spurned a new internal security debate in Germany, and a critical reconsideration of multiculturalist paradigms all across Europe. In a climate of increasing concerns over Islamist violence, "tolerance" toward public expressions of Islamic or nationalist beliefs can quickly become discredited as "soft liberalism" in the face of allegedly dangerous extremism. When Islamic or nationalist migrant producers appear as corporate political actors on the Open Channel, the limits of "diversity" in broadcasting are truly put to the test. This ethnic minority presence in German broadcasting is much more uncomfortable than the one that has been institutionalized in the public service domain or in commercial projects that have to try not to alienate part of their potential audience by endorsing partisan positions.[21]

Anthropologist Talal Asad has pointed out the functioning of multiculturalism as a mode of normalization within modern states in Western Europe, particularly with regard to Muslim immigrant populations (Asad 1990). The particular modes of managing ethno-cultural difference, somewhat differing from state to state and from one institutional domain to the other, nevertheless converge upon the inscription and regulation of appropriate spaces as well as forms of expression for such difference. The problem with Islamic and nationalist migrant broadcasters is that they appear to make use of a liberal democratic institution in a way that seems to undermine the very egalitarian principles it is based on. They therefore come to represent a threat to the sociocultural order into which they were meant to be integrated by means of learning "how to have political exchanges in a democratic society," as the OKB director has put it. These broadcasters mostly do not fit the ideal profile of a minority representative whose "speaking for" a particular ethnic group could advance the cause of multicultural integration and tolerance, even though Ramazan Ekici is a notable exception. Neither do they represent the kind of diversity that Open Channels would like to foster. Most of them indeed test the limits of the dominant notion of multiculturalism in Germany, which accepts diversity only within a tightly delineated frame.

7

Signifying with a Difference: Migrant Mediations in Local and Transnational Contexts

In the contemporary Western moment of globalized modernity, mobility has become a central cultural category. Mobility animates not only the public and commercial fascination with fluid identities and cultural practices of "hybridizing" and "mixing" (Holert 1998; Hutnyk 2000), but is taken to be both an adequate description of globally ruling capitalism in its new labor regimes and financial flows and a normative, highly sought-after quality (Urry 2000). Flexibility is marketable both as an individual asset and as a consumer product. Control over mobility increasingly comes to be a prime cultural marker of socioeconomic elites, whether it is tied to jet-set life styles, congestion charge zones in metropolitan city centers, body modification, or wireless access technologies.

While mobility appears as a desirable quality for some, the movements and identificatory frames of economically and culturally "poor" migrants are much more critically viewed and tightly regulated. A range of legal regulations and policy practices control the territorial movements of poor migrants and give differential access to entities such as "Fortress Europe." Differential access ranges from refugee camps, which are increasingly located outside of EU borders, to temporary work permits, from asylum seekers prohibited from wage labor to immigrants with permanent resident status (Diken 2004). Even though many immigrants from Turkey belong to the latter, most privileged category of permanent residents in Germany, they face limitations on their mobility in terms of having to spend at least half of each year within the country, and in terms of not always being able to freely choose their place of residence. The so-called *Zuzugssperren*, legal prohibitions on foreign nationals moving into certain Berlin city districts, are a case in point. They were temporarily imposed by the Berlin city government for different periods between 1975 and 1990 in order to avoid "ghettoization," as it was called.

Within the context of German integration politics that deem the "three T's" of travel, telecommunications, and television a hindrance to "becoming local," the mobility of migrants from Turkey is anything but applauded. As has been shown several times in this book, immigrants' engagement with transnational issues tends to be interpreted by German political authorities and academics alike as a sign of dissociation and ghettoization, at worst indicating a kind of "cultural schizophrenia." For former labor migrant populations, the older, classically modernist paradigms still rule, which expect migration processes to take place as a kind of "replanting" procedure: as a successive cutting off of roots in one place and eventual growing of roots in another (Malkki 1992).

Recent cross-disciplinary work on transnational migration, diasporas, and mobility has revealed that such expectations are mistaken in a globalizing world that is marked by the time-space compressions of new communication technologies and international travel, and by the need for disposable, underpaid migrant work forces in the increasingly neoliberal economies of the highly industrialized countries.[1] The ideological labor and policy work directed at turning certain immigrants into locals masks both the opting out of economic elites from local or nation-state–based notions of social solidarity, and the precarious situation of illegalized and temporary migrants whose transnationalism is a strategy of precarious survival. Multiculturalist policies that aim to integrate resident immigrants into a multiethnic community framework are thus not only problematic for their essentialization of ethno-cultural differences. They also block much-needed debates on the different forms of mobility that inform increasing socioeconomic polarizations in highly industrialized countries around the globe (Hannam, Sheller, and Urry 2006; Sassen 1999).

However, the example of the Open Channel in Berlin has shown that the very policies designed to facilitate local integration can be used by migrants to build and participate in transnational social spaces, by addressing the *vatandaşlar* (compatriots), criticizing the government in Turkey, or creating Muslim transnational audiences that draw viewers in Berlin into a wider network of religious learning and transmission of knowledge. While German integration experts and politicians regard migrant activities at the Open Channel as a means to further their identification with local community affairs, the actual programs can forge quite different kinds of identifications. What happens in many of the Turkish programs at the Open Channel Berlin goes beyond the confines of the local life that German policies and discourses tend to stipulate as the appropriate site for multicultural diversity (Vertovec 1996b).

In the case of *Saadet TV*, this transgression does not take overtly political forms. Yet, as has been shown, many other Turkish-language programs have a strong focus on what German political authorities consider to be "domestic" Turkish conflicts, thus presenting another challenge to multiculturalist paradigms. The issue of "keeping out" these conflicts has particularly since the 1990s been discussed at the highest political level. This included public appeals by Germany's Foreign Minister when Kurdish groups staged violent demonstrations all over the country and other parts of Western Europe, in response to the capture of PKK leader Öcalan. German political authorities are finding it difficult to stay clear of such "domestic" Turkish conflicts: the line between "internal" and "external" politics is becoming increasingly blurred. Eva Østergaard-Nielsen has studied the patterns of dialogue between German political institutions and migrant organizations, and argues that homeland and immigrant political agendas have in fact become inseparable (Østergaard-Nielsen 2003).

In the domain of broadcasting, very different patterns of incorporation or exclusion have emerged, depending on the compatibility of German political agendas with those of the respective migrant broadcasting initiatives, as could be seen in the case of Radio MultiKulti. Those migrant "voices" that find representation in public service and mainstream commercial domains of German broadcasting are the least interested in Turkey's contentious "domestic" conflicts. They also rarely discuss and never promote Islamic agendas, and tend to have a local or regional orientation. But since Open Channels are by definition inclusive institutions, they attract migrant groups and positions that cannot find access to public service and commercial broadcasting domains in Germany. Ironically, then, the very broadcasting institutions that were set up and intended as "grassroots" public spheres with a local orientation have become home to transnationally waged politics of cultural struggle.

It would be wrong, though, to characterize this particular transnationalization at Open Channels as merely an import of "foreign" conflicts and issues carried out on German territory. Migrant broadcasters at the Open Channel do not simply replicate debates and positions from Turkey, but modify them, add to them, and go beyond them. Many seek to articulate these conflicts in ways that respond to the migration context, and to their position at the intersection of different fields of cultural struggle. As has been shown in the last chapter, even Turkish nationalists can find ways to relate their quest for Pan-Turkish unity to minority politics in Germany, as when the German state is accused of promoting separatist tendencies among the migrant population from Turkey in order to push its own assimilation-ist agenda. Other migrant broadcasters at the Open Channel employ similarly complex and shifting strategies to deal with their multiple positioning in national and transnational frames.

Alevi Subaltern Broadcasting Strategies

Several Alevi television programs form a counterpart to the predominance of Hanafite-Sunni Islamic orientations at the Open Channel Berlin. Even though Alevis are usually described as a Muslim minority in predominantly Sunni-Islamic Turkey, producers of Alevi programs are not included in the definition of "Islamist" used by the Open Channel management, by virtue of being allegedly more tolerant and supportive of democracy than their Sunni fellow Muslims.

The problems with defining Aleviness, which will be explored in detail below, go beyond the question of mass media representation. There exists, in fact, no easily identifiable group of people who embody and claim Aleviness in any straightforward way. As a "reflexive social entity" with a history of persecution and marginalization in Turkey, Aleviness is constituted through mediation, but at the same time posited as unmediated in different fictions of "premediated existence" (Mazzarella 2004).[2]

There are nevertheless several characteristics on which self-identified Alevis and scholars of Islam agree. In religious terms, Alevis are usually described as a Shi'ite-derived minority that has developed in Anatolia, linked to Shi'ite Islam mainly through their shared reverence for Ali and his descendents. Ali was son-in-law of the Prophet Muhammed, regarded by Shi'ites and Alevis as the Prophet's only legitimate successor. Despite shared historical roots, Alevi belief developed in a separate direction, drawing upon sources of Turkish mystical Islam and Anatolian folk culture. Alevi sources generally claim that they constitute between 18 to 25 million among Turkish nationals, out of a current total population of an estimated 63 million, 99 percent of whom are Muslim. Non-Alevi sources give estimates between 4.6 to 18 million, indicating the difficulties of statistically measuring minority belonging in Turkey (Vorhoff 1995). However, Alevis constitute not simply a religious minority—claims to Alevi identity variously combine ethnic, national, religious, and explicitly political criteria in their self-definition (Vorhoff 1995; see also Ocak 1991; Seufert 1997). Determining the overall numbers of Alevis in Germany presents similar difficulties. Alevi organizations such as the German Federation of Alevi Communities (AABF) claim figures between 500,000 and 700,000, though these estimates seem a bit high in relation to the overall immigrant popula-

tion from Turkey. But opinions on whom to include or exclude in defini-
tions of *Alevilik* (Aleviness/Alevi people) vary widely.

Alevi television producers in Berlin similarly shift in their respective
emphasis on ethnicity, culture, religion, and politics in their representations
of *Alevilik*. Affiliated with different and partly competing Alevi organizations in the city, they all claim to represent—in the sense of embodying and
speaking for—the real *Alevilik,* true to its historical origins, religious beliefs,
and traditions. In order to make sense of their shifting representations, two
Alevi programs are discussed in more detail.

Al Canlar

The program *Al Canlar* has been broadcast on the Open Channel since
1993, and differs from other Alevi programs at the OKB mainly in terms of
its explicitly leftist political orientation. Literally translated, the title of the
program means "red souls," offering a play on the Turkish flag (*Al Sancak*)
and the dervish word for brother, friend, or disciple, *can*. It is common
Alevi usage to greet other Alevis as *canlar.*

Halit Büyükgöl, a construction worker in his early thirties, is the main
producer of the program. Initially, Büyükgöl simply wanted to provide Alevis in Berlin with images of familiar landscapes and faces, showing material
that he had filmed in Eastern Anatolia, near his hometown close to the city
of Muş. As a result of earthquakes and particularly the military offensive of
the Turkish state in the area, almost two-thirds of the population has fled
the region over the past twenty years. In 1993, Büyükgöl began to be active
at the Anadolu Alevi Kültür Merkezi, the Cultural Center of Anatolian Alevis in Berlin (AAKM). The date is no coincidence: it was the year of the
Sivas murders. A hotel in the town of Sivas, site of a conference held by
Alevi left-wing intellectuals and writers, was burnt down by an angry Sunni
mob. Many of the conference participants did not escape the flames, and
the event ignited a wave of Alevi activism both in Turkey and Europe in response. Members of the Cultural Center encouraged Büyükgöl to expand
his broadcasting at the Open Channel in order to publicize the activities of
the center and create a new media presence for Alevis, in explicit reaction to
the absence of such a presence in the mass media in Turkey.

In the following years, Halit Büyükgöl began to produce material himself and moved toward live programming. Inviting *bağlama* musicians from
Hannover, Alevi writers from Turkey, or local representatives of the AAKM,
he wanted to be able to respond to current affairs and also enter a more "dialogical" relationship with his audience. At the same time, he continued to
include material from Turkey—for example, the popular video clips of Alevi

musicians in Turkey that do not get shown on Turkey's music television channels because of their political implications.

His programs had a political dimension from the start: when *Al Canlar* broadcast the images of the Sivas event, anonymous letters arrived at the OKB threatening the producers with violence if they were to continue with allegedly "defaming" Islam. Halit Büyükgöl sees his position at the OKB as quite precarious, given the range of Turkish-language programming there: he deems himself to be one of the few producers who subscribes to democratic, left-leaning views. The Open Channel is not aware, he says, of the many programs that promote violence under the cover of a foreign language. These are either *şeriat kökenli,* Islamic programs that mobilize for the Sharia, or *sağ görüşlü,* the programs of Turkish nationalist right-wing extremists. *Al Canlar* is the only program that speaks for Anatolian Alevis, he claims, with an emphasis on Anatolian: by distancing himself from the label "Turkish," he seeks to emphasize the diversity of Alevis in the country, who have different ethnic backgrounds.

Other producers active at the Open Channel take a very different position, such as the *Hacı Bektaş Veli Kültür Cemiyeti.* Different from Büyükgöl's organization, the HBVKC stresses Turkishness, and their loyalty to Atatürk and his ideals. Consequently, Büyükgöl claims, the HBVKC cannot represent the unity of Alevis across ethnic differences, cannot include *bütün renkler,* all colors of Alevi culture. What is more, Halit Büyükgöl argues that since the very beginnings of the Alevi tradition, Alevis have always stood on the side of the oppressed: *mazlumdan yana* ("on the side of the oppressed"). This political stance dates back to the very origins of Alevi belief, he claims.

Alevis are adherents of Ali, son-in-law of the Prophet Muhammed, whom the latter had allegedly intended to become his successor. He eventually became Caliph in the year 644 A.D. but was murdered seventeen years later by adherents of Muawiya who installed himself as Caliph. Alevi sources claim that the followers of Muawiya called themselves "Sunnis," and that they were responsible also for the massacre of Ali's son Hüseyin and his family at Kerbela (Iraq). The date of Hüseyin's death continues to be remembered by Alevis up to this day. In later centuries, Alevis in Anatolia sometimes needed to go into hiding, as rulers tended to support Sunni Islam. Another massacre took place in 1514 when the Ottoman ruler Yavuz Sultan Selim is claimed to have killed more than 40,000 Anatolian Alevis (Gülçiçek 1996; Şener 1994). The founding of the Turkish Republic under Mustafa Kemal Atatürk promised to many Alevis the end of Sunni dominance, and many welcomed the secularization and modernization program enforced during the first decades of the Republic. While some Alevis continue to identify with Kemalist state traditions, others like Büyükgöl are critical of the state for its nationalist course of *Türkçülük,* Turkism. The name of Halit Büyükgöl's organization signals this criticism quite strongly: it is the cultural center of Anatolian Alevis, not of Turkish Alevis. While Anatolia does not geographically include the "European" part of Turkey's territory, the identification with *Anadolu* suggests primarily a refusal to identify with Turkishness, given the political connotations of the term. Büyükgöl also uses *Türkiyeli,* "stemming from Turkey," when he speaks of the migrant population, but never "Turk." From this state-critical perspective, the history of Alevis is marked by almost continuous suffering and oppression. A straight line can be drawn from the massacre of Kerbela and that of Sultan Selim to the contemporary events that have come to be known as "Sivas" and "Gaziosmanpaşa," places where Alevis have come under attack by violent Sunni Islamists and Turkish police forces.[3] It is particularly the Sivas event that led to a wave of Alevi mobilization both in Turkey and Western Europe, and the *Al Canlar* television program was created in its wake.

The introductory sequence to one of *Al Canlar*'s live broadcasts on the Open Channel in the first week of April 1998 indicates the importance of the Sivas event. The following is a description of what unfolds on the television screen during the first three minutes of the program:

1. A portrait of Ali is shown, set in a round frame. The frame remains present throughout the introduction, leaving a circle in the midst of a pink screen, while the mournful, mounting sound of violins creates tension.

2. A portrait of Hacı Bektaş Veli follows, the founder of the Anatolian Alevi-Bektaşi movement, with a text by famous Sufi poet Pir Sultan Abdal framing it: *Gelin canlar, canlar bir olalım. Dönen dönsün ben dönmezem yolumdan.* (Come you souls, let us be one. Those who turn back let them, I will not divert from my path.)

3. Images of a Cem ceremony are intercut with footage of a march in Berlin, featuring banners of the AAKM, and others declaring *yaşasın 1 Mayıs* (long live the first of May).

4. Cut to a small group of elderly men and women performing together the *Semah,* part of the *Cem* ceremony, in which they dance in a circle, circling also themselves, accompanied by Saz music and mystic songs.

5. Images of the Sivas fire, which is engulfing the remnants of a building in the dark.

6. Back to the march in Berlin. The pictures of people who died in the Sivas fire are carried on posters in the front rows of the demonstration.

7. The music has changed to a more upbeat rhythm, a song accompanies the images of the hotel burning in Sivas. The song speaks of persecution and struggle against the enemy, assuring:

Dost, senin derdinden ben yana yana. Ali, Ali, Ali, ben yana yana.
(Friend, your sorrow lets me burn. Ali, Ali, Ali, I am burning, burning.)

8. Meanwhile, one can see an excited and angry crowd that has gathered in front of the burning hotel in the town of Sivas. A small group of people is carrying off an injured person, looking for help.
9. The police is shown to be standing idle, looking on and not intervening.
10. The crowd is shown again, the flames of the fire now engulfing the entire building. Blending into this scene, images of the Semah performance are inserted, so that the men and women seem to be dancing in the flames.
11. Newspaper clippings are shown, and a headline states, *Sivas gergin* (Sivas in tension).

After this dramatic introduction, the program cuts to the live studio space of the OKB, with two men sitting at a simple desk. Behind them, the studio walls are adorned with posters that announce the fourth *Alevi Kültür Haftası,* the Alevi Week of Culture, with Cem ceremonies, concerts, and panel discussions. The young moderator, clean-shaven in a green shirt, introduces his guest, president of the AAKM Dr. Yüksel Özdemir. Both congratulate their viewers, since it is the day of *Kurban Bayramı,* the Feast of Sacrifice. The theme of the program is the upcoming Week of Culture. Özdemir explains the reasons behind the event, stating that Alevis have faced a long period of suppression in Turkey, but that after the murders of Sivas and the Gazi events, they have finally had enough and have begun to organize. He states that the failure of the state to recognize the richness of Alevi culture, philosophy, and belief in Anatolia is a loss for Turkey. To counter the restrictions and the ignorance concerning Alevis, they have founded the center so that they can organize and teach about Alevi philosophy and beliefs in Germany and all Europe.

Halit Büyükgöl stresses the importance of reaching German audiences as well, as when *Al Canlar* was broadcasting live in German from the International Broadcasting Fair (*Internationale Funkausstellung*) held each year in Berlin. During a visit to his home, Büyükgöl showed me excerpts of the broadcast: Alevi youngsters were asking one of the representatives of the center questions about *Alevilik* in German. It was obvious that the questions had been prepared in advance, and that they were geared toward countering potential preconceptions and prejudices that a German audience might be expected to harbor. As Büyükgöl explained, in Germany and Europe as a whole, Turkey is seen as an Islamic state associated with Sunni Islam, with Sharia rule, and with human rights violations and the oppression of women:

All of that is the Turkey that the flashy papers write about, that the state television is showing, the Turkey that is made public. But those who do a bit of research, they will see that Turkey is in fact beautiful Anatolia. They can see that this beautiful Anatolia is made up of different cultures, different religions, different minorities, different groups. In this mosaic of Anatolia, there are people with very different ethnic roots. Now if I say to a German or a European, there are 20 million Alevis in Turkey, they wonder, do these people really exist in Turkey? . . . But if they are told what Alevilik is about, see, it is this, it is liberal in its religious beliefs, it wants to build schools instead of mosques in the village. It is laicist, it respects human rights. . . . There is no division between men and women . . . . See, the Alevi woman does not wear a headscarf. She dresses any way she wants to. She is free. When I say that, they ask, does all of that exist in Turkey, in an Islamic state? They don't know that . . . .[4]

German and European audiences thus need to be shown that the negative stereotypes associated with Turks and Turkey do not apply to Alevis. When people in Germany find out that Büyükgöl comes from Turkey, they immediately make assumptions regarding his behavior toward women or his perspective on religion, he claims. But while these assumptions might be justified for the majority Sunni population of Turkey, he argues that Alevis share with Germans and Europeans a democratic, laicist, and egalitarian outlook. They do not pray five times a day, they do not go to mosques, nor do they regard the eating of pork or drinking of alcohol as a crime. According to Büyükgöl, Alevilik thus presents a culture, philosophy, and version of Islam that is perfectly compatible with, and in some respects even exemplary of, the ideals of Western secular societies. One function of Alevi media in the migration context is thus to promote this understanding among German and European audiences.

But Büyükgöl identifies another group that has prejudices concerning Alevis, namely non-Alevi people in Turkey and migrants from Turkey. Their prejudices differ from those of Germans and Europeans, since they have come into contact with a range of stereotypes commonly held among the Sunni majority population in Turkey. These stereotypes target Alevis as Alevis, not as Turks, and derive from misconceptions of Alevi cultural and religious practices that have long persisted among the Sunni population. It is necessary to dispel such prejudices among non-Alevis who could be allies because of their shared critical perspective on the state, Büyükgöl claims:

We want to reach those people in Turkey who are not Alevi and who still don't know us, the democratic, revolutionary people. There are liberal people there, definitely. We want to make people see those beautiful, nice dimensions of Alevilik that they don't know about. And definitely, even among those who know of us, we think there are some prejudices. To remove the prejudices, I don't know, the slander that has been leveled against Alevis, well, things like *mum söndü,* not distinguishing between mother and sister and such, to stop this ugly slander that people have picked up, there is a need for these broadcasts. We want them to learn about Alevilik not from others, not from the media of the state, not from the Alevis that are on the side of the state, but from the real Alevi people, from those who struggle for the original Alevilik!

"Candle extinguishing," *mum söndürme,* is an expression that refers to the alleged hidden polygamy and sexual looseness stereotypically thought to characterize Alevi mixed-sex gatherings (Vorhoff 1995). Even "liberal" and "revolutionary" (*devrimci*) people (the meaning of these attributes lies much closer together for the Turkish context than for a European or Anglo-American one, in that they signal a critical distance toward an authoritarian state) are suspected of harboring such prejudices, thus preventing potential alliances.

Depending on the audience one addresses, then, representing Alevilik to German or non-Alevi audiences from Turkey requires two different strategies: for German audiences, it is the libertarian and egalitarian dimension of *Alevilik* that is emphasized, while non-Alevi audiences from Turkey need to be primarily convinced of the moral and sexual integrity of Alevis. Certainly, there is a common ground in terms of the commitment to a laicist state and to the principles of democracy, central to both strategies. But *Al Canlar* and "true" (*asıl*) Alevi media are trying to intervene against *two* dominant regimes of representation, one carrying importance in the German, the other in the Turkish context.

The kinds of representations produced for an Alevi audience, however, introduce a third strategy: it is a political history of suffering that is invoked to mobilize Alevi solidarity, as could be seen in the introduction to the program discussed above. A second example of Alevi programming contextualizes and responds to this suffering in a different way.

Kırk Budak TV

İbrahim Alkan and his friends started their program *Kırk Budak TV* in 1997.[5] He and others used to go to the AAKM, but split off because they were unsatisfied with the organization's politics. They want to separate Alevi belief from politics, and though no one accused the AAKM directly, it became clear from Alkan's statements that they disagreed with the latter's support of minorities such as the Kurds. In the organization's headquarters, a small storefront in Berlin's immigrant neighborhood Neukölln, pictures of

Atatürk line the walls, indicating explicit identification with Turkey's republican national tradition. Unlike Halit Büyükgöl, İbrahim Alkan has no misgivings about identifying as a Turk: an Alevi Turk but Turkish nevertheless. Like the AAKM, however, their media representations are oppositional, in the sense that they have been constructed to counter and correct stereotypes, particularly among Sunni Muslims. Alkan explained the aims of his program to me:

> Unfortunately, the Sunnis have been told the wrong things about us, very wrong! . . . We say to them, look, you say this and that, but we are not like that, we are different. This is what we are trying to do. This is what we are like. For example, we Alevis don't go to the mosque five times a day, we don't go there at all! But that does not mean that we condemn them, that we dislike them, no! Those who want to go should go. But we organize Cems, once or twice a year. This is also worshiping.[6]

In a *Kırk Budak TV* program broadcast on the OKB in May 1998, an unidentified moderator introduced the topic of the program as follows:

> Now we want to show you some misconceptions that are widespread among the people, and we will try to learn about them from the most knowledgeable sources, if you permit, esteemed viewers. As you all remember, we have had a radio station for some time, Köln Radyosu. . . . In a recent broadcast there, there was a Sunni sister (*bacı*) who called, and this is what I heard from her: "I slaughtered the animal to be sacrificed (*kurban kestim*) and gave some meat to the Germans, some to the *kızılbaşlar*,[7] that is to the Alevis. Now I wonder, did I do injustice to the sacrifice?" How sad that we hear such dangerous fatwas, using modern technologies. Of course it is not the sister to be blamed, she has been taught like that. But so we will hear today from our *dede*[8] how it is that the Alevis and Bektaşi actually sacrifice their animals, listen closely.

As becomes evident, the program is structured mainly as a response to Sunni stereotypes of Alevis, assuming as its audience a Turkish-speaking population that is potentially hostile, or at least unfamiliar with Alevi beliefs and practices. The *Kırk Budak* program represents an effort to find common ground with Sunni Muslims under the roof of Islam, Alkan states.

> I think the importance of our program for the Turks here is this: we try to make ourselves known to those people that come from Islam, those who call themselves Muslim. We tell them, yes, there are differences between us, but there is only one Islam and only one right way! Let's find this way together, this is why we explain ourselves to them. Let's stop the enmity between us.

Alkan came to Germany in 1973 and does not speak German, like many of the visitors at the Hacı Bektaş Kültür Cemiyeti (HBKC). The HBKC has difficulties attracting younger members, as the group present for the interview agrees. It is thus mainly first-generation male labor migrants who are active at the OKB. This explains at least partially why they do not worry about representing *Alevilik* to a German audience—the language barrier cannot but orient them toward a Turkish-speaking audience. Alkan does not consider Germany as his home country (*memleket*) and insists that he will eventually return to Turkey. Still, it is easier to live as an Alevi in Germany, Alkan and his friends say, and Germans need to learn about *Alevilik* as well, and about what makes it different from other forms of Islam.

Other Alevi migrant forms of public representation, such as Web sites, journals, or conferences, are indicative of substantial efforts to also reach German nonimmigrant audiences. The double orientation toward fellow migrants and nonimmigrant audiences in Alevi media productions highlights the representational challenges that subaltern migrant media producers can face in their work. Marginalized for different reasons in both Turkey and Germany, both the producers of *Al Canlar* and of *Kırk Budak TV* focus much of their attention on countering the negative attitudes they suspect their audiences (migrant and nonmigrant) to harbor. Whereas Abdullah Güneş, producer of *Türk'ten Türk'e,* can speak with the confidence of someone whose convictions and taken-for-granted assumptions are backed up by dominant, state-supported discourses in Turkey, Alevi migrant positions do not have that support. Theirs is an attempt to signify "from the periphery of authorized power and privilege," as Homi Bhabha has put it in his analysis of minority cultural production (Bhabha 1994, 2). Yet, unlike the producers of *Saadet TV,* who place their faith in the conviction that their Sheikh is exclusively authorized and able to mediate the word of God for his audience regardless of their lifeworlds and whereabouts, Alevi producers feel the need to engage with the dominant horizons of meaning in which they see their audiences embedded.

Seeking to intervene in dominant stereotypical discourses that reproduce their marginalization, the problem of how to represent their own difference differently takes center stage. Representations of Alevi identity are thus created strategically by migrant producers, using the very semiotic material that forms part of their audiences' ideological horizons in an attempt to re-signify. What complicates this project of semiotic intervention is its transnational location in the margins of not just one but two nation-states and their arenas of cultural struggle. When seen through a multiculturalist lens that focuses on the allegedly more "benign" nature of Alevi Islam in Germany, the picture of *Alevilik* is very different from the one provided by a dominant Turkish perspective that tends to regard Alevi religious practices and beliefs as un-Islamic.

As demonstrated, Alevi broadcasters move among different target audiences, modifying their strategies of representation as they go along. It is only by taking into account the transnational dimensions of their cultural positioning in Germany that these modifications can be understood. Their representations of Alevi identity appear as disjointed and even contradictory, unless the different contexts of enunciation are made transparent and are situated with regard to the heterogeneous complexities that bring them forth. Alevi migrant television programs are intended by their producers as strategic interventions into overlapping fields of cultural struggle where the dominant terms have already been set, casting Alevis in each as a different kind of problematic minority. The interesting question is how migrant television "voices" grapple with the collusion of these different national fields in the migration context. Once contextualized, it is possible to understand the work of migrant producers at the OKB, their shifting strategies of representation, and their efforts to mobilize support from different audience groups as syncretic rather than contradictory. Studying the programs of Alevi producers opens up a perspective not just on ideological contradictions and conflict, but reveals them as tactical articulations. Alevi programs combine elements drawn from different contexts, in the interest of forming different kinds of shifting alliances (Becquer and Gatti 1991), as will be shown below.

Strategic Alliances

Despite the secularist traditions of the Turkish state, the rise of new Islamic elites in the late twentieth century has led to an increasing emphasis on Islam as a central dimension of the Turkish nation-building project. The Islam that is mobilized by state elites is almost invariably a form of Sunni Islam. Already in Ottoman times, religious and "ethnic" belonging had a political dimension, and in the context of the Turkish Republic, both became articulated as important elements of national identity.[9] To identify—or to be identified as—non-Sunni Muslim and ethnically non-Turkish has therefore come to signify distance from the national mainstream, and from the state that claims to represent its political embodiment. The dominant articulations of national identity in Turkey thus produce Alevi identity as subaltern, forcing those who identify as Alevis to constantly grapple with schemes of classification that assign to them a lesser place in the national community. Given the dominance of Sunni Islam in Turkey, Alevis have had to define their identity in oppositional-relational terms (Sökefeld forthcoming 2007). This becomes evident also in the media representations produced by Alevi migrants in Germany. They constantly involve Sunni Islam as a point of reference: as an audience that has misconceptions about Alevi belief and religious practice, as a historical legacy of oppression and persecution, and as a form of Islamic doctrine and practice from which Alevis diverge.

Yet, this subaltern position has opened up possibilities for alliances with other groups that similarly do not fit the ethno-political and religious criteria defined as mainstream in Turkey. While this mainstream has become contested particularly along the secularist/Sunni Islamist divide (Navaro-Yashin 2002), other groups have not been able to mount significant challenges. The historical continuity of Alevi oppositional identity vis-à-vis the state (both the Ottoman and the Turkish-Republican) has created a particular affinity between Alevis and the political Left in Turkey. Further potential allies can be those groups that insist on identities marginalized by the dominant Turkish-Islamic synthesis, and those demanding an end to the often violent suppression of criticism enacted by the state. In the realm of Turkish party politics, Alevis have joined forces with leftists, feminists, and Kurdish sympathizers in the *Özgürlük ve Dayanışma Partisi* (ÖDP, Freedom and Solidarity Party), founded in Turkey in 1994 with the aim to be the true representative of those marginalized by the state. In the migration context as well, there is a reservoir of potential allies that Alevi broadcasters need to actively tap into, as the producer of the Open Channel's only left-leaning Alevi television program stated.

But in order for alliance politics to work, Alevi attempts to create alliances—in Antonio Gramsci's sense of an oppositional "historical bloc"—still have to grapple with the stereotypical traits alleged to characterize Alevi culture in a Turkish context. These traits endanger the claim to moral worth necessary for a new (trans)national alliance in the name of democracy, *sevgi* (love) and *saygı* (respect) for the people. The love that unites this alternative alliance may not be tainted by the morally scandalous possibility of *mum söndürme* and incestuous relations alleged to prevail among Alevis in the stereotypical ascriptions that are part of the dominant scheme of categorical identities in Turkey. As a consequence, Alevi migrant producers such as those of the OKB program *Al Canlar* have to convince their potential allies among Turkish oppositional groups of the falseness of such stereotypes. What needs to be accomplished is a rearticulation of Alevi cultural traits that demonstrates both superior morality and superior suffering with regard to the alliance that is its political goal.

This is done by several tactical interventions: the egalitarian relationship claimed between the sexes, known to involve the mingling of men and women in religious ceremonies, is defused of its sexually explosive potential by the use of kinship terms. Alevis are united through bonds of *kardeşlik,* brother- or sisterhood, and women can participate in activities as *bacılar,* sisters, thus creating a setting of mixed-sex interaction that is permissible also by Sunni standards. This articulation of relationships allows women to participate in political struggle while leaving their sexual honor intact (Seufert 1997). The gendering of public spheres in Turkey, which leads to mostly separated and different forms of political activism for men and women except among Kemalist elites (Delaney 1995; Göle 1996), can thus be partially subverted through the introduction of bonds that pertain to the "private" sphere of the family. This is relevant to the migration context as well. Thus, as the *Kırk Budak* program has shown, "sister" can appear in Alevi migrant broadcasts as a generic term for fellow Muslim women with whom no personal relations have been established.

Another intervention concerns the symbolic importance of suffering for one's convictions, and for the nation's future: in terms of suffering, Alevis make a strong case for having been subjected and having fought continuous injustice in Turkey for centuries. Beginning with the mythical invocation of Ali and continuing with all other eleven Imams recognized by Alevis as legitimate heirs to the Caliphat, theirs is a history of assassinations, massacres, and poisonings.[10] The Sivas fire brought Alevis once again to the forefront of suffering for a different kind of Turkey. A history of suffering can thus be mobilized to give Alevis a central place in the oppositional "historical bloc" (in the Gramscian sense) that is forming against the Turkish establishment on the political Left, uniting those who measure the libertarian potential of parliamentary democracy in Turkey against its record of violent suppression of different kinds of opposition.

In the migration context, however, this history can also be invoked to stress the differences between *Alevilik* and Sunni Islam, articulating it for a different kind of cultural struggle that is shaped by dominant perceptions of Islam and immigrant minorities in Germany. Alevis are able to capitalize upon a peculiar "reversal of hierarchies" in the migration context, Ruth Mandel has remarked (Mandel 1989, 1990, 1996). While Alevis are in one sense "doubly liminal"—with regard to Sunni Turks as Alevis and with regard to Germans as "Turks"—their religious-cultural traits that are negatively valued by the dominant Sunni-Islamic perspective in Turkey take on a positive meaning in Germany.

As seen, Alevi organizations stress in their German-language representations of *Alevilik* the criteria that make them different from Sunni Muslims: not praying in mosques, women and men intermingling in religious ceremonies, women not wearing headscarves. All of these dimensions—which among Sunni Turks tend to be interpreted as morally suspect and non-Islamic—turn Alevi beliefs and practice into a kind of Islam that in the German context tends to be interpreted as progressive and tolerant. Alevi insistence on "internal qualities," the purity of the soul as opposed to alleged "externals" such as praying five times a day, approximates a "privatized," more secular understanding of religion prevailing in Germany that sees it as linked to the conscience of the individual and less appropriate for public, communal manifestations.

While in Turkey, the ideological dominance of the Turkish-Islamic synthesis renders Alevis "lesser Turks" whose cultural contributions to the nation are suspect, the German context provides different standards for the evaluation of such contributions. Measured by these standards, Alevi migrants appear as "less alien" than their Sunni counterparts. What Seufert (1997) has called the *Staatsferne,* distance from the state that characterizes Alevi identity in Turkey, becomes *Staatsnähe,* closeness to the state in Germany, insofar as the processes of nation-building prevailing there allow them to cast themselves as the representatives of a "benign" Islam and as a model minority.

It is therefore crucial to study the conjuncture of two national contexts within which different kinds of cultural hierarchies dominate. The migrants effectively partake and situate themselves in both. This double engagement cannot be regarded as a relic of "cultural baggage" brought along from Turkey that is bound to disappear, as classical paradigms of migration once posited. Transnational affiliations continue to be forged, linking Alevi migrants in Western Europe to communities of origin and to places of worship, but also to new political-organizational structures emerging in Turkey, structures that are actively supported and even built in the migration context.[11] Thus, the Sivas event, in which prominent participants at an Alevi conference of artists and intellectuals lost their lives, has mobilized Alevi migrants just as much as Alevis in Turkey. It serves as an important point of reference for current representations of Alevi identity among migrants all over Western Europe. In fact, it was only after the Sivas event that translocal Alevi organizations were founded, first in Germany and later across Europe in the form of the Federation of Alevi Communities in Europe (Sökefeld and Schwalgin 2000).

More than a decade after the event, Alevi migrant organizations regularly commemorate the *katliam* of Sivas, the Sivas massacre, and declare those who died martyrs of the Alevi cause. *Ağıttan umuda,* "from elegy to hope," was the 2006 motto of a yearly mass event that draws Alevi audiences from all over Germany and parts of Europe, organized by the Union of Alevi Communities in Germany (AABF). Almost 15,000 people came to the event in Cologne to commemorate the Sivas murders, but not just the events in Sivas alone: Alevi representatives wanted to state that they would be always be on the side of those threatened and weak, so that the experiences of Solingen, Sivas, Halabja, and Auschwitz would not be repeated.[12] Invited speakers and participants included representatives of most major German political parties, representatives of different faith groups, and famous Alevi artists and musicians. Internationally renowned Turkish conductor Betin Güneş directed the Symphonic Orchestra Cologne. Combining antiracist appeals for tolerance and harmony with a public *Cem* ceremony, live music, and poetry, organizers managed to present Alevis as spearheading a universal movement to overcome racism and interfaith and interethnic violence. Taking Sivas as their point of departure, they could simultaneously place themselves at the center of a wider suffering and struggle, and present *Alevilik* to different publics: "From Elegy to Hope is an Alevi saga that is addressed to our youth, to the German public, to the circles unfamiliar with Alevis and Alevilik, presenting Alevi history in Turkish and German, and in the universal language of art."[13]

Though issued with an invitation, the Turkish Islamic Union DİTİB, linked to Turkey's Office of Religious Affairs, did not send an Imam to join the other religious representatives. The official reason that was given had to do with the large size of the meeting—a dubious argument, as the General Secretary of the AABF stated in an interview with Turkey's daily *Evrensel*.[14] Given the political importance of Sivas as a signifier for Alevi oppression in Turkey, however, the organizers were most likely not surprised that their invitation was rejected. They could well afford an inclusive gesture that would have been unthinkable and probably ill-advised in the context of Turkey. It is highly unlikely that such a commemorative event could have taken place in Turkey at all.

Hegemonic Formations

In order to make sense of the different representational strategies that Alevi migrant broadcasters employ, they need to be placed in the context of wider discursive fields within which cultural schemes of classification and "rankings" are produced—fields that are tied to two different nation-states and their histories. These fields should by no means be regarded as autonomous and unrelated. They are connected both through the historical ties that link Turkey and Germany and through the wider regional and global cultural and economic contexts in which they are implicated. Yet, the dominant articulations of national identity and of how to be a full member of society, as well as the cultural production of legitimate and illegitimate differences from the national mainstream, differ widely in Turkey and Germany. What is more, these dominant articulations are also differently linked to the respective state's monopoly on violence, creating radically different conditions for cultural struggles and the production of hegemonic meanings, as can be seen in the case of Alevi organizing.

Dominant articulations of national identity in Turkey are continuously contested. More or less pronounced challenges arise both from within the political and military establishment that influences state politics, and from outside political actors who oppose the state-promoted versions of national identity and differentiation. A major problem facing the Turkish state today, Günter Seufert has rightly argued in his seminal study of political Islam in Turkey, is its inability to find a common denominator that could unite the different "cultural camps" that struggle over the definition of national identity (Seufert 1997). Kurds regard the state-promoted "Turkish-Islamic Synthesis" version of national identity as being too Turkish, Alevis find it to be Sunni-dominated, while many Sunni-Islamists find it much too secular.[15] All of these groups consequently see themselves in opposition to the state, as marginalized and as treated unfairly. As much as the solidity and homogeneity of the Turkish state might be a fiction (Navaro-Yashin 2002), it is nevertheless differentially concretized in a range of oppositional discourses.

In the 1990s, Turkey has seen an increasing polarization of cultural camps that define themselves in opposition to the state, and an increasing use of violence by state forces against oppositional groups. One can thus only speak of a weak Turkish hegemony, if at all. It is stabilized by direct state violence, but also by the mobilization of one line of conflict against another: Turkish state forces have supported the Islamist Hizbullah in Eastern Anatolia in order to fight PKK activists in the area, recent governments have turned publicly against Alevis in an effort to win Sunni-Islamist sympathies, and parts of the political Left as well as some Alevi groups align with Kemalist state elites whenever the secularist foundations of the Republic seem to be threatened. The Turkish case serves as a reminder that the concept of hegemony cannot indiscriminately be applied to each and every nation-state context, as much of the literature employing the term seems to imply.[16] Nevertheless, insofar as the Turkish state claims to be a parliamentary democracy and functions as such within certain limits, the concept is still useful, insofar as it indicates the importance of consent to political leadership and not just domination by force (Gramsci 1971). But in the case of contemporary Turkey, it is mainly a strategy of "divide and conquer," of mobilizing oppositional camps against each other rather than successfully incorporating them into the ruling "historical bloc," as Gramsci would have put it.

The German case, on the other hand, can in Gramscian terms be described as a rather successful "transformist hegemony," beginning with the Federal Republic after World War II. The West German Bundesrepublik Deutschland managed by and large to integrate its internal oppositional movements within the system of parliamentary democracy. For several decades, however, labor migrants were not targeted and remained outside the national community both as an imagined construct and as a factual population of citizens. Labor migrants from Turkey were—and still are, as recent surveys among nonimmigrant Germans have shown—considered to be the culturally most "alien" migrant group in Germany (Ogelman 2003). As a consequence, up until the mid-1990s, analysts as well as policymakers in Germany tended to characterize the situation of immigrants from Turkey as being "torn between two cultures" (Durgut 1993; Mandel 1990; Mushaben 1991; Salt 1985). They were seen to move uneasily between two different national contexts, unable to find acceptance and feel at home in either. *Ausländer* (foreigner) in Germany and *Alamancı* (like a German) in Turkey, migrants from Turkey were deemed to be "out of place," during their regular vacation visits to Turkey as much as in Germany. "Home" had become an imaginary construct, located wherever the migrant is not. This story of "in-betweenness" could not have a happy ending: caught in a vicious circle of marginalization and alienation, migrants were at best left with a revisionist nostalgia that had no actually existing point of reference outside their own imagination (Çağlar 1990).

Despite the significant changes that have taken place since the 1990s, including new citizenship legislation and government initiatives to integrate immigrants symbolically into a German national community, the potential "in-betweenness" of migrants continues to be seen as a problem. The task of integrating immigrant populations in cultural terms is high on the German political agenda, and transnational orientations of migrants tend to be interpreted as signs of failed integration. In a critique of multiculturalist paradigms, conservatives have claimed that the uncritical acceptance of cultural differences has led to "parallel societies" (*Parallelgesellschaften*) that now threaten to explode Western European nation-states from within. Like the multicultural paradigms they aim to criticize, conservative positions link culture to the identity of social groups, and thus regard symbolic markers of cultural difference such as the headscarf as major obstacles to immigrant integration.

Although there are significant differences, dominant discourses in Germany and Turkey converge on several points: Both conservative and multiculturalist discourses in Germany and the conflicts among different "cultural camps" in Turkey tend to implicitly reduce culture to a feature of group identity. Culture as an object of representation that denotes the ethnic, religious, and often national membership of migrants is all about "totemic capital," as Michael Kearney (1991) has put it. This "particular strategy of linking culture to the social" (Hannerz 2000, 7) is prevalent in discussions on the multicultural society and the "dialogue of cultures" in Germany, but also in other Western European countries. In a recent study of ethnic identity politics in Norway, Unni Wikan claims that culture has become a new concept of "race," guiding both public opinion and state policies vis-à-vis immigrant groups, and warns against the consequences of essentializing cultural difference in the New Europe (Wikan 2002).

A similar focus on culture as a marker of group identity and basis for political mobilization can observed in Turkey, although this focus is not guiding official state policies. Analysts of Turkey speak of strong "cultural camps" that face each other in the country's political arena, with the most important divides being religious/secular, Sunni/Alevi, left/right, nationalist Kurds/nationalist Turks. The contemporary face of political Islam in particular is described as one that is exceedingly concerned with representational issues (Göle 1996, 1997a; Navaro-Yashin 2002; Seufert 1997). As a consequence, the equation of group boundaries with boundaries of culture is of at least double relevance to Turkish migrants in Germany, who find their cultural practices constantly scrutinized for what they might represent vis-à-vis categorical identities and conflicts. My analysis of migrant broadcasting in Berlin demonstrates how immigrants from Turkey are themselves very much involved in representing these practices as markers of group identity, whether this identity coined in ethnic, religious, or national terms.

A second point of convergence between dominant discourses in Germany and Turkey pertains to the figure of the migrant, and his or her problematic relationship to culture. Prior chapters in this book have traced the changing figure of the migrant in Turkey's modernization process, and in the history of the postwar Federal Republic of Germany. In both national contexts, migrancy is deemed to unsettle cultural identity and render its reproduction and transmission precarious. Many migrant broadcasters consequently represent their activities as an educative tool and corrective intervention in a process of cultural (re-)production that has gone astray. Both the disruptive effects of migration and the assumed cultural background of those who came as labor migrants to Germany are identified as problematic for their ability to (re-)produce culture and maintain or form particular identifications. A statement of Abdullah Güneş, producer of the Turkish-

178 | Migrant Media

nationalist television program *Türk'ten Türk'e* (From Turk to Turk) on Berlin's Open Channel, can illuminate both of these dimensions:

> There is one issue in the *Türk'ten Türk'e* program that is particularly important to us, and that is explaining Turkish culture. . . . If you've been to Turkey, you know that the people who've come here generally stem from a rural background. . . . Now look at their children, the second generation. These people have not yet been able to teach Turkish culture to their children. . . . Because if the parents are ignorant, they can't teach them a thing. . . . So we are forced to mobilize all our possibilities for these children not to be lost, not to disappear.

Güneş describes a situation in which the "normal" generational transmission of culture cannot take place due to the lack of cultural competence among the parent generation, and in which the (Turkish) state cannot step into the void due to the conditions of migration. His views are echoed by many representatives of Turkish organizations and initiatives in Berlin who do not share the same right-wing political agenda, but equally lament the difficulties of cultural transmission in the absence of state influence. The most prominent among them is the *Almanya Atatürk Düşünce Derneği,* the Organization to Promote the Thought of Atatürk in the Federal Republic of Germany.

The transmission and maintenance of culture certainly constitutes a widespread concern for migrant populations in many locations across the globe. What renders the Turkish-German migrant case particular is the specific relationship between culture and state that has characterized the Turkish Republic since its inception, and the contemporary conceptualization of ethno-cultural distinctiveness that marks multicultural paradigms and most of its conservative critiques in Germany.

A much-quoted statement by Turkey's founder Atatürk has described culture as the very basis of the new Republic. The leaders of the Turkish Republic found a large part of its citizenry to be lacking in those dimensions of culture that were regarded as the central basis for nation-building. They therefore sought to bring new educational institutions to every remote and rural village of the country, founding schools and cultural centers that would promote a uniform national culture. Though less vigorous, such efforts continue into the present. Seen in this light, migration to Western Europe is problematic in a double sense: it puts a part of the Turkish population more or less out of the reach of state institutions, and it involves a part of the population that is seen to be least culturally productive and in greatest need of educative intervention. Labor migrants to Germany have been defined in Turkey as culturally lacking even *before* their actual migration, and to be put further at risk in an environment that lacks the appropriate institutions as well as the cultural influences to mitigate this void. In Germany, on the other hand, migration itself has long been understood as a process that cuts people off from their cultural resources and confronts them with a potential "crisis of identity." Participating in multiple discursive universes that are linked to two different nation-states, migrants are thus in both of them faced with the suspicion of "cultural lack." They are seen to be living under conditions of adversity that do not allow them to "keep their own culture," and are also deemed to lack the resources necessary to obtain a proper culture—and thereby identity.

For migrant broadcasters partaking in these different, colluding fields of cultural politics opened up by national histories and migration trajectories, the challenge and ambition is to intervene and produce alternative representations that will signify differently. Difference, articulated from almost always subaltern positions within these colluding fields, can mean tactical interventions into dominant discourses, switching strategies of alliance-building, or attempts to create new common ground beyond contention. The study of Turkish-language migrant media reveals a wide range of representational practices that articulate difference and reconcile multiple cultural struggles in different ways. What it does *not* support is an argument that posits mediated migrant "voices" as a simple addition to the pluralism or diversity of public spheres at local, national, or transnational levels.

The consequences of migrants' complex implications in the transnational "politics of cultural struggle" cannot be illuminated at the level of cultural theory. It is necessary to examine the concrete circumstances under which different kinds of transnational migrants live their lives and make sense of them. The study of migrant broadcasting provides rich material through which to analyze practices and representations central to such politics. However, while there is a growing interest in the topic of migrant and diasporic media, there are as of yet few empirically based studies available that address these as concrete practices and representations, particularly in the context of media production (Sreberny 2001).

Apart from the fact that migrant media engagement is both expanding rapidly and changing along with technological and geopolitical developments, it is also difficult to research. Empirical research on migrant media production poses in very stark terms the challenge that anthropologists and social scientists have in recent years faced up to—the need to rethink frames of reference that were often taken for granted, be it the community, the relationship between localities of different scale, or society (Castles 2003). As has been demonstrated above, a familiarity or at least willingness to engage with the different transnational or diasporic contexts in which migrant media production takes place—George Marcus's "multi-sited sensibility"—

is an absolute requirement for fruitful empirical research and theorizing in this area (Marcus 1995). Yet, attention to what many analysts describe as the "dual implicatedness" or "bifocality" of transnational migrants with regard to their country of origin and their country of residence is not enough. The complexities of diasporic involvement and engagement with multiple national contexts in migrant media production can be addressed only if the widespread supposition of migrants "speaking for themselves" is abandoned. Instead, several questions need to be asked: How is it that migrant "voices" come to be constructed, and for what purposes are they mobilized? And more importantly still, what are the possibilities for migrant broadcasters to engage in politics of representation that can make a difference, instead of being forced to simply represent difference in (multi)cultural terms?

8

Conclusion

In the preceding chapters, Turkish-language broadcasting as a form of cultural production among migrants in Berlin has emerged as a highly contested issue. State representatives, migration experts, and broadcasting officials, but also producers and audiences themselves, disagree on how migrant broadcasting can best be understood. While many of them share the basic premise that these media representations have the potential to influence the self-understanding and the cultural practices of migrant audiences, opinions are split over what kind of influence they actually have and should exercise.

Whereas German advocates of multiculturalism regard migrant broadcasting as an indicator and tool of local integration, Turkish state representatives worry about the transnational political activism of Kurds and Islamists who are seeking to challenge the current balance of power in Turkey. While migrant producers at Radio MultiKulti want to produce programs for Turks who identify as Berliners, migrant broadcasters such as *Saadet TV* at the Open Channel seek to reach their audience as part of a global Muslim *Umma*. Alevi producers and other migrant broadcasters might switch between different representational strategies, depending on the particular audience they want to reach. Kurdish producers tend to address their audience as part of a Kurdish diaspora exiled from their rightful homeland, and circulate Open Channel productions so that they can be broadcast via satellite to larger Kurdish audiences scattered across the Middle East and Western Europe. Turkish nationalist programs, on the other hand, have been shown to encourage migrant identifications with the Turkish state and nation, even beyond its territorial boundaries.

The exploration of Turkish-language broadcasting in Berlin has thus revealed a highly complex picture of migrant media production. The radio and television programs presented in this book emerge as simultaneously constrained and enabled by different institutional and political contexts, and they have been shown to employ a wide range of representational strategies. The various aims and agendas of broadcasters that have been outlined in the prior chapters are not just heterogeneous, but also often in direct conflict with each other. Yet, most migrant broadcasting projects tend to share an approach to culture that regards it as a marker of group identity, as well as the conviction that "having culture" is a matter of great importance. Migrant broadcasting in Berlin approaches culture primarily as a struggle over ascriptive and self-defined identities.

Ascriptive Identities

Presenting cultural practices and understandings as defining qualities and markers of social groups, broadcasters not only produce statements about migrant life and migrant identity, they also claim a particular authority in the sense of "speaking for" the constituencies they want to represent. As has been shown, it is through the collusion of these two meanings of representation that the project of giving ethnic minorities a "voice" in the media gains its particular political appeal, in Germany but also elsewhere. Radio and television produced by and for immigrants promises to redress the imbalance of representation in an increasingly central domain of public cultural production. The history of public service broadcasting for migrants in Germany and the more recent one of commercial and open-access migrant broadcasting have revealed the importance of this political promise for the development and ongoing support of Turkish-language radio and television in Berlin.

However, the widespread assumption that Turkish-language broadcasting offers migrants the opportunity to "speak in their own voice" has been shown to be deeply problematic. Such assumptions give migrant media representations not just the status of subject-predications but also imbue them with a particular kind of authenticity: the migrant subject exists not just in itself, but also for itself, as a self-aware subject that has a political voice. While Open Channels and institutions like Radio MultiKulti all pursue strategies to "give a voice" to ethnic minorities, the ethnographic material presented in this book has offered ample evidence of the difficulties associated with this promise.

At Radio MultiKulti, the "foreign voices" are constructed within a dictate of normative difference that posits ethnic identity as central to cultures, in the plural sense—that is, cultures that operate and confront each other on a strictly local terrain. Constructing cultural difference along ethnic lines, it is simultaneously "translated" and rendered sensible to nonimmigrant audiences in the German-language programs that dominate the station's broadcasting schedule. While foreign-language teams have a considerable degree of editorial autonomy, MultiKulti's Turkish-language program echoes the station's take on cultural difference, addressing its audience as an ethnic minority community co-existing with others within an urban territory. In the broadcasts of MultiKulti's Turkish Program, its audience is thought to simultaneously affirm their bonds with the city's multicultural community and maintain their ethno-cultural distinctiveness. It is precisely this double movement of local identification and ethnic minority identification that characterizes desired migrant responses in German hegemonic multiculturalist paradigms of integration.

The "foreign voices" on Berlin's open-access channel OKB, on the other hand, do not provide such desired contributions at all. Whereas Radio MultiKulti can enforce its hegemonic vision of multicultural difference in the migrant "voices" it constructs and circulates as authentic minority representations, the Open Channel provides an environment with much less institutional control. Instead, it opts for an "organic" broadcasting pluralism that is to emerge from the grassroots activism of marginalized social groups. The argument here has not been to claim that the OKB allows for the truly authentic voices of migrants to be heard and seen. Rather, the Open Channel can offer very different conditions and possibilities for the construction of migrant representations beyond Germany's hegemonic multiculturalism.

To take migrant radio and television programs as the authentic expressions of migrant "communities" has grave political consequences. Thus, the operation of "foreign voices" as audible indicators of ethnic minority participation in Radio MultiKulti's German programs rests precisely on what Spivak (1988) has called the complicity of the two central meanings of representation: *Darstellung* in the sense of subject predication, on the one hand, and *Vertretung*, in the sense of "speaking for" on the other. The station's claims to "give a voice" to ethnic minorities is therefore highly problematic and politically misleading. By taking every statement uttered with an accent that denotes immigrant origin as an ethnic statement, it in fact preempts the questions of actual minority participation and sharing of power.

The OKB, on the other hand, does live up to the central promise of open access channels: to provide broadcasting opportunities for those otherwise marginalized in public service and commercial broadcasting realms. The migrant positions articulated in the context of Open Channel television programming in Berlin could not be heard and seen elsewhere within the German broadcasting landscape. The main reason for this lies in the fact that Turkish-language broadcasters differ in terms of their relative distance from state-condoned ideological projects and norms of cultural iden-

184 | Migrant Media

tity. Their "ranking" and fit with the dominant cultural hierarchies promoted in the two national contexts of Turkey and Germany correlates with their institutional location in the realm of broadcasting: While migrant producers at Radio MultiKulti receive funds for the production of their programs in the public service domain, the so-called bad guys of Turkish-language broadcasting lack the economic resources and the political-institutional support to broadcast anywhere but at the Open Channel.[1]

The relative lack of control exercised over program contents does not mean that *all* positions and groups not represented elsewhere make use of the broadcasting opportunities at the OKB: the almost total lack of women as producers (even in Alevi programming) gives an indication of the extent to which power relations among migrants outside of broadcasting contexts influence decisions and possibilities to "speak out" in public. Kurdish programs and those with a decisively secularist Turkish orientation are the only ones who occasionally feature women as active speakers, beyond the occasional dance or musical interlude where women appear as silent performers. During the period of research for this study, not one of the Turkish-language programs at the OKB was registered under a female name. Such absences and silences indicate once again that the claim to "speak for" particular constituencies or communities bears no necessary relation to the authority of representation that makes such claims possible. Power relations operate with regard to the emergence of migrant "voices" in particular institutional contexts, but also with regard to "inner-group" decisions about who may legitimately raise his (*sic*) voice to speak on others' behalf. This group should not be equated with the "community" or constituency that broadcasters claim to be speaking for.

Even though this book has been centrally concerned with public representational claims regarding migrant identity and different kinds of community, I have tried to avoid operating with a preconstituted object of a given minority community, as is often the case in migration research. Rather, this study has taken a field of conflicting discursive articulations, practices, and institutions as its starting point, and has then proceeded to explain how different community and identity labels are situated within it. The notion of community is thus problematized as a contested and unstable subject claim in the politics of representation, and not taken for granted as a ready-made unit for sociocultural research (Amit and Rapport 2002). (Mis-)taking it for the latter, researchers run both the danger of entering into tautological reasoning—studying the agency and fate of a group that they themselves have helped to bring into being—and of missing the often highly ideological dimensions of the community concept as it is mobilized in different contexts.

As has been shown in the prior chapters, the unquestioned use of the term "ethnic community" to describe the individual components of the multicultural mix of Berlin helps to reify ethno-culture as a marker of group belonging, and enthrones ethnicity as the primary category at work in sociocultural processes that involve immigrants. "Community" of the explicitly national kind is at issue when Turkish state representatives and Turkish nationalists reach out to their migrant "compatriots," the *vatandaşlar,* to unite against Kurdish guerilla activities or against different kinds of injustice or disrespect shown by agents of the German state. It has also been shown to be a crucial element of Kurdish nationalism, which aims to create a Kurdish community via different media technologies among immigrants living in Western Europe. In Turkish Islamic Open Channel programming, the *Umma,* the community of Muslim believers, is often invoked to create a sense of responsibility among audiences for the fate and suffering of Muslim populations elsewhere, and not just in Turkey.

Questions of community and identity have thus been addressed by focusing on cultural production concerned with the representation of Turkish identity along ethnic, religious, and other lines. They have also been addressed through approaching the public sphere of electronic media utterances as a complex realm in which local, national, and transnational elements intersect to produce community claims and identity labels. I have thus tried to interrupt the circuitous logic that links the representation of categorical identities to "really existing groups out there,' whereby migrant broadcasting automatically exemplifies an instance of migrants "speaking for themselves." This is not to say that these categorical identities exist only as free-floating signifiers that remain without consequences for the lives of migrants. On the contrary, I have tried to show how diverse representational claims are linked to different institutional structures and motivate different political agendas as well as policies. There is a lot at stake in the struggle over categorical identities and their potential to signify. This study has also shown that not everybody is equally well disposed to intervene in this struggle.

Even if, as in the case of Open Channel broadcasting, most barriers to mass media production are removed, the dominant standards against which "difference" is measured or "sameness" is asserted cannot easily be suspended or reversed by subaltern migrant broadcasters. The modes of self-representation developed in various domains of Turkish immigrant broadcasting clearly reveal the importance of these standards. Their role has become particularly evident with regard to the modes of address and the imagined audiences that immigrant producers seek to reach. As has been shown, Alevi producers attempt to distance themselves from certain practices and attitudes that they believe (with good reason) that a German majority population associates with Islam. Yet, they also distance themselves from the alleged sexual immorality and religious laxity they tend to be accused of by a majority of Sunni Muslims in Turkey. Dominant standards are also invoked when PKK sympathizers present the Kurdish-nationalist struggle against the Turkish state purely as a matter of human rights, since a universalist human rights discourse plays an important role in the European Union negotiations on Turkish membership. Drawing upon dominant multicultural paradigms, the right to maintain one's cultural distinctiveness as an ethnic minority is invoked by Kurds and Alevis in their efforts to mobilize support for their political struggle in Germany. They are also invoked when Turkish nationalists seek to fill the alleged gaps of cultural reproduction among their fellow nationals abroad.

Similarly, the efforts of the Turkish editors at Radio MultiKulti to promote "pure Turkish" among the migrant population can be justified both in terms of preserving the cultural identity of an ethnic minority in Germany and in terms of supporting the modernization project of the Turkish state. In this instance, however, there is no need to switch between conflicting representational strategies, since the German multicultural project of ethno-cultural preservation and the Turkish national project of cultural modernization and standardization are able to converge in MultiKulti's broadcasts. Turkish producers at Radio MultiKulti can thus readily state, "I am a Berliner, I am multicultural, I listen to Radio MultiKulti every day." Listening to the broadcasts of MultiKulti's Turkish Program, their audience is thought to simultaneously affirm their bonds with the city's multicultural community and maintain their ethno-cultural distinctiveness by engaging with "pure Turkish." As said, this combination of local identification and ethnic minority identification ideally characterizes the kind of migrant integration aimed for in German multiculturalist paradigms, an ideal to which most Turkish-language broadcasting at the Open Channel forms a stark contrast.

In order to explain these conflictual dimensions of Turkish-language migrant media representations, I have argued in this book that they need to be related to the wider social and cultural fields within which both their producers and their audiences are situated. The authority of the positions and of the frames of reference employed in migrant broadcasts depends on the extent to which they can draw upon dominant meanings that are taken for granted or at least considered highly legitimate in those fields. This pertains above all to the categories of ethnic or religious identity and to the cultural hierarchies that are invoked in migrant broadcasts.

The existence of ethno-cultural differences, their interrelations, and the dynamics between them cannot be seen as a simple consequence of immigration to Germany. I have argued that it is necessary to ask how the standards against which cultural difference is measured come to be developed, and how ethno-cultural distinctions function in relation to different forms of stratification. The concept of hegemony has offered a way to understand ethno-cultural differences as categorical identities and forms of classification that are linked to stratification and struggle among different groups of national subjects. The multitude of ethnically defined cultures needs to be connected to what Joan Vincent once called the forms of "structured inequality" (Vincent 1974) within nation-states, and to the dominant discourses that render them legitimate. Arguments about cultural identity and practices are almost always linked to challenges to, or justifications for, power differences among competing interests (Williams 1989).

The recognition that ethnic and racialized groups differ in their ability to influence representations of themselves and, more generally, to influence dominant schemes of cultural classification has been an essential insight provided by anthropological studies of ethnic stratification, racialization, and national identity in the course of the 1990s (Fox 1990; Handler 1992; Williams 1993, 1995). As demonstrated in this book, this insight has particular relevance for the study of Turkish migrant media production in Germany. It is those groups at the bottom of cultural hierarchies (most often correlated with economic hierarchies as well) that also have the least power to control public representations of themselves. As Open Channel advocates in Germany have quite rightly pointed out, these "marginalized," low-status groups usually have little access to the mass media through which public representations are mainly produced and circulated. They are marginal both to the production process and to the targeted "mainstream" audience, whether the latter is packaged as the average citizen (as in the public service domain in Germany), as a national subject (as during the period of state-controlled broadcasting in Turkey), or as a standardized consumer (as in the domain of commercial broadcasting).

It is in light of this marginality that different strategies of representation at the Open Channel have to be understood. The phenomenon of switching among different representational strategies that depend on the respective target group they are aimed at cannot adequately be apprehended as different manifestations of "situational" or "plural" identities. It is not simply a matter of multiple and overlapping sets of loyalties and identifications that make for this context-dependent switching, but rather a question of tactical positioning in light of multiple dominant discourses.[2]

But once the search for the true "authentic voices" of migrants from Turkey has been abandoned, migrant programming at the Open Channel can be examined for the instructive disturbances it creates. Quite obviously,

Turkish "voices" no longer appear in the singular, as they do on Radio MultiKulti or even on the commercial radio station Metropol FM. The latter tries to avoid all conflict in order not to alienate a part of its already small target audience of Turkish-speaking Berliners. Turkish-language Open Channel programs, on the other hand, are decidedly oppositional. What is more, despite the OKB's self-understanding as a local institution and public media platform, programming at the channel demonstrates the salience of transnational issues of concern and conflict among migrants from Turkey. Some broadcasters articulate these issues with a strong focus on the former home country, practically creating and contributing to public spheres in exile (Naficy 1993, 1999). Others articulate their audience as part of different communities and sociocultural formations with local as well as transnational dimensions.

Transnational Dimensions

The material presented in this book has demonstrated that the context of a single nation-state does not suffice to explain the politics of representation in migrant broadcasting. In order to make sense both of conflicting representational claims and of the switching among different representational strategies, it is necessary to understand the dual implication of Turkish immigrants in dominant discourses that pertain to two different nation-states. Locally produced media representations of migrant life cannot be divorced from the respective schemes of classification and dominant categories of identity that prevail in both Germany and Turkey. As this book has demonstrated, migrant broadcasting operates precisely at the points of intersection between them.

Against the grain of still-dominant paradigms of ethnicity and "race" that posit the nation-state as the most appropriate framework for analyzing the representational struggles of (immigrant) minorities, a transnational perspective on such struggles needs to emphasize the importance of multiple ideological fields that collude in the lives of contemporary migrants across the globe. Social science research in the late twentieth century has mainly highlighted the hegemonic construction of nationhood as central to classificatory schemes of ethnicity and racial hierarchies. However, to seriously think through the consequences of contemporary developments pertaining to migration, travel, and cross-border communication technologies implies a significant challenge to perspectives centered on the nation-state. As the material presented in this book shows, the lives and representational practices of migrants from Turkey are informed by more than one national context, and face different challenges as well as opportunities linked to cross-border politics and the deployment of new media technologies by state and non-state actors.

The cultural consequences of such deployment, embedded in contexts of increasing cross-border flows of capital, consumer goods, and people between Turkey and Germany, cannot be generalized and attributed to a single overarching logic of cultural globalization (Tsing 2000). They can be understood only through a close analysis of the specific cultural politics through which migrants are constructed and also represent themselves as particular kinds of sociocultural beings.

In the flourishing anthropological literature on transnationalism and diasporas, transnationalist practices and identifications have often been invested with the hope that they might remove migrants from the hegemonic reach of nation-states, and open up utopian spaces for imagining and living progressive forms of community (Appadurai 1996; Clifford 1994; Kearney 1995). The material presented in this book does not substantiate such hopes. Transnational migrants remain in different forms subjected to the power of nation-states, both in terms of practical interventions—such as legal regulations, broadcasting infrastructure, financial support, or governmental pressure—and in terms of hegemonic articulations that classify groups and link culture to forms of entitlement and moral worth. Nor are their de-territorialized representations of community inherently progressive and nontotalizing, as the discussion of different primordialisms and essentialisms deployed in migrant media programs has shown. But there is nevertheless a peculiarity of transnational migrant media practices that relates to their different positioning: the discursive universes in which migrants participate and the structural influences to which they are subjected have two different nation-states as their referents. In turn, migrants' social networks, their strategies for economic survival, their cultural practices, and their forms of self-representation similarly extend across and build upon a transnational or "transstate" dimension.

Transnationalism, in the sense of a border-crossing expansion of spaces with regard to kinship groups, networks, communities, and organizations that have ties across state borders, offers a fascinating but challenging arena for anthropological research. The research strategies it calls for are for the most part diametrically opposed to the strong tradition of community studies in the discipline of anthropology that once concentrated on single localities.[3] The challenge for transnationalist research is precisely to trace different forms of circulations—of people, goods, money, cultural practices, and understandings—along routes and across spaces that belong to different nation-states (Appadurai 1991; Hannerz 1996). For many analysts, a number of criteria have to be fulfilled before we can speak of a transstate or transnational space, criteria that render the border-crossing dimension meaningful enough in terms of its extent and intensity. They look for clear spatial placement, definite actors and fields of engagement, a high speed of transactions, a complex infrastructure, and forms of institutionalization and regulation (see Faist 2000).

However, the starting point for this book has been a different one: rather than taking the border-crossing expansion of social and cultural spaces as its main focus of analysis, the transnational dimensions of migrant broadcasting have emerged as aspects of local media practices among Turkish migrants in the city of Berlin. At the level of organizational ties and circulation of people, money, and so forth, no full description of cross-border spaces could be provided. Taking a locally developed media landscape as my point of departure, I have outlined such spaces only in fragments. A full treatment would have required a different research focus and a much more limited analysis of a few select media productions.

The fragments do, however, provide ample evidence for the contention that local Turkish media production in Berlin cannot be understood within a local or national frame of reference alone. While this production is very much shaped and constrained by German institutional structures, integration politics as well as laws and regulations, it is also influenced by transnational factors that link it to Turkey. These transnational links have been shown, for example, with regard to the recruitment of staff, financial support, or the circulation of programs produced in different locations. The main focus of this book, however, has pertained to the *discursive* dimensions of transnational ties as they enter into and emerge in the locally produced mass media representations of Turkish migrant life. Addressing migrant broadcasting as a site for public discourses that articulate migrant life in different ways, the transnational elements in such discourses can be identified in the frameworks or points of reference through which migrant life is represented. Transnational points of reference do not require, but can include, directly traceable forms of border-crossings. More often, however, they appear as references to dominant discourses, common-sense notions, and contentious issues prevalent in Turkey that inform the representation of migrant life, without the exact path of their "crossing" ever becoming evident. In my conversations with migrant producers, in their broadcasting activities and in the programs they produce, these transnational references have surfaced as stated motivations or aims, as ways of imagining and addressing an audience, in the selection of "topics" to be dealt with and to be left aside, in styles of representation.

At first sight, paradoxically, diversity policies aiming at integration of immigrants at a local or national level might in some instances themselves create opportunities for transnational engagement. While it is often assumed that transnationalist orientations are advanced by repressive policies and discrimination in host countries, liberal policies in realms such as broadcasting can allow immigrants to uphold distinctiveness and maintain ties to the former homeland (Faist 2000). In a significant part of the literature on transnationalism and diasporic formations, transnational orientations are seen as a response to repression immigrants are facing in their country of residence, or as a resource to escape the hegemonic reach of national identities that disadvantage migrant groups in the national politics of cultural struggle.

The case of the Open Channel supports a different argument: Even though it is a liberal broadcasting institution, which sees its role for migrants as an integrative one by tying migrants closer to local community life and allowing them to participate in public debates at their place of residence, it has been shown that the Open Channel is used by migrants to build and participate in transnational social spaces. Its Turkish-language programs do contribute to new kinds of public spheres, but mostly not within a local framework as it has been hoped for and expected by German integration experts, broadcasting officials, and politicians. In their programs, they represent and address social groups that are not always tied to local forms of community, and are not necessarily territorially defined. Multiculturalist paradigms that regard immigrants as minorities within local or national contexts only are unable to account for the complexity of these representations.

In the anthropological literature on migrant transnationalisms, different concepts have been suggested to account for the complexity of migrants' cultural orientations across different national spaces and localities. Most of them refer to a duality that is united in migrants' outlooks and experiences: bifocality (Vertovec 2004) and dual frames of reference (Guarnizo 1997) have taken over from earlier, more negative characterizations of migrant existence as 'living between two cultures." The "neither here nor there" has been replaced in transnational perspectives with a "both here and there." Yet, such positive formulations still retain a dualistic frame that obfuscates rather than illuminates the complexities of migrants' transnational orientations. When reducing the complexities of cultural struggles in different national arenas to two implicitly unified and homogeneous locations, the differential positioning and movement of migrants and their practices of rearticulating different cultural elements within these arenas become difficult to grasp. The complexities of how migrants actually engage with the different interpellative "pulls" and cultural hierarchies that are implicated in this "both here and there" remain an open question.

But oppositional dualisms are pervasive also in the schemes of cultural classification that operate in the transnational field mapped out in Turkish migrant broadcasting. The here versus there, the foreigner versus German, the Turk versus Kurd, Islamist versus secularist—all of these pairs tend to block the investigation of how different kinds of antagonisms are articulated in much greater complexity than the logic of conflictual opposition can suggest. Migrant broadcasting practices reveal a multitude of positions vis-à-vis dominant discourses, characterized by different forms of alignment, displacement, switching, and evasion.

Going beyond the here and there, it is therefore important to recognize that the elements of migrant media representations have no necessary fixed belongingness, and that their differences are strategically reconstituted in an ongoing process of engagement. The different articulations of "being Muslim" and of "suffering" in Alevi migrant media representations are a case in point. Producers can present themselves as "benign" Muslims toward nonimmigrant German audiences, mobilize histories of suffering in left-of-center alliances with non-Alevis, or stress the compatibility of Alevi religious practices with Sunni Muslim standards of Islam. Both the overdetermination of conflicts that divide cultural camps and the noncontiguity of conflicts across national spaces allows for a range of articulations that propose alliances and construct different kinds of antagonisms. Turkish nationalists can mobilize German multicultural policies to their advantage in order to get support for cultural maintenance work, and at the same time turn racist attacks in Germany into a powerful incentive for galvanizing migrant audiences around a reactive minority nationalism. The hip-hop group Cartel was taken by surprise when faced with differing interpretations of their rallying cry for Turks to unite. Kurdish nationalists, on the other hand, increasingly turn toward international human rights discourses to find allies among nonimmigrant Germans, while focusing on the inalienable right of nations to sovereign statehood in their diasporic mobilization among migrants.

Such possibilities of tactical articulation, which draw upon and restructure elements that figure in dominant discourses, are not peculiar to transnational politics of representation.[4] Even within single (though not self-contained) national contexts, which still provide a central frame for the politics of cultural struggle, the overdetermination and non-fixity of cultural signifiers opens up possibilities for rearticulation that exceed the dualistic oppositions of left-right, Alevi-Sunni, Islamist-secularist, Turkish-German, and so on (Laclau and Mouffe 1985). But the confluence of cultural politics associated with two different national contexts increases both the number of hegemonic claims to authoritative signification and the room for maneuvering, switching, and rearticulation that migrant broadcasters can avail themselves of. Some can exploit the antagonisms between different cultural hierarchies, as the case of Alevi broadcasting has shown. At times, the differential insertion in discursive universes that pertain to two different nation-states can widen migrants' range of representational strategies, which, to use Pierre Bourdieu's term, allow them to maximize their "cultural capital" gains on different fronts (Bourdieu 1984; see also Çağlar 1995). While the systems of ethno-cultural classification that operate in the two national contexts both position Alevis as problematic minorities, Alevi migrants can strategically represent themselves as "less problematic Muslims" in the German context, while being able to emphasize other aspects in the Turkish context that suggest their contribution to and embodiment of Turkish national virtues. Others use broadcasting opportunities in the migration context to engage in politics of exile with a strongly homeland-oriented agenda, as in Kurdish Open Channel programs.

The transstate dimension allows for explicitly counter-hegemonic projects such as the Kurdish nationalist one to benefit from extended spaces for maneuvering. It is here that the hopes of some analysts regarding the potential of transmigrants and diasporas to "escape" the reach of nation-states is most closely realized—yet mainly with regard to the nation-state of origin. As has been discussed, both Kurdish nationalists and political Islamists use Germany and other diasporic locations as a base for political organizing. The Kurdish PKK and the Islamist Millî Görüş present examples of transnational organizations that—quite literally—escape the reach of the Turkish state by conducting political activities directed toward Turkey from abroad (Mertens 2000; Trautner 2000). However, this is not so much an issue of having escaped the hegemonic reach of Turkey: both organizations have initially developed their counter-hegemonic visions from within the country, and struggle not only on a discursive terrain but also, in the case of the PKK, by violent means for the realization of these visions. The Kurdish PKK sympathizers and Islamist Millî Görüş members do not need to be outside Turkey to develop an identity that opposes state-condoned, dominant articulations of Turkic and secular nationalism. They do need to be outside of Turkey, however, in order to engage in organizational activities, fundraising, member recruitment, and the like, which are prohibited and more easily curtailed within the country. They also need to be outside the territorial boundaries of Turkey to effectively circulate political messages via mass media. At the same time, migrant life in the diaspora has certainly influenced the political projects pursued in Turkey, so that particularly in the Kurdish case, the nationalist project is nowadays importantly shaped by diaspora activities. Elements of Turkey-oriented politics can also appear in close articulation with "local" contents pertaining to life in Berlin, as in educational or dress-code debates in Islamic programs on the OKB. And yet others, like the producers of *Saadet TV,* use the Open Channel opportunities to introduce contents, modes of address, and aesthetics that are radically marginal in both national cultural arenas. Instead, they draw upon long traditions of mystical Islam that are revitalized and continued by means of new communication technologies in a global context.

While arguing, then, that migrant media representations cannot be made sense of without understanding their relationship to dominant cultural politics in two different nation-states, this recognition can only be a starting point for further analysis. Some caution is called for in order to avoid instating transnational cultural affiliations as something akin to a "whole way of life," as Raymond Williams once famously sought to define culture. Orientational bifocality, once examined in its complexities, falls apart into a wide range of migrant engagements and representational practices that are interesting precisely because "here" and "there" signify in so many different ways, and can indicate a multitude of locations. The study of transnational cultural phenomena requires the analyst's familiarity with politics of culture in different national contexts, but they do not simply add onto one another, nor do they disappear with cross-border movements.

Muslims in Europe

While part of this book deals explicitly with Islam in the context of migrant broadcasting, almost all of the migrants from Turkey discussed in these chapters identify on some level as Muslims. For some, this is a central dimension of their identity and a focal point of their broadcasting activism. For many, it is a rather small aspect of their lives, and other dimensions take center stage.

It is in fact the *noncentrality* of religion in the lives of many Muslims in Western Europe that cannot be stressed enough in the terror-dominated contemporary climate of "moral panics" regarding Islam and Muslim populations. In Germany, migrants from Turkey constitute the large majority of Muslim residents, estimated to number around 3.1 million people in total. Many of them do not actively practice their religion, and they support secularist principles as were once implemented by Kemalism in Turkey. Those who do actively practice their religion nevertheless embrace a wide range of affiliations and identifications. As is the case for lived Christianity in Europe, there is a multitude of ways in which Muslims relate to religion in their daily lives, from vague cultural orientations and secularist outlooks to much more rare devout practices that may or may not find political articulation (Nonneman et al. 1996). As the different examples of Islamic engagements at the Open Channel in Berlin has shown, religious instruction, debate, and passing on the word of God via mass media can take very different forms, which do not necessarily have explicit political dimensions. Approaching Islam in Europe through the lens of migrant broadcasting in Berlin, however, the focus in this book is of course already on those groups, individuals, and networks that have been seeking to "go public" with their message.

Having drawn attention to the noncentrality of Islam in the lives of Muslim migrants, it is equally necessary to stress the complexity of existing Islamic religiosities in Western Europe, of their transnational dimensions and of their relationship to politics. This complexity is in danger of disappearing from view in current Western discourses on Muslim immigrants, which are characterized by a growing focus on terrorism, intolerance, and violence. Violence in different forms—as produced by foreign military interventions, such as in Afghanistan and Iraq, but also in the form of terrorist attacks—is contributing to a growing polarization that dangerously positions Muslims as a unified category against the "West" (Amin 2004). In the context of the European Union, there is a danger that Muslims are becoming the Other of what is claimed as European civilization, on the basis of an alleged incompatibility of Islam with basic values of tolerance and democracy (Bunzl 2005).

After the suicide bombings that targeted the London public transport system in July of 2005, Muslim representatives in Britain were called upon to distance themselves from the perpetrators, despite the fact that Muslims were also among the victims. While Britain's Prime Minister Tony Blair spoke of the suicide bombers as "perverting the religion of Islam," Muslim immigrants were nevertheless expected to react and speak out publicly against extremists in their midst. The discursive logic at work here exemplifies once again the dilemmas of representation for immigrant minorities that are associated with hegemonic processes of othering: whereas dominant identity positions (such as, depending on the specific contexts, white, heterosexual, nonimmigrant German, Christian, or secular)[5] tend to become highlighted only through the negative foil of an "other," and usually function as the naturalized and normative base upon which other kinds of identity positions unfold, the categorical identities of minorities stick to them like glue.

Even though the paradigms of multiculturalism discussed in this book promote the equal worth of all ethno-cultural groups, each of them signaling and contributing a different part of diversity (including the majority population), it is the minorities that are forced to signify and embody diversity as the "other" of the mainstream. On Radio MultiKulti, the slogan "we speak with an accent" most succinctly captures this embodiment of difference. It is also instructive, however, to look beyond the station's programming and examine how it is situated as part of wider multicultural policies and institutional frameworks in Berlin. The ways in which German discourses and broadcasting institutions distinguish between cultural diversity as a multiplicity of coexisting ethno-cultures and culture (*Kultur*) in the singular show how the cultural practices and representations of immigrants are both reified as markers of ethnic group identity and excluded from other domains of cultural production.

Dominant processes of "othering," which not only ascribe categorical identities to minority groups but also foreground this identity to the exclusion or diminishing of all other possible identity positions, thereby aid the conflation between different aspects of representation. If every Muslim immigrant is first and foremost representing ethno-religious difference, then violent attacks carried out in the name of Islam have to be publicly denounced by each and every one who falls into the category of Muslim. Representing Muslims in the sense of an inescapable *Darstellung,* she or he then also has to *speak for* them, and for the truth of Islam. In a climate of growing antagonism in which Islamist violence is identified as a main threat facing Western nation-states today, it becomes ever more difficult to question this logic of both "othering" and representation, and to address a different complexity of contemporary Muslim lives and representational struggles in Western Europe today. This book will hopefully nevertheless make such a contribution, against a climate that is increasingly characterized by fear, polarization, and the breakdown of communication.[6]

Constructive interventions also cannot afford to ignore the transnational dimensions of the current crisis. When Home Office representatives in Britain diagnosed the failure of multicultural laissez-faire paradigms in the wake of the London terror attacks, and called for a more interventionist approach with regard to Muslims and immigrant communities, they in fact continued the widespread political disregard for transnational dimensions of immigrant life in Western European nation-states. Instead of linking the terror attacks to the British military engagement in Iraq and to the history of Western military intervention in Afghanistan and the Middle East, they located the causes in the alleged failures of "internal," nation-bound social and cultural policies. Regardless of one's take on British foreign policy, to dismiss any link between the rise of terrorist violence in Western nation-states and their military as well as political interventions appears as a dangerous misrecognition of the contemporary realities associated with "transnationalism." There is an urgent need to realize that it is not simply the preachings of Islamist fundamentalists that promote anti-Western sentiments in the name of Islam, but also feelings of shared empathy with Muslim victims of military intervention on the Asian subcontinent and in the Middle East. This empathy does not, of course, lead itself to the condoning of violence, but it creates a situation in which cross-border solidarities are mobilized. Different forms of migrant media play an important role in providing different narratives and images of suffering that counteract CNN-type stories of the "war on terror" among immigrant populations in Western countries.

Anthropologist Pnina Werbner has called British Muslim diasporas "transnational communities of co-responsibility" (Werbner 2002). Reflecting on the responses of British Pakistanis to the September 11 attacks, she has pointed out the tragic dilemma produced by the escalating antagonism between the alleged poles of Islam and the West: called upon to declare their "loyalty" to their country of residence and to distance themselves from goals or utopias that Islamist struggles support, it becomes more and more difficult for Muslim immigrant populations to reconcile their diasporic and transnational affiliations with their plight as British citizens. While their diasporic commitments to concrete or imagined Muslim communities elsewhere and their religious practices could once coexist with the classic interests of immigrant minorities—prosperity, equal rights, freedom of expression—these are increasingly placed against each other as mutually exclusive choices (Werbner n.d.). In the antagonism of Islam versus the West that is promoted by Western "moral panics" and by Islamist extremism alike, diasporic religious commitments now seem to run counter to the full participation of immigrants in their countries of residence. Yet, measures such as citizenship ceremonies (as they were recently instituted in Britain) will do little to create loyalties at the expense of transnational and diasporic affiliations. At a time when documented immigrants to Western Europe enjoy relative ease of travel and access to media and communication technologies on an unprecedented scale, such affiliations are not just here to stay, but are likely to increase.

Diasporic identifications, transnational political mobilization, and social ties that link immigrants in the "West" to conflict regions in other parts of the world will doom to failure any narrowly inward-looking governmental strategy of response in Western Europe. This is especially the case for regions where the interventions of Western powers do not adhere to the same principles of legality, human rights, and compassion that are applied within their own territories. There is nothing that renders transnational and diasporic affiliations inherently antagonistic to a responsible participation in different kinds of communities and sociopolitical formations at one's place of residence—be it a neighborhood, the city of Berlin, Germany, or even the European Union. But it will be difficult to invite participation and avoid further alienation if foreign military interventions accord much less value to a human life that forms part of a transnational "community of co-responsibility" outside the West than to human lives inside. Alienation is not simply a product of radical Islamists preaching extremism to young and impressionable immigrants, as much of the journalistic output on the causes of terrorist violence suggests.

In the case of Turkish Muslim migrants in Germany, ties to other Islamist organizations in the Middle East do exist, but the bulk of organizing in the name of Islam is oriented toward Turkey. Islamic programming on the Open Channel has shown the continued relevance of issues related to Turkey, but also efforts to overcome any place-bound aspects of belief and focus instead on the individual-oriented transmission of what is claimed as a divine message. It is not my intention to dispute the growing orientation of many Islamic migrant organizations toward questions and concerns pertaining to the migration context, and toward the project of "making a place for Islam," as it was put by contributors noting the *New Islamic Presence in Western Europe* in the 1980s (Gerholm and Lithman 1988). However, this orientation goes hand in hand with a continued or renewed interest in so-called home country affairs, as well as with attempts to establish transnational and diasporic networks and orientations. These attempts are being made at different levels, such as that of the European Union, in connection with Turkey, or in translocal patterns that can bridge several different continents.

The case of the Kurdish nationalist satellite television station MED-TV and the Turkish state response has shown most explicitly that the transnationalist constellations arising through migrant media practices are not simply border-crossing phenomena, but transformative in a much deeper sense. They affect the lives of migrants in complex ways, and form part of new cultural orientations, economic possibilities, social affiliations, and political practices. But they also impact the territorial political formations whose boundaries they span, most obviously in the Turkish case where Kurdish migrant satellite television has prompted a reorientation of state laws, policies, and cultural politics. The transnational media landscape allows migrants not only to stay in touch with home country affairs, it allows them to influence these affairs themselves and transform the ways in which domestic politics are understood.

The impact upon countries of residence such as Germany is less obvious, and this is at least partially due to the dominant politics of integration that aim to "localize" migrants as members of ethnic communities within multicultural social formations. Years before the change in state politics that redefined Germany as a country of immigration and opened new avenues for immigrant identification at a national level, major cities such as Berlin already encouraged resident "foreigners" to integrate themselves as a distinctive part of multiethnic urban formations. Radio MultiKulti offers the best example of this integrationist agenda being translated into a public service broadcasting strategy, with its framing of ethnic difference in multicultural terms. Other examples in the domain of cultural politics have been pointed to, such as the city's yearly Carnival of Cultures or the institutional provisions for supporting immigrants' cultural activities (Kosnick 2004).

Other countries have pursued different paths of integration. The most obvious example is France, where state politics have for some time insisted upon nationalizing immigrant minorities and enforcing secularist state culture in all but private domains of immigrant life (Brubaker 1992; but see Kiwan and Kosnick 2006). Despite their significant differences, governmental strategies of integration in Germany and France converge upon both ignoring and discouraging the transnational engagements of migrant populations. In the French case, this strategy also serves to dissociate the nation-state from its colonial past, similar to Britain where debates about immigration frame the country as just another nation-state under siege, thus by and large repressing the British colonial experience. In Germany, there is next to no public awareness that German colonies ever existed. Verena Stolcke pointed out more a decade ago the similarities among the anti-immigrant discourses dominant across Western Europe in the late twentieth century. These discourses have tended to deemphasize formerly central arguments about the alleged "racial" inferiority of unwanted newcomers, and instead focus on cultural incompatibilities and the cultural-territorial integrity of the nation (Stolcke 1995). Immigrants are to go "back to where they came from," and back to where they "rightfully belong." The more recent calls for protecting the alleged integrity of "European civilization" against seemingly incompatible cultural and religious influences brought on by non-European immigration retain this focus on a wider scale. Following this logic, Turkey's place cannot be in Europe—neither because of its economic situation nor because of its human rights situation, but because of its apparently innate cultural antagonisms.

For the historical moment of the early twenty-first century, the rhetoric of national and European retrenchment with regard to non-European immigration serves well the double agenda of fortified borders and foreign intervention that characterizes the politics of many states in the European

Union, most importantly Britain, Spain, and Italy. Such an agenda is not incompatible with multiculturalist paradigms influencing social and cultural policies "internally," as the case of Britain shows with particular clarity.[7] What unites most of these policies is a disregard for, or active discouragement of, transnational affiliations among immigrants, which are seen as an indicator of failed integration or as an illicit import of "foreign" conflicts, as for example in the case of Kurdish nationalist activism in Germany (Øestergaard-Nielsen 2003).

Terrorist violence in Western Europe, a most distinctively transnational political phenomenon, could be seen as the most tragic reminder of the fact that the distinction between "internal" and "foreign" politics is increasingly put into question by transnational identifications and forms of activism. The deliberate or implicit misrecognition of the latter in multicultural paradigms and policies is likely to block a better understanding of both the cultural dynamics and forms of political activism that cross nation-state borders in the present moment of globalization. Yet, those who now diagnose the failure of multiculturalism and advocate a strong assimilationist approach to immigrant "communities" in order to procure certain cultural commitments and democratic orientations similarly ignore transnational realities. Efforts to turn migrants into locals (and locals only) will remain futile, whether as ethnic minorities within a multicultural society or as newcomers who have to adapt to a *Leitkultur*, the German term for the cultural orientations deemed normative for and characteristic of a particular nation-state. Nevertheless, such efforts do have palpable effects. To ignore transnational affiliations or to treat them as obstacles toward equal participation in nation-state contexts further marginalizes migrants, and renders the possibilities of their cultural projects to signify with a difference and to intervene in dominant politics of culture increasingly remote. Under such circumstances, it becomes ever more difficult to address the vexed issue of minority media as tools for the self-expression of subordinated social groups, in contexts of subordination that condition not just their access to the material resources of media production but also their lack of control over the very schemes of classification that label and constitute them as particular kinds of minorities or national subjects.

NOTES

1. Introduction

1. None of the personal names mentioned in this study are pseudonyms, except where explicitly requested by informants. I have not, however, provided full names of informants in cases where the publication of their statements could have negative consequences for them.

2. There is a lot of conceptual confusion concerning the terms "transnational" and "diasporic." I use the former term to describe cross-border ties and processes that do not need to involve more than two nation-states, and reserve the latter to refer to cross-linkages among migrant populations that have settled in different countries. While migrants from Turkey have come to reside in several, mostly Western European nation-states, the links among them are still weak, with the exception of those who identify as Kurdish. Given the extent of Kurdish organizing across Europe and the Middle East, it makes sense to speak of a Kurdish diaspora, whereas Turkish migrant ties to Turkey are for the most part best described as transnational rather than diasporic.

3. A notable exception is Berlin's monthly magazine *Merhaba,* which survives on advertising revenues and is available free of charge in many Turkish shops and restaurants across the city. It covers local "community" affairs, gossip, and articles connected to the respective sponsors of an issue. Efforts to establish similar and more ambitious publications have all failed for financial reasons. Most notable are the much-publicized startup of the monthly lifestyle magazine *Etap,* aimed at young Turkish Germans, and the biweekly *8. Gün* (which translates as "the eighth day"), a paper aiming to present critical journalism on integration and other political issues that was started by a group of Germany-based correspondents working for several of Turkey's major daily papers. Neither publication was able to attract enough sponsors, advertising, and circulation revenues to keep afloat.

4. http://www.destatis.de/basis/d/bevoe/bevoetab4.php; accessed December 20, 2004.

5. Figure as of December 31, 2005, *Statistisches Landesamt Berlin.* Only 9 of the 191 United Nations member countries were not represented.

6. In Berlin, so-called *Zuzugssperren,* limitations regarding the movement of immigrants into certain neighborhoods, were imposed by the city government between 1975 and 1990, in order to stop the formation of "ghettos." At the time, the districts of Kreuzberg, Wedding, and Tiergarten were home to 46 % of all foreign nationals living in the city. Exceptions were made on a case-by-case basis, leading to a huge number of applications that eventually exhausted the capacity of district bureaucracies. An additional step—this time encouraging rather than restrictive—was taken in 1980, when social housing corporations were forced to give at least 15% of their rental space in outer districts such as Britz, Mariendorf, and Lichtenrade to foreign nationals.

7. For media marketing strategies that target the former citizens of the GDR, see Boyer 2001.

8. For a trenchant early critique of such thinking in German academic writing on migration, see Ayşe Çağlar 1990.

9. *Cem evis* are special buildings where Alevi Muslims congregate for the *cem* ceremony; see chapter 6.

10. Leader of all Muslims, a position the Turkish state abolished in 1925.

11. Two different successor parties emerged, with the AKP Justice and Development Party forming the latest Turkish government in the November elections of 2002. In Germany, efforts have been made to outlaw Millî Görüş, following the terrorist attacks of September 11, 2001 in New York and Washington, which prompted "antiterrorist legislation: in Germany as in other Western nation-states.

12. But there is also the subversive use of "small media" like tapes, photocopied flyers, etc. that challenge or at least escape centralized control. See Armbrust 1996; Caton 1990; Sreberny-Mohammadi and Mohammadi 1994.

2. The History of Broadcasting for Migrants in Germany

1. An earlier version of this chapter has been published as "Building Bridges—Media for Migrants and the Public-Service Mission in Germany" (Kosnick 2000). All quotations in this chapter are the author's translations from German, except where noted otherwise.

2. Extent refers to the number of readers/viewers, whereas intensity refers to the time spent using a particular mass medium.

3. The Mercedes-Benz research concluded that 20% of Turkish buyers in Germany preferred a Mercedes and proceeded to produce a television commercial showing a Mercedes car at the center of attention during a traditional wedding in a Turkish village. The car that was featured in the spot was not one of the latest models, but an older, larger type that advertisers deemed to meet migrant tastes for flashy display. Stereotypes of migrants' preference for conspicuous consumption abound in both Turkey and Germany. The figure of the well-off but ignorant *Alamancı,* a term with negative connotations coined for migrants living in Germany who return for the summer holidays, is a well-known cliché in Turkey. It has been most succinctly captured in the 1993 road movie *Mercedes, Mon Amour,* featuring the famous comedian Ilyas Salman as a Turkish guestworker who takes his brand-new gold-colored Mercedes from Germany back to his Turkish village in order to impress relatives back home. His eagerness to impress finally leads him to crash the car, symbolizing the futility of migrants' efforts to transform their hard-earned financial capital into cultural capital (in Pierre Bourdieu's sense of the term, Bourdieu 1984).

4. The decision as to what programs to transmit was made by the respective broadcasting corporations based on the regional composition of the labor migrant population. In a federal state like the Saarland, where during the 60s the migrant population was by and large Italian, only the Italian program of the WDR was transmitted.

5. For different accounts of this *Ätherkrieg* (war on the airwaves), see Holzweißig 1989 and more recently Koch and Glaser 2005.

6. While the corporations retained their independence, the ARD came to operate West Germany's first television channel, established in 1953. A second television channel, the ZDF, was added in 1961, centrally organized unlike the ARD, but still structured as a public service corporation.

7. In an article by an unnamed author published by the weekly political journal *Der Spiegel,* "Im Kreise herum," September 4, 1972, 70–71.

8. Ibid.; Siegfried Hanni, "Weitere Wortmeldungen im Rundfunkstreit," *Süddeutsche Zeitung,* June 22, 1972, 15.

9. Only the Italian broadcasting service RAI cooperated closely with the Italian ARD program and provided about 10% of its content (Rissom et al. 1977, 32).

10. Even though public service broadcasting relies financially mainly on service fees that every user of broadcasting has to pay, advertising revenue has begun to play a greater role in public service budgets. What is more, the repeated political challenges to public service broadcasting—the claim that it is becoming irrelevant—can only be refuted by pointing to audience ratings as an indication of continued interest.

11. The analysts nevertheless argued that the feared isolation was not taking place, pointing to the figure of 72.5% of people who were switching between Turkish and German media when taking into account radio and newspaper use as well. Heinemann and Kamcılı likewise argue that such fears are unfounded, and are ultimately based on a problematic assumption of media effects (Heinemann and Kamcılı 2000). A more recent 2003 study by the Zentrum für Türkeistudien came to the conclusion that despite the continued preference for imported Turkish television, over 90 % of migrants switched between German and Turkish mass media.

12. The relatively scarce data on actual program preferences all indicate that program imports from Turkey continue to play a preeminent role in media use. In a 2003 survey carried out in Berlin by the Zentrum für Türkeistudien, only 31% of respondents stated that they watched more German than Turkish television.

13. Proponents of this argument include Becker 1998a; Goldberg 1998; Greiff 1995; Heitmeyer, Müller, and Schröder 1998; Okkan 1998.

14. In 1997, a survey established the number of listeners per day at 147,000. Conventional surveys exclude "foreign" households from their respondent group. The actual number of listeners is thus likely to be much higher, the station estimates. In order to have a sense of MultiKulti's acceptance among at least one minority, MultiKulti has commissioned surveys, the latest among Turkish Berliners in 1996. Of the respondents, 12% claimed to know the station, and about 4% would listen on an average day. This was interpreted as a positive sign of acceptance (Mohr 1996).

15. For discussions of the German *jus sanguinis* and its consequences, see Bauböck 1994; Brubaker 1992; Räthzel 1990.

16. In the sense of both light-skinned and/or intelligent, an intentional play on the German term "helle."

17. See also Baumann 1999. Not all multiculturalist approaches are guilty of essentializing, however—see for a counter example the Parekh Report published by the Commission of the Future of Multi-Ethnic Britain, which attempts very explicitly to avoid the reification of ethnic culture (Commission on the Future of Multi-Ethnic Britain/Runnymede Trust 2000; also Vertovec 2001).

18. Analogous arguments were made in approaches that studied the production of class-related cultures (Bourdieu 1984; Thompson 1968; Willis 1977), gender differences (Delaney 1995; De Lauretis 1987; Kandiyoti 1991), youth subcultures (Hebdige 1979), sexuality-related differences (Alexander 1991; Halley 1993; Mosse 1985), and racial differences (Gilroy 1991; Hall 1986; Harrison 1995; Omi and Winant 1994), to list but a few.

19. Such is also the basic assumption in Charles Taylor's influential essay on multiculturalism (Taylor 1992).

20. Though at times so-called indigenous populations, first peoples, and others, such as "deviants," are also symbolically placed outside, or placed quite forcibly in what Foucault has called "heterotopias of deviance" (Foucault 1985–1986).

3. Foreign Voices

1. Before 2003, Radio MultiKulti formed part of the Sender Freies Berlin (SFB), the regional public service corporation for Berlin only. It has been merged with its East German partner ORB, which served the surrounding federal state of Brandenburg, to form the RBB.

204 | Notes to pages 56–72

2. There are exceptions, such as the two second-generation moderators of Turkish pop music programs on Radio MultiKulti, Erci E. and Aziza A., who both achieved moderate celebrity status as hip-hop stars in the 1990s. Erci E. used to host Berlin's first Turkish pop music program on a pirate radio station, and became famous as a member of the group Cartel before embarking on his career as a solo artist. Both Erci E. and Aziza A. have local reputations that render a foreign accent unnecessary.

3. I thank Charlotte L. Sever for drawing my attention to this important question.

4. This is not to subscribe to an assimilationist view of language change, presuming that migration backgrounds will leave no linguistic trace. There is ample evidence to suggest that postmigrant youths develop "mixed" codes and forms of slang that incorporate Turkish elements (Hieronymus 2003). However, such codes are at present too subaltern and fluid to fully function as signifiers for Radio MultiKulti's target audience. What is more, young people *without* a migration background similarly adopt such codes and slang terms, particularly in working-class urban settings.

5. After the break-up of the Soviet bloc and large-scale immigration to Germany from Eastern Europe and Russia, this has been changing since the early 90s, judging from my own experience. While my first and last name has never been much of an issue until this period, I am now being questioned as to my background on a fairly regular basis in Germany.

6. "Up to now we have not been able to attract enough foreign colleagues [*ausländische Kollegen*] for the German-language program, the lingua-franca part" (Voß 1996, 6).

7. One of them was about to complete her term at the station when I came to visit for the first time. Having spent part of her childhood in Germany as a second-generation migrant from Turkey, she felt that she did not fit the profile that was initially targeted for the Grimme initiative. However, she reported that they had trouble finding enough first-generation women who could master the high expectations of language competence in German, and this is how she got in. She was dissatisfied with work at MultiKulti—while she thought that training ethnic minority women as journalists was a worthwhile effort, she did not want to be working on "ethnic" issues all the time. It seemed much more desirable to her to work in other contexts of German broadcasting, and she felt offended by expectations that the appropriate place for ethnic minority journalists was MultiKulti.

8. Barry Dornfeld makes a similar point regarding audience expectations in his ethnography *Producing Public Television, Producing Public Culture* (1998).

9. Religious festival at the end of Ramadan. The name "Sugar Holiday" derives from the tradition of giving sweets to children.

10. Author's interview with Emine Gül (pseudonym), February 2001, translation from German.

11. As approximately 98% of the population in Turkey are.

12. I suggest this expression to denote the problematic celebration of the concept of hybridity as an antidote to all forms of essentialism.

13. Author's interview with Emine Gül, February 2001, translation from German.

14. The reification, Baumann claims, is very much due to the British political system, which recognizes essentialist notions of ethnic communities and puts them in relations of competition with each other. "Rather than thinking in terms of civil rights and a culture-transcending equal treatment for all, the system encourages the representation and public servicing of minorities that can organize themselves to prove their cultural distinctiveness" (Baumann 1999, 123).

15. Author's interview with Cem Dalaman, February 1998, translation from German.

16. In the first decades of its existence, this replacement mainly took the form of expelling Arabic and Persian influences from the language and replacing them with words that have—imagined or factual—Turkic roots (Lewis 1968). The transformation was presented as a return to the language of the people, as opposed to the assumed "Ottoman" of former state elites. Şerif Mardin has shown that Turkish already played an important role as an ele-

ment of distinction for Ottoman elites, wanting to differentiate themselves from other languages of the Empire (Mardin 2002). Language change in the Turkish Republic has also not been unidirectional: Martin Stokes has drawn my attention to a reverse process of language replacement in the early 1980s, much to the dismay of TRT television announcers and newsreaders who had to contend with new word lists on a weekly basis. While this reveals a much more unstable and conflictual process of enforcing linguistic change, in conversations with me the Turkish editors at Radio MultiKulti continuously referred to *öztürkçe* as an uncontested and stable standard against which they judged migrants' shortcomings.

17. Author's interview with Emine Gül, February 2001, translation from German.

18. The commercial radio station Metropol FM in Berlin is grappling with the same problem: even though it presents itself as radio made by Turkish Berliners, the majority of its staff was born and educated in Turkey.

19. This double competence is however not to be confused with other forms of cultural syncretism and hybridity often claimed to characterize immigrant life in Germany. The "Kanak Sprak" celebrated by the well-known "migrant" writer Feridun Zaimoğlu, referring to the emergence of a kind of Creole language that mixes German with Turkish influences, constitutes a very different kind of combining cultural repertoires that have different nation-state origins (Zaimoğlu 2000). It has a definite class belonging, and if its users do not simultaneously have command of those linguistic repertoires defined as correct in Turkey or particularly in Germany, it in fact hinders their upward social mobility. It is those individuals who have full command of these "high cultural" repertoires who can benefit from switching and combine them in advantageous ways.

20. Author's interview with Cem Dalaman, February 1998, translation from German.

21. Author's interview with Atife Öztürk, January 1999, translation from German.

22. In anthropology, scholars have up to now concentrated not so much on migrant or ethnic minority media as on "indigenous media," as a particular form of local cultural activity in community contexts of "first peoples" (Ginsburg 1991, 1993; Michaels 1994; Tini Fox 1993; Turner 1990, 1991, 1992). As in the literature on ethnic media, this activity has mainly been conceptualized as a sign of vitality and opposition on the part of locally rooted cultures against obliterating national or even transnational influences. Yet, anthropologists have also taken note of contrary evidence that complicates the notion of authentic cultural (re-)production. Research on indigenous media production presents evidence both of the appropriation of media technologies for projects of cultural "survival," and of the influence of dominant media environments—sometimes coming to define what is to qualify as indigenous cultural production, sometimes being dealt with strategically by indigenous producers (Ginsburg, Abu-Lughod, and Larkin 2002).

23. Gramsci's notion of the "traditional intellectuals" also allows for them to have historically outlived the "organic" structural position they once occupied in a different hegemonic context (Boyer 2005a). Though never dominant, Turkish migrant labor activists might be described as traditional intellectuals in this sense, given their role in the German union movement of the 1970s and 80s, and its contemporary decline. They played an important role in politicizing the labor migrant population beyond class consciousness, and were often involved in establishing migrant organizations with Leftist sympathies, such as those of Alevis, Kurds, educational lobbies, etc.

24. This is not to deny that sharing experiences related to one's position in a hierarchical scheme of ethnic or racial classification is without consequence for representation, merely to criticize the inside-outside distinction that disregards differences "within" ethnic minority groups and turns every statement of an "ethnic" into an ethnic statement.

25. This tends to be the assumption even of thinkers such as Laclau and Mouffe, who seek to open up the concept of hegemony by claiming a possible plurality of political spaces in a general "field of discursivity" (Laclau and Mouffe 1985).

4. The Gap between Culture and Cultures

1. Hito Steyerl has drawn attention to recent attempts that mobilize immigrant cultural production in a new way, turning migrant artists into cultural ambassadors to represent Germany abroad through a "marketable brand of façade cosmopolitanism" (Steyerl 2004). Such efforts, although significant in terms of new developments within a limited part of the German *Kultur* establishment, do not represent the "high cultural" mainstream.

2. In the 1960s and 70s, some popular German singers without immigrant backgrounds took on names such as Rex Gildo (famous for his songs "Hossa," "Fiesta Mexicana," "Der letzte Sirtaki") or Roy Black. Many others sang songs romanticizing exotic women, longing for a lost home, and foreign poverty in different disguises. In the 1970s, singer Paola could revive a 1940s song, "Capri Fischer," Katja Ebstein praised "Der Stern von Mykonos," Michael Holm "My Lady of Spain," and duo Cindy and Bert sang of "Spaniens Gitarren." Singing with accents that would have mustered Radio MultiKulti review, popular "foreign" singers could cross national lines, especially westward. Roberto Blanco landed a huge success at the Eurovision Song Contest with his "Samba si! Arbeit no!," Bata Illic could sing "Bahia Blanca," and Karel Gott "Das Mädchen von Athen," despite his Czech origins. For an exploration of how Spanish and Latin American exoticism figured in the twentieth century *Schlager* genre, see the work of Wolfgang Dietrich (Dietrich 2002).

3. See Coşkun 1995a, 1995b; "Turkish Pop: The Rise of Spontaneous Synthesis," *Turkish Daily News,* November 13, 1995, B1.

4. A notable exception is Kool Savaş, a young rap musician who has collaborated with many German and international artists and has also acted in Thomas Arslan's 1997 film *Geschwister—Kardeşler.*

5. See also below.

6. House of World Cultures, mission statement, 2004, http://www.hkw.de/external/en/profil/das_hkw/wirueberuns_1.hmtl, accessed January 2004.

7. http://www.hkw.de/external/en/profil/das_hkw/c_index.html, accessed July 8, 2003.

8. Author's interview with Hans Georg Knopp, August 21, 2003, translation from German.

9. http://www.werkstatt-der-kulturen.de/index2.htm, translated from German, accessed August 5, 2003.

10. To give an example, the director of the WdK Andreas Freudenberg co-organized the Second Federal Congress for Cultural Politics, "inter.kultur.politik.—kulturpolitik in der multiethnischen gesellschaft," Berlin, June 26–27, 2003.

11. The figures were published online: http://www.senwisskult.berlin.de/4_kultur/inhalt/ 1_kulturpolitik/4_haushalt/eckdatenLUVkultur2003ff.pdf, accessed April 16, 2003.

12. The term "foreigner" has been all but dropped from public language and official documents dealing with immigrant groups. Its continued appearance in the culture budget gives additional support to the argument that immigrants have yet to "arrive" in the domain of dominant culture and cultural funding in Berlin.

13. Senatsverwaltung für Wissenschaft, Forschung und Kultur 2003, translation from German.

14. Karcı 2002, translation from Turkish.

15. Author's interview with Manfred Fischer at the Senatsverwaltung für Wissenschaft, Forschung und Kultur, May 20, 2003.

16. Mousse T. has written songs such as "Sex Bomb" for Tom Jones, the 1998 hit single "Horny," and is known for remixes such as the dancefloor version of "Sing It Back" for the band Moloko. All of them were huge international commercial successes.

17. The company had little idea of what was to follow, otherwise I would certainly not have been asked to do the job. But once chosen to translate, I had the opportunity to follow the film's magical transformation in the German mainstream media from "guestworker cinema" (labeled as such at the first press conference following the initial press screening) to "rock 'n roll" (as one of the international jury members stated in their announcement of selecting the film for the prime award) to the best German film in decades (as proud commentators stated when the film went on to also claim the European Film Award a year later). Turkey's main daily newspapers immediately hailed the film as a Turkish success instead. Despite such claims, questions around representational authority and accuracy continued in Germany. While Akın claims to have simply wanted to tell a compelling story, the question of whether he had accurately represented the fate of second-generation migrants in Germany was endlessly debated by film critics and migration experts alike.

18. Author's interview with Werner Felten, June 11, 2003, translated from German.

19. To give a few examples, the quarrels between different Turkish theater groups in the city has received public attention even in the German media (Kosnick 2003). Also notorious is the conflict between two institutions seeking state recognition as academies for Turkish music (so far in vain), the Conservatory for Turkish Music (*Berliner Konservatorium für Türkische Musik*) and its rival, the German-Turkish Music Academy (*Deutsch-Türkische Musikakademie*), and the infighting in the more or less inactive Turkish Cultural Council of Berlin (*Türkischer Kulturrat Berlin*).

5. Bringing the Nation Back In

1. Literally, "with crazy blood," term used to describe young, unmarried men in Turkey.

2. *Nokta,* 13, no. 33 (1995):72–73, author's translation from Turkish.

3. *Hürriyet,* September 23, 1995, 18.

4. The close connections between right-wing terror and police as well as secret service forces have been documented from a number of different political and institutional perspectives both within and outside of Turkey. In official contexts, the Susurluk Report has to be named, which was commissioned by then Prime Minister Mesut Yılmaz and investigated the entanglement of state actors with drug traders and right-wing assassins. Investigations began after a car crash on November 3, 1996, which involved a high-ranking police official, a member of parliament, and the infamous Abdullah Çatlı. Çatlı had held leading positions in fascist organizations during the 70s and later became an internationally sought terrorist with close connections to Turkey's secret service *MİT* (Savaş 1998). Other reliable sources include Amnesty International's yearly evaluation of human rights violations in Turkey and the documentation on the Turkish state's fight against Kurdish separatism (Berger et al. 1998).

5. *Türkiye,* "*Kültür milliyetçileri,*" August 17, 1995, 4, translated from Turkish.

6. *Sabah,* "*Avrupa'daki Türkler'in Sesi—Cartel,*" August 2, 1995, 16.

7. Neither could they be integrated into the economic project of modernization, as Çağlar Keyder has pointed out (Keyder 1999). The employment that rural migrants could find in cities like Istanbul tended to be in the rapidly expanding informal sector, rendering them marginal or illegal with regard to both housing and work.

8. Interestingly, German depictions of labor migrants' fates tended to echo this vision, as, for example, Helma Sanders-Brahms's film *Shirin's Wedding* (*Shirins Hochzeit,* 1976), in which the protagonist, a young Anatolian peasant woman, moves from German factory floors on to prostitution. Films produced in Turkey mostly depicted migration in negative terms, but Tunç Okan's *Otobüs* (1974), following the bus journey of labor migrants from Sweden to Turkey, was an important exception.

9. *Hürriyet*, August 28, 1995, *kelebek* section, "*İşte, Rafet El Roman: Tarkan, Ahmet ve Cartel'den sonra Almanya'dan son transfer.*"

10. *Turkish Daily News*, November 13, 1995, "Turkish Pop: The Rise of a Spontaneous Synthesis," section 2, B1.

11. Lale Yalçın-Heckmann has drawn attention to a similar change in media representations of Turkish migrants in Germany, a change that is generationally specific. It is only the younger generation that is seen to develop "hybrid" identities, and doing so by revolting against a parent generation presented as culturally conservative (Yalçın-Heckmann 2002). Ayşe Çağlar has described aspects of such revolt in the consumption practices of second- and third-generation German Turks (Çağlar 2002).

12. I thank Martin Stokes for drawing my attention to Navaro-Yashin's work.

13. Jenny White provides a telling example of such strategies in her discussion of an Islamist Virtue Party rally in İzmit, when the secularist ruling elites were represented as ignoring the plight of the poor and living a life of luxury. While the party used such strategies to demonstrate its own "classless" commitment to the people, Islamic symbols such as styles of dress are at the same time reclassified as cultural markers of the new Islamist elites, as when it comes to the *tesettür* fashion popular among upwardly mobile Islamist women (White 2002; see also Navaro-Yashin 2002).

14. The name of MED-TV was derived from the Meder people who are believed to have lived in Mesopotamia 4,000 years ago, and whom Kurdish nationalists regard as their ancestors.

15. This was in fact not his real name, he told me quite openly. He did use it, however, in connection with all of his production activities at the OKB as well as in our encounters.

16. Apart from broadcasting, print, and nonpublic forms of communication, the Internet plays a growing role for Kurdish activism, ranging from public portals to chat rooms and newsgroups with restricted access and membership. It is difficult to gain an overview of the wide range of Internet sites and forums dedicated to Kurdish issues. What can be said, however, is that its contents elude the control of state forces even more so than satellite television does. Larger portals seem to have contributors from across Europe, and Web content is often presented in various languages, including Western European, Turkish, and Kurdish dialects. It is evident that the Internet allows Kurdish groups to "jump scales," to form new political alliances translocally and to reach out to new publics. Accessible media such as the Internet and widened mass-media possibilities thus provide new conditions for "grassroots" politics—they need not be tied to a particular locality. The grassroots can be anywhere.

17. *Turkish Daily News*, November 15, 2000.

18. *Hürriyet*, November 28, 2000, 1, translation from Turkish.

19. *Turkish Daily News*, "Coalition Clash over Kurdish Broadcasts," November 15, 2000; article posted as electronic edition at http://www.turkishdailynews.com.tr/archives.php?id=20530, accessed January 2007.

20. *Mehmetçik* is a term of endearment widely used for Turkey's soldiers.

6. Coping with "Extremism"

1. The latter three all have mass media networks in Turkey that include newspapers, television channels, and radio stations, leading Günter Seufert to claim that Islamic communities have "veiled" themselves as modern institutions to enter and restructure Turkey's public space (Seufert 1997, 145–49).

2. Open Channels in areas with large immigrant populations report similar problems, such as the Open Channel Hamburg and Frankfurt/Offenbach.

3. Author's interview with Susanne Gramms, December 1997.

4. While I did not conduct a formal survey to determine the television and radio habits of Berlin's Turkish migrant population, I did make some attempts in this direction. Together with my friend Hülya Karcı, I set out on some weekends to ring the doorbells of people with Turkish-sounding names in Kreuzberg. Armed with a catalog of questions, we asked particularly about their opinion of locally produced Turkish-language programs. These outings would usually end with both of us being invited into the living room and chatting for hours, not very conducive to producing relevant statistical results. One of the most interesting observations we made in this context, however, pertained to peoples' reactions to Open Channel broadcasts. While the large majority of respondents claimed that they did not watch OKB programs at all because of their amateur qualities and politically doubtful orientations, almost everybody knew exactly what was "on," and could even name several programs they deemed particularly offensive or funny.

5. "Anayasada yer alan hak ve hürriyetlerden hiçbiri, Devletin ülkesi ve milletiyle bölünmez bütünlüğünü bozmak, . . . amacıyla kullanılamazlar." ("None of the rights and freedoms stated in the constitution may be used . . . for the purpose of destroying the indivisible integrity of the state and nation," Article 14, *Türkiye Cumhuriyeti Anayasası* 1995).

6. Due to repeated state interventions banning the party, it was reconstituted several times under different names, starting as the National Order Party and most recently splitting into two, the Party for Justice and Development (AKP), currently in power, and the Wellbeing Party (*Saadet*).

7. This last program name takes up a slogan promoted by the journal *Bozkurt* in the 1970s, organ of the Nationalist Action Party (Landau 1995).

8. *İmam Hatip* schools are semi-private secondary schools in Turkey that offer Islamic instruction. While state-sponsored in the 1960s in order to better monitor rising Islamic activism and to counter "leftist" ideologies, secularist forces in the Turkish government and military have reacted to their growing popularity by expanding compulsory primary education to eight years instead of five in 1998. This move has forced *İmam Hatip* schools to cut down their seven-year curriculum to four years, and take in students at a much later age.

9. Author's interview with Jürgen Linke, December 1997.

10. A commentator made this charge in the *Offenbach-Post* newspaper, May 12, 1998.

11. http://www.bok.de/referat3.html, accessed April 2002.

12. Author's interview with Abdullah Güneş, June 3, 1998. All the quotes that follow stem from the same interview, and are translations from Turkish, except where noted otherwise.

13. Literally meaning "older brother," used as a friendly yet respectful term among men of different age groups.

14. Ramazan Ekici talking to a live caller on the OKB, June 2000, translated from Turkish.

15. Author's interview with Ramazan Ekici, July 1998, translation from Turkish.

16. Translated from Turkish.

17. I thank Gerdien Jonker for sharing some of her observations regarding the Open Channel and her knowledge of Islamic life in Berlin with me (see Jonker and Kapphan 1998).

18. "Bağımsız kalmazsam ben, *frei* düşünemem. Sizinle bir grup olursam ben, siz de benim şefim olursanız, ne yapacağım ben? . . . ben bağımsız kalmazsam, bizim grubu *pflegen* yapacağım, öbürlerine *schlagen* yapacağım, ya? Onun için, ben bağımsız kalmak istiyorum ki, *Wahrheit Sieger* olsun" (German terms in the original).

19. Interview with managing director Werner Felten, June 11, 2003. I followed the station's attempts to obtain a license from the start, reporting several times for Radio Multi-Kulti on its progress, and interviewed myself for a job as editorial staff member. My Turkish was not good enough—and several applicants with Turkish backgrounds but raised in Ber-

lin were rejected for the same reason. Metropol FM thus faces the same problem as the editorial staff of Radio MultiKulti's Turkish program, and almost all of its moderators and editors have completed a large part of their education in Turkey.

20. Sympathizers of Millî Görüş form an exception: the mixed-use commercial *Spreekanal* hosted for several years the Turkish-language broadcasts of TFD, Turkish Television Germany, despite the activities of other groups at the Open Channel that were at least loosely associated with the organization. The existence of TFD indicates the wealth of financial resources members or sympathizers of Millî Görüş were able to mobilize for their outreach work. It is unlikely, though, that TFD would have been given a license for twenty-four-hour programming, particularly after the September 11 events.

21. This is quite a challenge for locally based commercial Turkish-language radio and television ventures such as the radio station Metropol FM and the cable television station TD-1, given the massive conflicts among their target audience along the lines of religion, ethnicity, and Left versus Right.

7. Signifying with a Difference

1. The literature most widely acknowledged in anthropology includes Appadurai 1996; Basch et al. 1994; Brah 1996; Clifford 1994; Glick Schiller et al. 1992; Hannerz 1996; Portes 1998; Sassen 1991; Vertovec 1999.

2. William Mazzarella employs these terms to describe the fundamental dilemma and recursive doubling of identity formation processes.

3. Gaziosmanpaşa is a poor neighborhood in Istanbul whose inhabitants are predominantly Alevis. In 1995, fifteen Alevis were killed in clashes with police forces after unidentified gunmen had opened fire on a teahouse. For the Sivas fire, see below.

4. This and the following quotes stem from author's interview with Halit Büyükgöl, June 1998, translated from Turkish.

5. *Kırk Budak*, literally "forty branches," refers to the forty saints that the Prophet Muhammed met according to Alevi interpretation during his ascent to heaven (*miraç*).

6. Author's interview with İbrahim Alkan, April 1998, translated from Turkish.

7. The term *kızılbaş*, "redhead," has become a widespread pejorative term for Alevis in Turkey. It emerged in the early sixteenth century in the Ottoman Empire as a label for heterodox Muslims, and is traced back to the red turban of Ali, but also to the traditional headgear of Türkmen populations.

8. *Dede* literally means grandfather, but is also an Alevi name for the intermediate rank of male spiritual leaders who transmit religious and cultural knowledge and decide community grievances.

9. The Ottoman Millet system was an administrative apparatus that gave far-reaching autonomy to religious and ethnic minorities in the Ottoman Empire while incorporating them into its political and economic structures. This approach to religious and particularly ethnic difference was sharply reversed in the Turkish Republic.

10. According to Shi'ite and Alevi sources, all Imams except the last one who became "invisible" have been murdered.

11. Such as when, for example, the son of the famous secularist writer Aziz Nesin mobilizes Alevi audiences in Berlin to donate money for the building of a boarding school for Alevi orphans in Turkey.

12. The German translation of the AABF announcement lists Srebrenica rather than Auschwitz in this list of places that are associated with different atrocities: http://www.alevi.com/pressemeldung+M517cec622ce.html, accessed August 2006. Halabja is a Kurdish town in Northern Iraq where hundreds of people died in a poison gas attack by Iraqi

soldiers in 1988. Solingen is a German town associated with the racist arson attack that led to the death of five Turkish women and girls in 1993.

13. http://www.alevi.com/etkinlik+M5ea83c8af92.html, accessed August 2006.

14. *Evrensel,* June 19, 2006.

15. This is not to say that these cultural camps represent mutually exclusive groups within the population, or even mutually exclusive categories of identification, as the existence of, for example, Kurdish Alevi organizations can indicate.

16. Antonio Gramsci himself was much more careful in his use, deploying the concept for the analysis of historically specific situations pertaining to Italy, without attempting to place it at the center of a general theory.

8. Conclusion

1. One might want to challenge this argument by pointing to the activities of Turkish nationalists at the Open Channel, or the broadcasts of the television project TFD in the commercial domain of local cable television. The former claim to represent the ideals and interests of the Turkish nation-state, yet broadcast in a marginal institutional setting. The latter belongs to the group of "Islamist" broadcasting deemed problematic both in the Turkish and in the German context. However, the Turkish nationalist positions articulated in Open Channel broadcasts belong to the Extreme Right—not moderate enough for Turkey's state and private television imports, and politically unacceptable in Germany. The ability of the television project TFD to broadcast on commercial cable in Berlin is above all an indication of the economic strength of the "Islamist" cultural camp represented politically by the former Welfare (Refah) and later Virtue (Fazilet) Party in Turkey, and outside the country by its foreign branch, the İGMG. Financial capital can thus partly make up for the relative lack of cultural capital and distance from state-condoned articulations of religious and cultural identity in both countries.

2. In the sense of dominant, institutionalized uses of language and other sign systems that are supported and (re-)produced by nation-state institutions as well as those classified under the rubric of "civil society" (see Bauböck 1994).

3. This tradition posed particular problems for early Europeanist anthropologists, since they faced the challenge to deal with "complexity," once thought to be a specific feature of Western fieldsites. For much research in Europe, rural communities offered a seemingly acceptable equivalent to non-Western "intimate" settings. In the 1970s, as anticolonial movements on the colonial periphery struggled for independence in predominantly nationalist terms and newly formed governments began the project of nation-building, anthropologists generally were alerted to the relations between local and national structures. As the former colonies appeared to grow in "complexity," the conceptual reorientation within the discipline of anthropology provided a new rationale for fieldwork in Europe. The idea that the once-preferred objects of anthropological study such as tribes and relatively isolated communities were being transformed into ethnic groups (Cohen 1974) rendered Europe as a fieldsite less marginal, given that the concept of ethnicity had been long in use there to describe mostly minority groups within nation-states. Given the new prominence of ethnicity and nation-state frameworks, contributors to Jeremy Boissevain and John Friedl's volume *Beyond the Community* (1975) could thus confidently advocate the study of national and supranational processes for the discipline as a whole.

4. This is a stronger sense of tactics than Michel de Certeau's clandestine practices of the oppressed, which he situates in the realm of "consumption," never managing to rise beyond a "quasi-invisibility" (De Certeau 1984). The migrant media producers described here are actively engaged in the production of representations, not just in their clandestine ma-

nipulation. This does not mean that they can ignore dominant ideologies, but the practices described here suggest a much more complex sense of cultural struggle than De Certeau's bipolar model of domination and resistance (Frow 1991).

5. These dimensions tend to be particularly relevant in categorizing numerical minorities as "other" within social formations such as nation-states, though class and gender differences can be mobilized along similar lines.

6. This breakdown of communication is unfortunately and paradoxically supported by Open Channel decisions to require German transcripts for foreign-language broadcasts, and to limit the number of Islamic programs by having them compete for "religious" programming slots, as happened with the OKB's so-called *Sendeschienen*. This has effectively resulted in a steep drop in Islamic broadcasts. Comparable measures were taken at Open Channels in Frankfurt-Offenbach and in Hamburg, with similar results.

7. See the Parekh Report commissioned by the Runnymede Trust (Commission on the Future of Multi-Ethnic Britain 2000). Neither is this agenda incompatible with a range of labor immigration regimes that are tolerated or even explicitly encouraged by Western European governments, with people on temporary work permits and undocumented migrants creating an underpaid labor force that can be recruited and disposed of at will. In Britain, the case of the National Health Service (NHS) employing migrant nurses and cleaning personnel at substandard wages has made modest headlines recently, as well as its "brain drain" of highly qualified medical personnel from Germany and Eastern Europe.

BIBLIOGRAPHY

Abdullah, M. Salim. 1995. "Muslims in Germany." In *Muslim Minorities in the West,* ed. Syed Abedin and Ziauddin Sardar, 67–77. London: Grey Seal.

Abu-Lughod, Lila. 2005. *Dramas of Nationhood: The Politics of Television in Egypt.* Chicago: University of Chicago Press.

Aksoy, Asu, and Kevin Robins. 1993. "Gecekondu-Style Broadcasting in Turkey: A Confrontation of Cultural Values." *Intermedia* 21, no. 3: 15–17.

———. 2000. "Thinking across Spaces: Transnational Television from Turkey." *European Journal of Cultural Studies* 3, no. 3: 343–65.

———. 2002. "Banal Transnationalism: The Difference that Television Makes." *Transnational Communities Working Paper Series,* http://www.transcomm.ox.ac.uk/working%20papers/WPTC-02–08%20Robins.pdf, accessed May 5, 2003.

Alexander, M. Jacqui. 1991. "Redrafting Morality: The Postcolonial State and the Sexual Offences Bill of Trinidad and Tobago." In *Third World Women and the Politics of Feminism,* ed. Chandra T. Mohanty, Ann Russo, and Lourdes Torres, 133–52. Bloomington: Indiana University Press.

Alonso, Ana Maria. 1994. "The Politics of Space, Time and Substance: State Formation, Nationalism, and Ethnicity." *Annual Review of Anthropology* 23: 379–405.

Amin, Ash. 2004. "Multi-Ethnicity and the Idea of Europe." *Theory, Culture & Society* 21, no. 2: 1–24.

Amiraux, Valérie. 1997. "Turkish Islamic Associations in Germany and the Issue of European Citizenship." In *Islam in Europe: The Politics of Religion and Community,* ed. Steven Vertovec and Ceri Peach, 245–59. Basingstoke and London: Macmillan.

Amit, Vered, and Nigel Rapport. 2002. *The Trouble with Community: Anthropological Reflections on Movement, Identity and Collectivity.* London: Pluto.

Amnesty International. 1996. *Türkei—Unsichere Zukunft ohne Menschenrechte.* Bonn: Amnesty International.

Anderson, Bendedict. 1983. *Imagined Communities: Reflections on the Origin and Spread of Nationalism.* London: Verso.

Ang, Ien. 1989. "Wanted: Audiences—on the Politics of Empirical Audience Studies." In *Remote Control: Television, Audiences, and Cultural Power,* ed. Ellen Seiter et al., 96–115. London and New York: Routledge.

Appadurai, Arjun. 1991. "Global Ethnoscapes: Notes and Queries for a Transnational Anthropology." In *Recapturing Anthropology,* ed. Richard G. Fox, 191–210. Santa Fe, N.M.: School of American Research Press.

―――. 1996. *Modernity At Large: Cultural Dimensions of Globalization.* Minneapolis: University of Minnesota Press.

Armbrust, Walter. 1996. *Mass Culture and Modernism in Egypt.* Cambridge: Cambridge University Press.

Arslan, Emre. 2004. "Turkish Ultra-nationalism in Germany: Its Transnational Dimensions." In *Transnational Social Spaces: Agents, Networks and Institutions,* ed. Thomas Faist and Eyüp Özveren, 111–39. Aldershot, U.K.: Ashgate.

Asad, Talal. 1990. "Multiculturalism and British Identity in the Wake of the Rushdie Affair." *Politics & Society* 18, no. 4: 455–80.

Ausschuss für Kulturelle Angelegenheiten. 2003. *Wortprotokoll der 25. Sitzung.* Berlin: Abgeordnetenhaus Berlin.

Ayata, Sencer. 1996. "Patronage, Party, and State: The Politicization of Islam in Turkey." *Middle East Journal* 50, no. 1: 40–56.

Aydaş, Osman Tuncay, Bilin Beyaptı, and Kıvılcım Metin-Özcan. n.d. "Determinants of Workers' Remittances: The Case of Turkey." Working Papers, Department of Economics, Bilkent University, Ankara, Turkey, 1–27.

Bagdikian, Ben H. 2004. *The New Media Monopoly.* Boston: Beacon.

Bakojannis, Pavlos. 1972. "Zensur im Äther." *Die Zeit,* no. 36: 5.

Barth, Frederik. 1956. "Ecological Relationships of Ethnic Groups in Swat, North Pakistan." *American Anthropologist* 58: 1079–89.

―――, ed. 1970. *Ethnic Groups and Boundaries: The Social Organization of Cultural Difference.* London: Allen and Unwin.

Basch, Linda G., Nina Glick Schiller, and Cristina Szanton Blanc. 1994. *Nations Unbound: Transnational Projects, Postcolonial Predicaments, and Deterritorialized Nation-States.* Langhorne, Pa.: Gordon and Breach.

Bauböck, Rainer, ed. 1994. *From Aliens to Citizens: Redefining the Status of Immigrants in Europe.* Aldershot, U.K., and Brookfield, Vt.: Avebury.

Baumann, Gerd. 1999. *The Multicultural Riddle: Rethinking National, Ethnic, and Religious Identities.* New York and London: Routledge.

Bax, Daniel. 1999. "Türkische Küsse." *Zeitschrift für Kulturaustausch,* no. 3: http://www.ifa.de/zfk/themen/99_3_hysterie/dbax.htm. Accessed June 2000.

―――. 2003. "Her mit den jungen Türken." *taz,* October 24, Berlin ed.

Beauftragte der Bundesregierung für Migration, Flüchtlinge und Integration. 2004. *Strukturdaten der Ausländischen Bevölkerung.* http://www.integrationsbeauftragte.de/download/Strukturdaten.pdf. Accessed May 2006.

―――. 2005. *Bericht über die Lage der Ausländerinnen und Ausländer in der Bundesrepublik Deutschland.* http://www.integrationsbeauftragte.de/download/LageberichtInternet.pdf. Accessed May 2006.

Becker, Jörg. 1998a. "Die Ethnisierung der deutschen Medienlandschaft—Türkische Medienkultur zwischen Assoziation und Dissoziation." In *Deutschland im Dialog der Kulturen: Medien, Images, Verständigung,* ed. Siegfried Quandt and Wolfgang Gast, 295–302. Konstanz: UKV Medien.

———. 1998b. "Multiculturalism in German Broadcasting." *Media Development,* no. 3: 8–12.

———. 2001. "Zwischen Integration und Abgrenzung: Anmerkungen zur Ethnisierung der türkischen Medienkultur." In *Zwischen Abgrenzung und Integration: Türkische Medienkultur in Deutschland,* ed. Jörg Becker and Reinhard Benisch, 9–24. Loccum: Evangelische Akademie Loccum.

Becquer, Marcos, and José Gatti. 1991. "Elements of Vogue." *Third Text,* nos. 16/17: 65–81.

Belge, Murat. 1990. "Toplumsal Değişme ve 'Arabesk.'" *Birikim* 17: 16–23.

Berger, Andreas, Rudi Friedrich, and Kathrin Schneider. 1998. *Der Krieg in Türkei-Kurdistan.* Göttingen: Lamuv.

Berger, Hartwig. 1990. "Vom Klassenkampf zum Kulturkonflikt: Wandlungen und Wendungen der Westdeutschen Migrationsforschung." In *Ethnizität: Wissenschaft und Minderheiten,* ed. E. Dittrich and O. Radtke, 119–38. Opladen: Westdeutscher Verlag.

Bhabha, Homi K. 1994. *The Location of Culture.* London and New York: Routledge.

Bloomfield, Jude. 2003. "'Made in Berlin': Multicultural Conceptual Confusion and Intercultural Reality." *International Journal of Cultural Policy* 9, no. 2: 167–83.

Blumer, Jay G., and Wolfgang Hoffmann-Riem. 1992. "New Roles for Public Television in Western Europe: Challenges and Prospects." *Journal of Communication* 42, no. 1: 20–35.

Boissevain, Jeremy, and John Friedl, eds. 1975. *Beyond the Community: Social Process in Europe.* The Hague: Department of Educational Science, The Netherlands.

BOK. 2000. *Was sind Offene Kanäle?* http://www.bok.de/was.html: Bundesverband Offene Kanäle Deutschland. Accessed September 2001.

Bolter, Jay D., and Richard Grusin. 1999. *Remediation: Understanding New Media.* Cambridge, Mass.: MIT Press.

Bourdieu, Pierre. 1977. *Outline of a Theory of Practice.* Cambridge, U.K., and New York: Cambridge University Press.

———. 1984. *Distinction: A Social Critique of the Judgement of Taste.* Cambridge, Mass.: Harvard University Press.

Boyer, Dominic. 2001. "Media Markets, Mediating Labors, and the Branding of East German Culture at Super Illu," *Social Text* 19, no. 3: 9–33.

———. 2005a. *Spirit and System: Media, Intellectuals, and the Dialectic in Modern German Culture.* Chicago: University of Chicago Press.

———. 2005b. "Welcome to the New Europe." *American Ethnologist* 32, no. 4: 521–23.

Brah, Avtar. 1996. *Cartographies of Diaspora.* London and New York: Routledge.

Breuer-Ücer, Ulya, and Gualtiero Zambonini. 1996. "Hörfunksendungen für Ausländer in Deutschland." *Media Perspektiven,* no. 8: 462–65.

Breunig, Christian. 1998. "Offene Fernseh- und Hörfunkkanäle in Deutschland." *Media Perspektiven,* no. 5: 236–49.

Brubaker, Rogers. 1992. *Citizenship and Nationhood in France and Germany.* Cambridge, Mass.: Harvard University Press.

Brüning, Jens B., and Wilfried Nax. 1975. "Integration durch Information? Zur Situation der ausländischen Arbeitnehmer und der Angebote der Massenmedien." *Medium—Zeitschrift Für Hörfunk, Fernsehen, Film, Bild, Ton* 5, no. 12: 3–8.

Bundeszentrale für politische Bildung. 1987. *Ausländer und Massenmedien. Bestandsaufnahmen und Perspektiven.* Bonn: Bundeszentrale für politische Bildung.

Bünger, Reinhard. 1995. "Offen für Neues." *Agenda,* no. 18: 46–47.

Bunzl, Matti. 2005. "Between Anti-Semitism and Islamophobia: Some Thoughts on the New Europe." *American Ethnologist* 32, no. 4: 499–508.

Burul, Yeşim. 2003. "The World of Aziza A.: Third Spaces in Identities." *New Perspectives on Turkey,* nos. 28–29: 209–28.

Busch, Brigitta. 2004. *Sprachen in Disput. Medien und Öffentlichkeit in multilingualen Gesselschaften.* Klagenfurt and Celovec: Drava Verlag.

Busch, Jürgen C. 1994. *Radio Multikulti: Möglichkeiten für lokalen Ethnofunk Berlin—Deutschland—Großbritannien.* Berlin: Vistas.

Çağlar, Ayşe. 1990. "Das Kultur-Konzept als Zwangsjacke in Studien zur Arbeitsmigration." *Zeitschrift Für Türkeistudien* 3, no. 1: 93–105.

———. 1995. "German Turks in Berlin: Social Exclusion and Strategies for Social Mobility." *New Community* 21, no. 3: 309–23.

———. 1998. "Verordnete Rebellion. Deutsch-türkischer Rap und türkischer Pop in Berlin." In *Globalkolorit: Multikulturalismus und Populärkultur,* ed. Ruth Mayer and Mark Terkessidis, 41–56. St. Andrä/Wördern: Hannibal Verlag.

———. 2002. "A Table in Two Hands." In *Fragments of Culture: The Everyday of Modern Turkey,* ed. Deniz Kandiyoti and Ayşe Saktanber, 294–307. New Brunswick, N.J.: Rutgers University Press.

———. 2004. "Mediascapes, Advertisement Industries and Cosmopolitan Transformations: German Turks in Germany." *New German Critique,* no. 92: 39–61.

Calhoun, Craig, ed. 1992. *Habermas and the Public Sphere.* Cambridge, Mass.: MIT Press.

Castles, Stephen. 1984. *Here for Good: Western Europe's New Ethnic Minorities.* London: Pluto.

———. 2003. "Towards a Sociology of Forced Migration and Social Transformation." *Sociology* 37, no. 1: 13–34.

Caton, Steven. 1990. *"Peaks of Yemen I Summon": Poetry as Cultural Practice in a North Yemeni Tribe.* Berkeley: University of California Press.

Cheesman, Tom. 1998. "Polyglot Politics: Hip Hop in Germany." *Debatte* 6, no. 2: 191–214.

Clifford, James. 1994. "Diasporas." *Cultural Anthropology* 9, no. 3: 302–38.

Cohen, Abner. 1974. "The Lesson of Ethnicity." In *Urban Ethnicity,* ed. Abner Cohen, ix–xxiii. London: Tavistock.

Commission on the Future of Multi-Ethnic Britain/Runnymede Trust. 2000. *The Future of Multi-Ethnic Britain: Report of the Commission on the Future of Multi-Ethnic Britain.* London: Profile Books.

Coşkun, Zeki. 1995a. Ağlama diye diye ağlatan müzik (Music which makes you cry by saying "don't cry"). *Cumhuriyet,* August 6, 14,.

———. 1995b. "Beyaz Türklerin türküsü." *Cumhuriyet,* August 7, 15.

———. 1995c. "Rap beni yarım, rap beni!" *Cumhuriyet,* August 27, 15.

———.1995d. "Türkü lazımsa, onu da biz yaparız!" *Cumhuriyet,* August 9, 12.

Cottle, Simon, ed. 2000. *Ethnic Minorities and the Media.* Buckingham, U.K.: Open University Press.

Coulmas, Peter. 1975. "Der Rundfunk: Keine Schule der Gastarbeiter." *Materialien zur Politischen Bildung,* no. 2: 84–92.

Çürükkaya, Selim. 1997. *PKK: Die Diktatur des Abdullah Öcalan.* Frankfurt a.M.: Fischer.

Darkow, Michael, Josef Eckhart, and Gerhard Maletzke. 1985. *Massenmedien und Ausländer in der Bundesrepublik Deutschland.* Schriftenreihe Media Perspektiven, ed. Arbeisgemeinschaft Rundfunkwerbung. Frankfurt a.M.: Alfred Metzner Verlag.

Das, Veena. 1995. "On Soap Opera: What Kind of Anthropological Object Is It?" In *Worlds Apart: Modernity through the Prism of the Local,* ed. David Miller, 169–89. London: Routledge.

De Certeau, Michel. 1984. *The Practice of Everyday Life.* Berkeley: University of California Press.

De Lauretis, Teresa. 1987. *Technologies of Gender: Essays on Theory, Film, and Fiction.* Bloomington: Indiana University Press.

Delaney, Carol. 1995. "Father State, Motherland, and the Birth of Modern Turkey." In *Naturalizing Power: Essays in Feminist Cultural Analysis,* ed. Sylvia Yanagisako and Carol Delaney, 177–99. New York and London: Routledge.

Deutscher Städtetag, ed. 1992. *DST-Beiträge Zur Bildungs- und Kulturpolitik: Fünf Jahrzehnte Kommunale Kulturpolitik.* Vol. C. Köln: Deutscher Städtetag.

Diaz-Diaz, Pablo. 1989. "Brücke zur Heimat mit neuer Aufgabe—Ein Interview mit Manuel Moral." *Informationsdienst Zur Ausländerarbeit,* no. 2: 18–20.

Dickey, Sara. 1997. "Anthropology and Its Contributions to Studies of Mass Media." *International Social Science Journal,* no. 153: 413–27.

Dietrich, Wolfgang. 2002. *"Samba Samba": Eine politikwissenschaftliche Untersuchung der fernen Erotik Lateinamerikas in den Schlagern des 20. Jahrhunderts.* Strashof: Vier-Viertel-Verlag.

Diken, Bülent. 2004. "From Refugee Camps to Gated Communities—Biopolitics and the End of the City." *Citizenship Studies* 8, no. 1: 83–106.

Diller, Ansgar. 1975. "25 Jahre ARD—Daten und Fakten." *ARD Jahrbuch 75*, no. 7: 38–56.

Dornfeld, Barry. 1998. *Producing Public Television, Producing Public Culture*. Princeton, N.J.: Princeton University Press.

Durgut, Gülay. 1993. "Gündüz Almanya—gece Türkiye: Almanya'da Türk basını." In *Deutsche Türken—Türk Almanlar: Das Ende der Geduld—Sabrın Sonu*, ed. Claus Leggewie and Zafer Senocak, 231–39. Reinbek: Rowohlt Verlag.

Duyar, Akın, and Nesrin Çalağan. 2001. "94,8 Metropol FM—Das erste türkischsprachige Radio in Deutschland." In *Zwischen Abgrenzung und Integration: Türkische Medienkultur in Deutschland*, ed. Jörg Becker and Reinhard Behnisch, 85–98. Loccum: Evangelische Akademie Loccum.

Dyer, Richard. 1993. *The Matter of Images: Essays on Representation*. London: Routledge.

———. 1997. *White*. London: Routledge.

Ebers, Michael, and Tayfun Erdoğmus. 1975. "Die Ausländer schauen in die Röhre." *Medium—Zeitschrift Für Hörfunk, Fernsehen, Film, Bild, Ton* 5, no. 12: 9–12.

Eckhardt, Josef. 1987. "Ausländer als Zielgruppe der Massenmedien." In *Ausländer und Massenmedien—Bestandsaufnahme und Perspektiven*. Bundeszentrale für politsche Bildung, 93–96. Bonn: Bundeszentrale für politische Bildung.

———. 1991. "Massenmedien und Ausländer in Nordrhein-Westfalen." In *Programme gegen Fremdenfeindlichkeit—2. Radioforum Ausländer bei uns*, ed. Martin A. Kilgus and Karl-Heinz Meier-Braun, 41–62. Baden Baden: Nomos Verlagsgesellschaft.

———. 1996. "Nutzung und Bewertung von Radio- und Fernsehsendungen für Ausländer." *Media Perspektiven*, no. 8: 451–61.

Eisenstein, Elizabeth L. 1980. *The Printing Press as an Agent of Change*. Cambridge, U.K.: Cambridge University Press.

Erzeren, Ömer. 1997. *Der lange Abschied von Atatürk*. Berlin: ID-Verlag.

Faist, Thomas, ed. 2000. *Transstaatliche Räume: Politik, Wirtschaft und Kultur in und zwischen Deutschland und der Türkei*. Bielefeld: transcript Verlag.

Finkel, Andrew. 2000. "Who Guards the Turkish Press? A Perspective on Press Corruption in Turkey." *Journal of International Affairs* 54, no. 1: 147–66.

Foucault, Michel. 1985–1986. "Of Other Spaces: Utopias and Heterotopias." *Lotus International*, nos. 48/49: 9–17.

Fox, Richard G., ed. 1990. *Nationalist Ideologies and the Production of National Cultures*. Washington, D.C.: American Anthropological Association.

Frachon, Claire, and Marion Vargaftig, eds. 1995. *European Television: Immigrants and Ethnic Minorities*. London: John Libbey.

Frankenberg, Ruth. 1993. *White Women, Race Matters: The Social Construction of Whiteness*. Minneapolis: University of Minnesota Press.

Fraser, Nancy. 1992. "Rethinking the Public Sphere: A Contribution to the Critique of Actually Existing Democracy." In *Habermas and the Public Sphere,* ed. Craig Calhoun, 109–42. Cambridge, Mass.: MIT Press.

Frei, Kerstin. 2003. *Wer sich maskiert, wird integriert. Der Karneval der Kulturen in Berlin.* Berlin: Hans Schiler.

Frow, John. 1991. "Michel de Certeau and the Practice of Representation." *Cultural Studies* 5, no. 1: 52–60.

Gerholm, Tomas, and Yngve Georg Lithman, eds. 1988. *The New Islamic Presence in Western Europe.* London: Mansell.

Gilroy, Paul. 1991. *"There Ain't No Black in the Union Jack": The Cultural Politics of Race and Nation.* Chicago: University of Chicago Press.

Ginsburg, Faye. 1991. "Indigenous Media: Faustian Contract or Global Village?" *Cultural Anthropology* 6, no. 1: 92–112.

———. 1993. "Aboriginal Media and the Australian Imaginary." *Public Culture* 5, no. 3: 557–78.

Ginsburg, Faye, Lila Abu-Lughod, and Brian Larkin, eds. 2002. *Media Worlds: Anthropology on New Terrain.* Berkeley: University of California Press.

Glick Schiller, Nina, Linda Basch, and Cristina Blanc-Szanton, eds. 1992. *Towards a Transnational Perspective on Migration: Race, Class, Ethnicity, and Nationalism Reconsidered.* Vol. 645. New York: Annals of the New York Academy of Science.

Gökalp, Ziya. 1968. *The Principles of Turkism.* Leiden: E. J. Brill. Originally published in 1923.

Goldberg, Andreas. 1998. "Mediale Vielfalt versus mediale Ghettoisierung. Türkischsprachige Medien in Deutschland." *IZA, Zeitschrift Für Migration Und Soziale Arbeit,* no. 2: 35–42.

Göle, Nilüfer. 1996. *The Forbidden Modern: Civilization and Veiling.* Ann Arbor: University of Michigan Press.

———. 1997a. "The Gendered Nature of the Public Sphere." *Public Culture* 10, no. 1: 61–81.

———. 1997b. "Secularism and Islamism in Turkey: The Making of Elites and Counter-Elites." *Middle East Journal* 51, no. 1: 46–58.

Gramsci, Antonio. 1971. *Selections from the Prison Notebooks,* ed. Quintin Hoare and Geoffrey N. Smith. New York: International Publishers.

Greiff, Nannette. 1995. *Türkische Medien in Deutschland.* Berlin: Media Watch.

Greve, Martin. 2002. "Der Marsch in die Institutionen: Auf der Suche nach deutsch-türkischer Musikausbildung." *Üben & Musizieren,* no. 1: 16–22.

———. 2003. *Die Musik der imaginären Türkei. Musik und Musikleben im Kontext der Migration aus der Türkei in Deutschland.* Stuttgart: J. B. Metzler.

Greve, Martin, and Tülay Çınar. 1997. *Das Türkische Berlin.* Berlin: Die Ausländerbeauftragte des Senats.

Grillo, Ralph D. 2003. "Cultural Essentialism and Cultural Anxiety." *Anthropological Theory* 3, no. 2: 157–73.

Guarnizo, Luis E. 1997. "The Emergence of a Transnational Social Formation and the Mirage of Return Migration among Dominican Transmigrants." *Identities* 4, no. 2: 281–322.

Guglielmi, Guiseppe. 1998. "'Funkhaus Europa' liegt vorerst auf Eis." In *Migration und Medien,* ed. Adolf-Grimme-Institut, 17–18. Marl: Adolf-Grimme-Institut.

———. 1999. "Brücke zur neuen Heimat: Die muttersprachlichen Radio-Angebote der ARD." *Menschen Machen Medien* 48, no. 3: 10–11.

Gülçiçek, Ali Duran. 1996. *Der Weg der Aleviten (Bektaschiten).* Köln: Ethnographia Anatolica.

Halberstam, Judith. 2005. *In a Queer Time and Place: Transgender Bodies, Subcultural Lives.* New York: New York University Press.

Hall, Stuart. 1982. "The Rediscovery of 'Ideology': Return of the Repressed in Media Studies." In *Culture, Society and the Media,* ed. Michael Gurevitch et al., 56–90. London and New York: Routledge.

———. 1986. "Gramsci's Relevance for the Study of Race and Ethnicity." *Journal of Communication Inquiry* 10, no. 2: 5–27.

Halley, Janet. 1993. "The Construction of Heterosexuality." In *Fear of a Queer Planet: Queer Politics and Social Theory,* ed. Michael Warner, 82–102. Minneapolis and London: University of Minnesota Press.

Handler, Richard. 1992. "High Culture, Hegemony, and Historical Causality." *American Ethnologist* 19, no. 4: 818–24.

Hannam, Kevin, Mimi Sheller, and John Urry. 2006. "Editorial: Mobilities, Immobilities and Moorings." *Mobilities* 1, no. 1: 1–22.

Hannerz, Ulf. 1996. *Transnational Connections: Culture, People, Places.* London and New York: Routledge.

———. 2000. "Flows, Boundaries and Hybrids: Keywords in Transnational Anthropology." *Transnational Communities Working Paper Series* htttp://www.transcomm.ox.ac.uk, no. 2: 1–25. Accessed May 2003.

Harrison, Faye V. 1995. "The Persistent Power of 'Race' in the Cultural and Political Economy of Racism." *Annual Review of Anthropology* 24: 47–74.

Hartigan, John. 1997. "Establishing the Fact of Whiteness." *American Anthropologist* 99, no. 3: 495–505.

Harvey, David. 1989. *The Condition of Postmodernity.* Oxford: Basil Blackwell.

Hebdige, Dick. 1979. *Subculture: The Meaning of Style.* London: Methuen.

Heinemann, Lars, and Fuat Kamcılı. 2000. "Unterhaltung, Absatzmärkte und die Vermittlung von Heimat. Die Rolle der Massenmedien in deutsch-türkischen Räumen." In *Transstaatliche Räume: Politik, Wirtschaft und Kultur in und zwischen Deutschland und der Türkei,* ed. Thomas Faist, 113–57. Bielefeld: transcript Verlag.

Heinrichs, Werner. 1997. *Kulturpolitik und Kulturfinanzierung.* Munich: C. H. Beck Verlag.

Heitmeyer, Wilhelm, Joachim Müller, and Helmut Schröder. 1998. "Islamistische Expansionspropaganda: Mediennutzung und religiös begründete Machtansprüche bei türkischen Jugendlichen." In *Politisierte Religion,* ed. Heiner Bielefeldt and Wilhelm Heitmeyer, 256–79. Frankfurt a.M.: Suhrkamp Verlag.

Heper, Metin. 1997. "Islam and Democracy in Turkey: Toward a Reconciliation?" *Middle East Journal* 51, no. 1: 32–45.

Hieronymus, Andreas. 2003. *"Ibo, Lan, das ist der Kral!" Qualitativ-heuristische Explorationen in urbane Lebenswelten. Vielsprachige Jugendliche in Sankt Pauli und Altona.* http://www.imir.de/DissHieronymus/. Accessed January 2004.

Hoffmann, Hilmar, and Wolfgang Schneider, eds. 2002. *Kulturpolitik in der Berliner Republik.* Köln: Dumont.

Holert, Tom. 1998. "Mischkalkulationen und Gesichter der Zukunft." In *Globalkolorit: Multikulturalismus und Populärkultur,* ed. Ruth Mayer and Mark Terkessidis, 25–39. St. Andrä/Wördern: Hannibal Verlag.

Holler, Wolfgang. 1997. "Radio MultiKulti gefährdet?" *UNESCO Heute,* nos. 1–2: 15–16.

Holzweißig, Gunter. 1989. *Massenmedien in der DDR.* Berlin: Holzapfel.

Human Rights Watch. 1999. *World Report 1999.* http://www.hrw.org/worldreport 99/europe/turkey.html. Accessed October 2004.

———. 2004. "Turkey: Progress on Human Rights Key to EU Bid." *Human Rights News* http://hrw.org/english/docs/2004/10/04/turkey9434.htm. Accessed October 2004.

Humphreys, Peter J. 1990. *Media and Media Policy in West Germany.* Oxford: Berg.

Hunwick, John Owen. 1998. "Tassawwuf." *Encyclopedia of Islam.* Vol. 10, 313–40. Leiden: Brill.

Husband, Charles, ed. 1994. *A Richer Vision: The Development of Ethnic Minority Media in Western Democracies.* Paris: UNESCO.

———. 2005. "Minority Ethnic Media as Communities of Practice: Professionalism and Identity Politics Interaction." *Journal of Ethnic and Migration Studies* 31, no. 3: 461–79.

Huth, Lutz. 1981. *Medien und ausländische Arbeitnehmer aus Italien und den ehemaligen Anwerbeländern. Forschungs- und Diskussionsstand.* Marl: Adolf-Grimme-Institut.

Hutnyk, John. 2000. *Critique of Exotica: Music, Politics and the Culture Industry.* London: Pluto.

IPA Plus. 1994. *Türken in Deutschland 1994: Markt-Media-Studie.* Frankfurt a.M.: IPA.

İş Rehberi. 1999. *Altın Sayfalar.* Berlin: Karma Verlag.

Jarren, Otfried, Thorsten Grothe, and Roy Müller. 1994. *Bürgermedium Offener Kanal.* Berlin: Vistas Verlag.

Jonker, Gerdien. 2000. "Islamic Television 'Made in Berlin.'" In *Paroles d'Islam: Des nouveaux Discourses islamiques en Europe,* ed. Felice Dassetto, 267–80. Strasbourg: Gallimard.

———. 2002. *Eine Wellenlänge zu Gott. Der Verband der Islamischen Kulturzentren in Europa.* Bielefeld: transcript Verlag.

Jonker, Gerdien, and Andreas Kapphan, eds. 1998. *Moscheen und islamisches Leben in Berlin.* Berlin: Die Ausländerbeauftragte des Senats.

Jordanova-Duda, Matilda. 1997. "Schwierige Messung." Vol. 4. *Medienspiegel* 21, no. 8: 5.

Kammann, Uwe. 1997. "Ausländerprogramme als Zankapfel: eine Chance." *Epd Medien,* no. 45: 5–8.

Kandiyoti, Deniz, ed. 1991. *Women, Islam and the State.* London: Macmillan.

Karakasoğlu, Yasemin. 1996. "Turkish Cultural Orientations in Germany and the Role of Islam." In *Turkish Culture in German Society Today,* ed. David Horrocks and Eva Kolinsky, 157–79. Providence and Oxford: Berghan Books.

Karcı, Hülya. 2002. "Egzotik olmanın dayanılmaz hafifliği . . ." *Tiyatro Bülteni,* no. 7: 7.

Kaya, Ayhan. 2001. "Rhizomatic Diasporic Space—Cultural Identity of the Berlin-Turkish Working-Class Youth." *Summer Institute Working Paper,* ed. Thomas Faist and Eyüp Özveren. Bremen and Ankara: INIIS and IIBF.

———. 2002a. "Aesthetics of Diaspora: Contemporary Minstrels in Turkish Berlin." *Journal of Ethnic and Migration Studies* 28, no. 1: 43–62.

———. 2002b. *"Sicher in Kreuzberg": Constructing Diasporas: Turkish Hip-Hop Youth in Berlin.* Bielefeld: transcript Verlag.

Kearney, Michael. 1991. "Borders and Boundaries of State and Self at the End of Empire." *Journal of Historical Sociology* 4, no. 1: 52–74.

———. 1995. "The Local and the Global: The Anthropology of Globalization and Transnationalism." *Annual Review of Anthropology* 24: 547–65.

Kelek, Necla. 2005. *Die Fremde Braut: Ein Bericht aus dem Inneren des Türkischen Lebens in Deutschland.* Köln: Kiepenheuer and Witsch.

Kern, Stephanie. 1996. "Mercedes spricht auch Türkisch." *W & V—Werben und Verkaufen,* no. 46: n,p.

Keskin, Hakki. 1989. "Die Türkei und die Türken im Ausland." In *1. Radioforum Ausländer bei Uns.* ed. Ausländerredaktion Süddeutscher Rundfunk, 57–66. Stuttgart: Landeszentrale für Politische Bildung.

Keyder, Çağlar, ed. 1999. *Istanbul Between the Global and the Local.* Lanham, Md.: Rowman and Littlefield.

Kilgus, Martin A., and Karl-Heinz Meier-Braun, eds. 1991. *Programme gegen Fremdenfeindlichkeit: Tagungsbericht zum 2. Radioforum Ausländer bei Uns vom 8. bis 10. Oktober in Stuttgart.* Baden-Baden: Nomos Verlagsgesellschaft.

King, Russell, and Nancy Wood, eds. 2001. *Media and Migration: Constructions of Mobility and Difference.* London: Routledge.

Kiwan, Nadia, and Kira Kosnick. 2006. "The 'Whiteness' of Cultural Policy in Paris and Berlin." In *Transcultural Europe: Cultural Policy in a Changing Europe,* ed. Ulrike H. Meinhof and Anna Triandafyllidou. Basingstoke: Palgrave Macmillan.

Klitzke, Dietrich, ed. 1980. *Das Medienangebot für die Bevölkerung aus der Türkei in Berlin (West).* Preprints zur Medienwissenschaft 1980/2. Berlin: Technische Universität.

———. 1981. "Türkçe Video Kasetler—oder: das Geschäft mit dem mangelnden Programmangebot." *Migration* 1, no. 1: 94–102.

Koch, Hans Jürgen, and Hermann Glaser. 2005. *Ganz Ohr. Eine Kulturgeschichte des Radios in Deutschland.* Köln: Böhlau Verlag.

Kolland, Dorothea. 2003. "Kiez International" in der "Contact Zone": Interkulturelle Konzepte in Berlin-Neukölln. Berlin: Jahrbuch Beitrag.

Koschinski, Michael. 1986. *Fernsehprogramme als Mittel der Integration. Eine Untersuchung interkultureller Kommunikationsprobleme der türkischen Minderheit in der Bundesrepublik Deutschland.* Essen: Verlag Die Blaue Eule.

Kosnick, Kira. 2000. "Building Bridges—Media for Migrants and the Public-Service Mission in Germany." *European Journal of Cultural Studies* 3, no. 3: 321–44.

———. 2003. *Reaching Beyond the Local: A Study of Turkish Migrant Broadcasting in Berlin, Germany.* Ph.D. diss., New School for Social Research.

———. 2004. "The Gap between Culture and Cultures: Cultural Policy in Berlin and Its Implications for Immigrant Cultural Production." EUI Working Papers, European University Institute, RSCAS No. 41.

———. 2005. "Selecta at the Door: Queer 'Oriental' Space and the Problem of Getting the Mix Right at Gayhane HomOriental Clubnights." *Berliner Blätter—Ethnographische und Ethnologische Beiträge,* no. 37: 126–31.

Krätke, Stefan. 2001. "Berlin: Towards a Global City?" *Urban Studies* 38, no. 10: 1777–99.

Lachmann, Günther. 2005. *Tödliche Toleranz. Die Muslime und unsere Offene Gesellschaft.* München: Piper.

Laclau, Ernesto, and Chantal Mouffe. 1985. *Hegemony and Socialist Strategy: Towards A Radical Democratic Politics.* London: Verso.

Landau, Jacob. 1995. *Pan-Turkism: From Irredentism to Cooperation.* Bloomington: Indiana University Press.

Leidinger, Christiane. 2003. *Medien, Herrschaft, Globalisierung: Folgenabschätzung zu Medieninhalten im Zuge transnationaler Konzentrationsprozesse.* Münster: Verlag Westfälisches Dampfboot.

Lendzian, Bettina. 1999. "Die Erhöhung der Duisburger Müllgebühren auf türkisch und italienisch: Ausländerprogramme im NRW Hörfunk." *Menschen Machen Medien* 48, no. 3: 14–15.

Lewis, Bernard. 1968. *The Emergence of Modern Turkey.* Oxford: Oxford University Press.

Linke, Jürgen. 1997. "You Are Me—Integration Model Open Channel." In *Handbuch Medien. Offene Kanäle,* ed. Ulrich Kamp, 44–47. Bonn: Bundeszentrale für Politische Bildung.

Lohrmann, Reinhard, and Klaus Manfrass, eds. 1974. *Ausländerbeschäftigung und internationale Politik.* München: Oldenbourg Verlag.

Malkki, Liisa. 1992. "National Geographic: The Rooting of Peoples and the Territorialization of National Identity among Scholars and Refugees." *Cultural Anthropology* 7, no. 2: 24–44.

———. 1995. "Refugees and Exile: From 'Refugee Studies' to the National Order of Things." *Annual Review of Anthropology* 24: 495–523.

Mandel, Ruth. 1989. "Ethnicity and Identity among Migrant Guestworkers in West Berlin." In *Conflict, Migration, and the Expression of Ethnicity,* ed. Nancie Gonzales and Carolyn McCommon, 60–74. Boulder, Colo.: Westview.

———. 1990. "Shifting Centres and Emergent Identities: Turkey and Germany in the Lives of Turkish Gastarbeiter." In *Muslim Travellers: Pilgrimage, Migration, and the Religious Imagination,* ed. Dale Eickelmann and James Piscatori, 153–74. London: Routledge.

———. 1994. "'Fortress Europe' and the Foreigners Within: Germany's Turks." In *The Anthropology of Europe: Identity and Boundaries in Conflict,* ed. Victoria A. Goddard, Josep R. Llobera, and Cris Shore, 113–24. Oxford and Providence, R.I.: Berg.

———. 1995. "Second-Generation Non-citizens: Children of the Turkish Migrant Diaspora in Germany." In *Children and the Politics of Culture,* ed. Sharon Stephens, 265–81. Princeton, N.J.: Princeton University Press.

———. 1996. "A Place of Their Own: Contesting Spaces and Defining Places in Berlin's Migrant Community." In *Making Muslim Space in North America and Europe,* ed. Barbara Metcalf, 147–66. Berkeley: University of California Press.

Mankekar, Purnima. 1999. *Screening Culture, Viewing Politics. An Ethnography of Television, Womanhood, and Nation in Postcolonial India.* Durham, N.C., and London: Duke University Press.

Marcus, George E. 1995. "Ethnography in/of the World System: The Emergence of Multi-sited Ethnography." *Annual Review of Anthropology* 24: 95–117.

Mardin, Şerif. 2002. "Playing Games with Names." In *Fragments of Culture: The Everyday of Modern Turkey,* ed. Deniz Kandiyoti and Ayşe Saktanber, 115–27. New Brunswick, N.J.: Rutgers University Press.

Massey, Doreen. 2005. *For Space.* London: Sage.

Mazzarella, William. 2004. "Culture, Globalization, Mediation." *Annual Review of Anthropology* 33: 345–67.

McChesney, Robert W., and Dan Schiller. 2003. "The Political Economy of International Communications: Foundations for the Emerging Global Debate about Media Ownership and Regulation." *Technology, Business and Society Programme.* Geneva: United Nations Research Institute for Social Development.

McLeod, Kembrew. 1999. "Authenticity within Hip-Hop and Other Cultures Threatened with Assimilation." *The Journal of Communication* 49: 134–50.

Medienwerkstatt Frankfurt. 1998. *Zielsetzung des Offenen Kanals.* http://www.mefi-ffm.de/offkanal.htm. Accessed January 2000.

Mertens, Ilja. 2000. "Von einer 'Inneren Angelegenheit,' die auszog, Europa das Fürchten zu lehren. Transstaatliche politische Mobilisierung und das 'Kurdenproblem.'" In *Transstaatliche Räume: Politik, Wirtschaft und Kultur in und zwischen Deutschland und der Türkei,* ed. Thomas Faist, 159–99. Bielefeld: transcript Verlag.

Metcalf, Barbara, ed. 1996. *Making Muslim Space in North America and Europe.* Berkeley: University of California Press.

Michaels, Eric. 1994. *Bad Aboriginal Art: Tradition, Media, and Technological Horizons.* Minneapolis: University of Minnesota Press.

Mohr, Inge. 1996. "SFB 4 MultiKulti: Öffentlich-rechtliches Hörfunkangebot nicht nur für Ausländer." *Media Perspektiven,* no. 8: 466–72.

Morley, David. 2000. *Home Territories: Media, Mobility and Identity.* London and New York: Routledge.

Morley, David, and Kevin Robins. 1995. *Spaces of Identity.* London: Routledge.

Mosse, George L. 1985. *Nationalism and Sexuality: Middle-Class Morality and Sexual Norms in Modern Europe.* Madison: University of Wisconsin Press.

Müller, Roswitha. 1990. "From Public to Private: Television in the Federal Republic of Germany." *New German Critique,* no. 50: 41–55.

Mushaben, Joyce M. 1991. "A Crisis of Culture: Isolation and Integration among Turkish Guestworkers in the German Federal Republic." In *Die Zweite und Dritte Ausländergeneration: Ihre Situation und Zukunft in der Bundesrepublik Deutschland,* ed. Konstantin Lajios, 125–50. Opladen: Westdeutscher Verlag.

N. N. 1995. "SFB 4—Radio MultiKulti." *UNESCO Heute,* no. 3: 176–77.

Naficy, Hamid. 1993. *The Making of Exile Cultures: Iranian Television in Los Angeles.* Minneapolis: University of Minnesota Press.

———, ed. 1999. *Home, Exile, Homeland: Film, Media, and the Politics of Place.* London: Routledge.

Navaro-Yashin, Yael. 2002. *Faces of the State: Secularism and Public Life in Turkey.* Princeton, N.J.: Princeton University Press.

Negt, Oskar, and Alexander Kluge. 1993. *Public Sphere and Experience: Toward an Analysis of the Bourgeois and Proletarian Public Sphere.* Minneapolis and London: University of Minnesota Press.

Nikolinakos, Marios. 1973. *Politische Ökonomie der Gastarbeiterfrage. Migration und Kapitalismus.* Reinbek: Rowohlt Verlag.

Nonneman, Gerd, Timothy Niblock, and Bogdan Szajkowski, eds. 1996. *Muslim Communities in the New Europe.* Reading, N.Y.: Ithaca Press.

Nowell-Smith, Geoffrey, and Tana Wollen, eds. 1991. *After the Wall: Broadcasting in Germany.* London: British Film Institute.

Ocak, Ahmet Yaşar. 1991. "Alevilik ve Bektaşilik Hakkında Son Yayınlar Üzerine (1990) Genel Bir Bakış ve Bazı Gerçekler." *Tarih Ve Toplum,* no. 91: 20–25.

Ogan, Christine. 2001. *Communication and Identity in the Diaspora: Turkish Migrants in Amsterdam and Their Use of Media.* Lanham, Md.: Lexington Books.

Ogelman, Nedim. 2003. "Documenting and Explaining the Persistence of Homeland Politics among Germany's Turks." *International Migration Review* 37, no. 1: 163–93.

Oguntoye, Katharina, May Opitz, and Dagmar Schultz, eds. 1986. *Farbe bekennen. Afro-deutsche Frauen auf den Spuren ihrer Geschichte.* Berlin: Orlanda.

Ohliger, Rainer, and Ulrich Raiser. 2005. *Integration und Migration in Berlin: Zahlen, Daten, Fakten.* http://www.berlin.de/imperia/md/content/sengsv/intmig/doku/zahlen_daten_fakten.pdf. Accessed August 2006.

Okkan, Osman. 1998. "Anmerkungen zum Projekt 'Europäisches Migranten-TV.'" In *Migration und Medien,* ed. Adolf-Grimme-Institut, 14–16. Marl: Adolf-Grimme-Institut.

Omi, Michael, and Howard Winant. 1994. *Racial Formation in the United States: From the 1960s to the 1990s.* New York and London: Routledge.

Öncü, Ayşe. 1995. "Packaging Islam: Cultural Politics on the Landscape of Turkish Commercial Television." *Public Culture* 8: 51–71.

———. 2000. "The Banal and the Subversive: Politics of Language on Turkish Television." *European Journal of Cultural Studies* 3, no. 3: 296–318.

Østergaard-Nielsen, Eva. 2003. *Transnational Politics: Turks and Kurds in Germany.* London: Routledge.

Otan, Ümit. 1995. *bâbitelli.* Izmir: İzmir Kitaplığı.

Portes, Alejandro. 1998. "Globalization from Below: The Rise of Transnational Communities." *Transnational Communities Working Paper Series.* http://www.transcomm.ox.ac.uk, no. 1: 1–26. Accessed June 2003.

Poster, Mark. 1995. *The Second Media Age.* New York: Blackwell.

Räthzel, Nora. 1990. "Germany: One Race, One Nation?" *Race & Class* 32, no. 3: 31–48.

Refiğ, Halit. 1996. "Türkiye'de Televizyon Yayıncılığı üzerine bazı Görüşler." In *2000'li Yıllara Doğru: Türkiye'de TV,* ed. Emir Turam, 127–33. Istanbul: Altın Kitaplar.

Regierung Online. 2001. Vertrag zur Kulturfinanzierung in der Bundeshauptstadt 2001–2004. June 13. http://www.Bundesregierung.de. Accessed May 2003.

Rex, John. 1991. "The Political Sociology of a Multi-cultural Society." *Journal of Intercultural Studies* 2, no. 1: 7–19.

Riggins, Stephen Harold, ed. 1992. *Ethnic Minority Media: An International Perspective.* Newbury Park, Calif.: Sage.

Rissom, Hans-Wolf, Jens Brüning, Wilfried Nax, Karsten Renckstorf, and Rainer Thissen. 1977. *Ausländische Arbeitnehmer und Massenmedien in der Bundesrepublik Deutschland.* Köln: Deutsche Unesco Kommission.

Robbins, Bruce, ed. 1993. *The Phantom Public Sphere.* Minneapolis and London: University of Minnesota Press.

Röll, Hans-Heinz. 1985. "Zur ZDF Sendung 'Nachbarn in Europa—Nachrichten und Informationen für Ausländer und Deutsche'." In *Massenmedien und Aus-*

länder in der Bundesrepublik Deutschland, ed. Michael Darkow, Josef Eckhardt, and Gerhard Maletzke, 111–17. Frankfurt a.M.: Alfred Metzner Verlag.

Rose, Tricia. 1994. *Black Noise: Rap Music and Black Culture in Contemporary America.* London: Wesleyan University Press.

Roters, Gunnar. 1990. *Publikum ohne Programm? Eine repräsentative Studie zur Mediennutzung und -beurteilung der türkischen Bevölkerung von Berlin.* Berlin: Vistas Verlag.

————. 1991. "Wie Türken in Berlin die Medien nutzen." In *Programme gegen Fremdenfeindlichkeit—2. Radioforum Ausländer bei Uns,* ed. Martin A. Kilgus and Karl-Heinz Meier-Braun, 63–108. Baden-Baden: Nomos Verlagsgesellschaft.

Rotter, Erich. 1969. "Freunde, nicht Fremde. Die Gastarbeitersendungen der Landesrundfunkanstalten." *ARD Jahrbuch* 69: 96–102.

Sağnak, Mehmet. 1996. *Medya-Politik: 1983–1993 Yılları Arasında Medya-Politikacı İlişkileri.* Istanbul: Eti Kitapları.

Şahin, Haluk, and Asu Aksoy. 1993. "Global Media and Cultural Identity in Turkey." *Journal of Communication* 43, no. 2: 31–41.

Salt, John. 1985. "West German Dilemma: Little Turks or Young Germans?" *Geography,* no. 70: 162–68.

Sassen, Saskia. 1991. *The Global City: New York, London, Tokyo.* Princeton, N.J.: Princeton University Press.

————. 1999. *Globalization and Its Discontents: Essays on the New Mobility of People and Money.* New York: New Press.

Savaş, Kutlu. 1998. "Susurlukbericht der Inspektionsbehörde beim Ministerpräsidialamt, Kutlu Savaş." In *Bandenrepublik Türkei? Der Susurlukbericht des Ministerialinspektors Kutlu Savaş,* ed. Internationaler Verein für Menschenrechte der Kurden e.V., 1–63. Berlin: Papiertiger.

Schiffauer, Werner. 1999. "Islamism in the Diaspora: The Fascination of Political Islam among Second-Generation Turks." *Transnational Communities Working Paper Series.* http://www.transcomm.ox.ac.uk, no. 6: 1–21. Accessed December 2002.

————. 2003. "Muslimische Organisationen und ihr Anspruch auf Repräsentativität: Dogmatisch bedingte Konkurrenz und Streit um Institutionalisierung." In *Der Islam in Europa: Der Umgang mit dem Islam in Frankreich und Deutschland,* ed. Alexandre Escudier, 143–75. Göttingen: Wallstein Verlag.

Schweitzer, Helmuth. 1998. "Wir haben unsere Stimme noch nicht laut gemacht." In *Migration und Medien,* ed. Adolf-Grimme-Institut, 7–8. Marl: Adolf-Grimme-Institut.

Seidel-Pielen, Eberhard. 1996. *Aufgespießt: Wie der Döner über die Deutschen kam.* Hamburg: Rotbuch Verlag.

Senatsverwaltung für Wissenschaft, Forschung und Kultur. 2003. *Merkblatt—Projektförderung im Bereich der Kulturaktivitäten von Bürgerinnen/Bürgern aus-*

ländischer Herkunft für das Jahr 2003. Berlin: Senatsverwaltung für Wissenschaft, Forschung und Kultur.

Şener, Cemal. 1994. *Yaşayan Alevilik.* Istanbul: Anadolu Matbaası.

Seufert, Günter. 1997. *Politischer Islam in der Türkei: Islamismus als symbolische Repräsentation einer sich modernisierenden Muslimischen Gesellschaft.* Istanbul: Franz Steiner Verlag.

—. 1999. "Die Türkisch-Islamische Union der türkischen Religionsbehörde—Zwischen Integration und Isolation." In *Turkish Islam and Europe: Europe and Christianity as Reflected in Turkish Muslim Discourse and Turkish Muslim Life in the Diaspora,* ed. Günter Seufert and Jacques Waardenburg, 261–93. Istanbul: Franz-Steiner Verlag Stuttgart.

SFB 4—MultiKulti. 1995. *Project Description.* Berlin: Sender Freies Berlin.

Silverstone, Roger, and Myria Georgiou. 2005. "Editorial Introduction: Media and Minorities in Multicultural Europe." *Journal of Ethnic and Migration Studies* 31, no. 3: 433–41.

Smith, M. G. 1969. "Some Developments in the Analytical Framework of Pluralism." In *Pluralism in Africa,* ed. L. Kuper and M. G. Smith, 415–58. Berkeley: University of California Press.

Sökefeld, Martin. Forthcoming 2007. "Aleviten in Deutschland—von *takiya* zur alevitischen Bewegung." In *Aleviten in Deutschland,* ed. Martin Sökefeld. Bielefeld: transcript.

Sökefeld, Martin, and Susanne Schwalgin. 2000. "Institutions and their Agents in Diaspora: A Comparison of Armenians in Athens and Alevis in Germany." Paper presented at the biennial conference of the European Association of Social Anthropologists (EASA). Cracow, July 26–29.

Soysal, Levent. 1999. *Projects of Culture: An Ethnographic Episode in the Life of Migrant Youth in Berlin.* Ph.D. diss., Harvard University.

—. 2002. "Beyond the 'Second Generation': Rethinking the Place of Migrant Youth Culture in Berlin." In *Challenging Ethnic Citizenship: German and Israeli Perspectives on Immigration,* ed. Daniel Levy and Yfaat Weiss, 121–36. New York: Berghan Books.

Spitulnik, Debra. 1993. "Anthropology and Mass Media." *Annual Review of Anthropology* 22: 293–315.

—. 1998. "Mediating Unity and Diversity: The Production of Language Ideologies in Zambian Broadcasting." In *Language Ideologies: Practice and Theory,* ed. Bambi Schieffelin, Kathryn Woolard, and Paul Kroskrity, 163–88. Oxford: Oxford University Press.

Spivak, Gayatri Ch. 1988. "Can the Subaltern Speak?" In *Marxism and the Interpretation of Culture,* ed. Larry Grossberg and Cary Nelson, 271–313. Urbana: University of Illinois Press.

Sreberny, Annabelle. 2001. "The Role of the Media in the Cultural Practices of Diasporic Communities." Research Position Paper 6. In *Differing Diversities:*

Transversal Study on the Theme of Cultural Policy and Cultural Diversity, ed. Tony Bennett, 155–67. Strasbourg: Council of Europe Publishing.

Sreberny-Mohammadi, Annabelle, and Ali Mohammadi. 1994. *Small Media, Big Revolution: Communication, Culture, and the Iranian Revolution.* Minneapolis: University of Minnesota Press.

Stelzle, Walter. 1980. "Das Ausländerprogramm der ARD." *ARD Jahrbuch 80,* no. 12: 55–67.

Steyerl, Hito. 2004. "Gaps and Potentials: The Exhibition *Heimat Kunst*—Migrant Culture as an Allegory of the Global Market." *New German Critique,* no. 92: 159–68.

Stokes, Martin. 1992. *The Arabesk Debate: Music and Musicians in Modern Turkey.* Oxford, U.K.: Clarendon.

———. 1999. "Sounding Out: The Culture Industries and the Globalization of Istanbul." In *Istanbul: Between the Global and the Local,* ed. Çağlar Keyder, 121–39. Lanham, Md.: Rowman and Littlefield.

Stolcke, Verena. 1995. "Talking Culture: New Boundaries, New Rhetorics of Exclusion in Europe." *Current Anthropology* 36, no. 1: 1–24.

Tabak, Hikmet. 2001. "The Kurdish Television Station MED-TV." In *Zwischen Abgrenzung und Integration: Türkische Medienkultur in Deutschland,* ed. Jörg Becker and Reinhard Behnisch, 149–72. Rehburg-Loccum: Evangelische Akademie Loccum.

Taylor, Charles. 1992. *Multiculturalism and "The Politics of Recognition."* Princeton, N.J.: Princeton University Press.

Thompson, Edward P. 1968. *The Making of the English Working Class.* Harmondsworth, U.K.: Penguin.

Tibi, Bassam. 2002. *Islamische Zuwanderung. Die gescheiterte Integration.* Stuttgart/München: Deutsche Verlags-Anstalt.

Tini Fox, Derek. 1993. "Honouring the Treaty: Indigenous Television in Aotearoa." In *Channels of Resistance: Global Television and Local Empowerment,* ed. Tony Dowmunt, 126–37. London: British Film Institute.

Trautner, Bernhard. 2000. "Türkische Muslime, islamische Organisationen und religiöse Institutionen als soziale Träger des transstaatlichen Raumes Deutschland-Türkei." In *Transstaatliche Räume: Politik, Wirtschaft und Kultur in und zwischen Deutschland und der Türkei,* ed. Thomas Faist, 57–86. Bielefeld: transcript Verlag.

Treibel, Annette. 1990. *Migration in modernen Gesellschaften. Soziale Folgen von Einwanderung und Gastarbeit.* Weinheim and Munich: Juventa Verlag.

Troltsch, Klaus. 2002. "Migranten und Migrantinnen in Deutschland: Ein Vergleich zur Bildungsbeteiligung und -chancen junger Erwachsener mit Migrationshintergrund." *Bundesinstitut Für Berufsbildung.* http://www.bibb.de/dokumente/pdf/pr_pr-material_2002_migranten_migr_troltsch.pdf. Accessed April 2004.

Tsing, Anna. 2000. "The Global Situation." *Cultural Anthropology* 15, no. 3: 327–60.

Turam, Emir, ed. 1996. *"2000'li Yıllara Doğru" Türkiye'de TV.* Istanbul: Altın Kitaplar.

Türkeş, Alparslan. 1965. *Dokuz Işık.* Istanbul: Dokuz Işık Yayınları.

Türkoğlu, Sevim. 2003. "Die kurdische und türkische Theaterlandschaft in Berlin." Unpublished manuscript, Berlin.

Turner, Terence. 1990. "Visual Media, Cultural Politics, and Anthropological Practice: Some Implications of Recent Uses of Film and Video among the Kayapo of Brazil." *Commission on Visual Anthropology Review* (spring): 8–13.

———. 1991. "Representing, Resisting, Rethinking: Historical Transformations of Kayapo Culture and Anthropological Consciousness." In *Colonial Situations: Essays on the Contextualization of Ethnographic Knowledge,* ed. George W. Stocking, 285–313. Madison: University of Wisconsin Press.

———. 1992. "Defiant Images: The Kayapo Appropriation of Video." *Anthropology Today* 8, no. 6: 5–16.

Ünüz, Hanzade. 1998. "Türklerin yüzde 81'i Türkçe TV seyrediyor." *Hürriyet,* February 14, sec. Avrupa Gazetesi, 14.

Urry, John. 2000. *Sociology beyond Societies: Mobilities for the Twenty First Century.* London: Routledge.

Van Bruinessen, Martin. 2000a. *Kurdish Ethnonationalism versus Nation-Building States.* Istanbul: ISIS Press.

———. 2000b. "Transnational Aspects of the Kurdish Question." *EUI Working Papers, European University Institute,* no. 22: 3–33.

Vertovec, Steven. 1996a. "Berlin Multikulti: Germany, 'Foreigners' and 'World-Openness.'" *New Community* 22, no. 3: 381–99.

———. 1996b. "Multiculturalism, Culturalism and Public Incorporation." *Ethnic and Racial Studies* 19: 49–69.

———. 1999. "Conceiving and Researching Transnationalism." *Ethnic and Racial Studies* 22, no. 2: 447–62.

———. 2000. "Fostering Cosmopolitanisms: A Conceptual Survey and a Media Experiment in Berlin." *Transnational Communities Working Paper Series.* http://www.transcomm.ox.ac.uk/working%20papers/Vertovec.pdf. Accessed November 2001.

———. 2001. "Transnational Challenges to the 'New' Multiculturalism." *Transnational Communities Working Paper Series.* http://www.transcomm.ox.ac.uk/working%20papers/ WPTC-2K-06%20Vertovec.pdf. Accessed December 2002.

———. 2004. "Migrant Transnationalism and Modes of Transformation." *The International Migration Review* 38, no. 3: 970–1001.

Vincent, Joan. 1974. "The Structuring of Ethnicity." *Human Organization* 33, no. 4: 375–78.

Voloshinov, V. N. 1973. *Marxism and the Philosophy of Language.* New York: Seminar.

Vorhoff, Karin. 1995. *Zwischen Glaube, Nation und neuer Gemeinschaft: Alevitische Identität in der Türkei der Gegenwart.* Berlin: Klaus Schwarz Verlag.

Voß, Friedrich. 1995. "Radio MultiKulti: Babylon auf dem Äther." *FU:N,* nos. 8–9: 23.

———. 1996. "Low Budget and High Level." *Wort, Bild & Ton,* no. 1: 6.

Wahlbeck, Östen. 1998. "Transnationalism and Diasporas: The Kurdish Example." http://www.transcomm.ox.ac.uk/working%20papers/Wahlbeck.pdf, no. WPTC-98–11. Accessed November 2001.

Warner, Michael. 2002. "Publics and Counterpublics." *Public Culture* 14, no. 1: 49–90.

Warner, Michael, ed. 1993. *Fear of a Queer Planet: Queer Politics and Social Theory.* Minneapolis and London: University of Minnesota Press.

Weiß, Hans-Jürgen, and Joachim Trebbe. 2001. *Mediennutzung und Integration der türkischen Bevölkerung in Deutschland: Ergebnisse einer Umfrage des Presse- und Informationsamtes der Bundesregierung.* Potsdam: GöfaK Medienforschung GmbH.

Werbner, Pnina. 1997. "Essentialising Essentialism, Essentialising Silence: Ambivalence and Multiplicity in the Constructions of Racism and Ethnicity." In *Debating Cultural Hybridity: Multi-Cultural Identities and the Politics of Anti-Racism,* ed. Pnina Werbner and Tariq Modood, 226–54. London: Zed Books.

———. 2002. *Imagined Diasporas among Manchester Muslims.* Santa Fe, N.M.: SAR.

———. n.d. The Predicament of Diaspora and Millennial Islam: Reflections in the Aftermath of September 11. http://www.Ssrc.Org/Sept11/Essays/Werbner.htm. Accessed July 2005.

White, Jenny B. 2002. "The Islamist Paradox." In *Fragments of Culture: The Everyday of Modern Turkey,* ed. Deniz Kandiyoti and Ayşe Saktanber, 191–217. New Brunswick, N.J.: Rutgers University Press.

Wikan, Unni. 2002. *Generous Betrayal: Politics of Culture in the New Europe.* Chicago: University of Chicago Press.

Williams, Brackette F. 1989. "A Class Act: Anthropology and the Race to Nation across Ethnic Terrain." *Annual Review of Anthropology* 18: 401–44.

———. 1993. "The Impact of the Precepts of Nationalism on the Concept of Culture: Making Grasshoppers of Naked Apes." *Cultural Critique,* no. 24: 143–91.

———. 1995. "Classification Systems Revisited: Kinship, Caste, Race, and Nationality as the Flow of Blood and the Spread of Rights." In *Naturalizing Power: Essays in Feminist Cultural Analysis,* ed. Sylvia Yanagisako and Carol Delaney, 201–36. New York and London: Routledge.

Williams, Raymond. 1971. *Culture and Society, 1780–1950.* London: Penguin.

Willis, Paul. 1977. *Learning to Labour: How Working Class Kids Get Working Class Jobs.* New York: Columbia University Press.

Yalcin-Heckmann, Lale. 2002. "Negotiating Identities: Media Representations of Different Generations of Turkish Migrants in Germany." In *Fragments of Culture: The Everyday of Modern Turkey*, ed. Deniz Kandiyoti and Ayşe Saktanber, 308–21. New Brunswick, N.J.: Rutgers University Press.

Yang, Mayfair Mei-Hui. 1997. "Mass Media and Transnational Subjectivity in Shanghai: Notes on (Re)Cosmopolitanism in a Chinese Metropolis." In *Ungrounded Empires: The Cultural Politics of Modern Chinese Transnationalism*, ed. Aihwa Ong and Donald M. Nonini, 287–319. New York and London: Routledge.

Yengin, Hülya. 1994. *Ekranın Büyüsü: Batıda Değişen Televizyon Yayıncılığının Boyutları ve Türkiye'de Özel Televizyonlar*. Istanbul: Der Yayınevi.

Zaimoğlu, Feridun. 2000. *Kanak Sprak: 24 Mißtöne vom Rande der Gesellschaft.* Hamburg: Rotbuch Verlag.

Zambonini, Gualtiero, and Mario Barbi. 1987. "Muttersprachliche und Zielgruppenspezifische Sendungen." In *Ausländer und Massenmedien,* ed. Bundeszentrale für Politische Bildung, 99–103. Bonn: Bundeszentrale für Politische Bildung.

Zentrum für Türkeistudien. 1992. *Ergebnisse einer Untersuchung zum Fernsehverhalten in Türkischen Haushalten.* Essen: ZfT.

———. 1997. *Kurzfassung der Studie zum Medienkonsum der türkischen Bevölkerung in Deutschland und Deutschlandbild im türkischen Fernsehen.* Essen: ZfT.

INDEX

KIRA KOSNICK is Junior Professor of
Cultural Anthropology and European Ethnology
at the Johann Wolfgang Goethe University
in Frankfurt, Germany.